As Good As A Dog

As Good As A Dog

David Rathman

ISBN: 978-1-4269-5804-5 (sc)
ISBN: 978-1-4269-5805-2 (e)

Trafford rev. 02/15/2011

 www.trafford.com

North America & international
toll-free: 1 888 232 4444 (USA & Canada)
phone: 250 383 6864 ✦ fax: 812 355 4082

WALKING THE STREETS OF READING

POINTS OF INTEREST:

- COUNTY SERVICES BUILDING, #1
- BERKS COUNTY COURTHOUSE, #2
- RACC, #3
- YMCA, #4
- LINCOLN PLAZA HOTEL, #5
- YOP AT 5TH AND PENN, #6
- BERKS BAR ASSOCIATION, #7
- DAUTRICH LAW OFFICE, #8
- FIRST PRESBYTERIAN CHURCH, #9
- PEANUT BAR & RESTAURANT, #10
- PAULINE'S SOUP CAFÉ, #11
- SOVEREIGN PERFORMING ARTS, #12
- SOVEREIGN CENTER, #13
- STATE OFFICE, #14
- READING EAGLE NEWSPAPER, #15

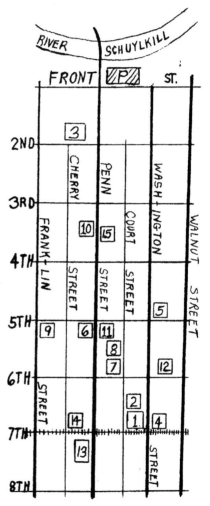

My Walk on August 26, 2008

My parking spot for RACC was located on the opposite side of Penn Street from the building where I taught my classes. I could walk under the bridge from the parking lot to get to my classroom. I walked from the lot to the courthouse (#2) on the morning of the custody trial. Later, I ran from the courthouse (#2) and to FPC (#9) and back to (#2). I had to make it from (#2) to (#3) before noon to start teaching my math class. At 2:30, I ran down the steps at (#3) and to the RACC parking lot. I walked from there to (#2) to take the witness stand. The trial for the afternoon had been moved to a courtroom in the County Service's Building (#1). I walked to (#1) and took the witness stand. At 4:15, I walked from (#1) to the parking lot at RACC. I drove home.

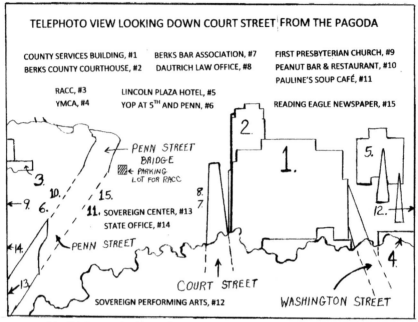

TELEPHOTO VIEW LOOKING DOWN COURT STREET FROM THE PAGODA

COUNTY SERVICES BUILDING, #1   BERKS BAR ASSOCIATION, #7   FIRST PRESBYTERIAN CHURCH, #9
BERKS COUNTY COURTHOUSE, #2   DAUTRICH LAW OFFICE, #8   PEANUT BAR & RESTAURANT, #10
                                                                 PAULINE'S SOUP CAFÉ, #11

RACC, #3   LINCOLN PLAZA HOTEL, #5
YMCA, #4   YOP AT 5TH AND PENN, #6   READING EAGLE NEWSPAPER, #15

PENN STREET BRIDGE
← PARKING LOT FOR RACC
SOVEREIGN CENTER, #13
STATE OFFICE, #14
PENN STREET
COURT STREET
SOVEREIGN PERFORMING ARTS, #12
WASHINGTON STREET

#1. Kristen worked here from 1997-2001 in Domestic Relations as a Conference Officer. Home of BCCYS and place where PFA's are filed. Harry went to both. The custody trial was conluded here.

#2. Kristen worked here from 2001-2003 in the Prothonotary Office. Custody trial started in a courtroom of this building.

#3. I taught here the day of the custody trial, my first day of classes.

#4. I taught here for the Youth Outreach Program in 2007. Left here to go to the Courthouse (#2) where I caught Harry lying to Kristen.

#5. In 2003, I received the "City on the Hill Award" here from the RBCC. Seated at our table were Judge Lash and his wife.

#6. Taught YOP here from 2003-2006 on the second floor above McDonald's. We ducked into this place to shake the private eye.

#7. Went here to get a referral for a lawyer for Kristen and later ourselves. Kristen got Jamie. We got nobody.

#8. The Law Office of Kristen's lawyer. We watched the private eye from the window. Double parked, policeman questioned him.

#9. The site of the church where I was Children's Ministry Director.

#10. Was the site of my meeting with Dr. Keevil, pastor of FPC.

#11. Was the site of many of my lunches when I taught for YOP.

#12. Was the site where my wife and I performed in the musical "Joseph and the Amazing Technicolor Dreamcoat."

#13. Is the home of the Reading Royal's ice hockey team. I led my ensemble BRASS IN PRAISE in a performance on the opening weekend of the arena for an ecumenical concert.

#14. Held here were the two expungement hearings in May and July of 2007. The "gang of four" were seen in its elevator.

#15. I did not get past the rear gate in my two attempts in finding someone to listen to my story.

LAUGH, LEARN, AND LOVE

The late Rev. Stacy Myers told the congregation at West Lawn United Methodist that he was given two gems of advice from his father concerning preaching. He was also a pastor and a preacher. The first gem was to demonstrate that you had a sense of humor. Stacy, with various degrees of success, tried to get that over with in the first few moments of each sermon. The second gem was to keep the sermon to only three major points. If you have more than three points, the people will not remember them. I find that statement to be amusing, even funny. That being said, my three major points are that you laugh, learn, and love while you read <u>As Good As a Dog</u>. Actually, I hope you can read better than a dog.

For my last semester in college I was a student teacher for senior high math. On my last day of classes a student gave me a little hand crafted and hand written booklet. Simply put, it was a collection of some of my sayings in math class. I only remember two of them, one being, "Cool it!" The other was a bit longer. It was, "having fun in school is okay as long as you're learning while you're laughing." More than forty years later, one of my students in College Algebra wrote the following comment on a teacher evaluation form. The student wrote, "I hate math, but I loved coming to math class. He made it fun. I actually came to math class and learned some math." Notice, the students get to evaluate their teachers. Perhaps, plaintiffs, defendants, and witnesses should evaluate and rate their lawyers and the judge.

This story is about a serious issue, just like math. However, I consider it my task to make it enjoyable reading. If I could write a serious letter to the judge and have lawyers laugh out loud, then I must have the gift. If you can't find humor somewhere in what I have written, God didn't create the "funny bone." Trey hit his elbow the other day and came out with an, "Ouch!" I asked him if he hit his "funny bone." He said, "No, it hurt." I laughed. Trey didn't. I hope you get to laugh.

I am a teacher. I will get the reader involved through questions. You may have to pause to think. If I did a good job of teaching you will come up with questions? The same event may be described in a different context in another chapter. Review is good. In one sense, I feel it is better to let you discover as you learn. Read the chapter titles for an inkling of what you might learn. I also hope through reading them you will be intrigued. Another hope is that you learn things you did not expect to learn. In writing math competencies, each statement of the competency starts with the phrase, "the student will be able to."

I give you three competencies describing what you will learn from reading this book. Anymore than that you will not remember. Did you laugh? Anyway, the reader will be able to:

- Understand the steps involved in custody determination.
- Recognize that "dirty tactics" are used to win in divorce and custody battles.
- Join in the fight against the use of these "dirty tactics" by the unscrupulous in the court system of family law.

We use the word "love" in many different ways. We say there are things we "love" to do. The boys love to ride bike. I love to play basketball. We say there are things of the "corporeal" that we love. We love the things of creation. But there are also the intangibles. My wife loves history. History is intangible. When you visit a place like Independence Hall, history can be experienced. The intangible becomes corporeal. It is said of God that he "so loved the world that he gave—." Love was the impetus for God to act. Liberty is intangible. People have loved liberty enough to fight and die for it. I love "justice" and hate "injustice." I love "justice" enough to write a book about seeking it. Love inspires action. So, laugh, learn, and love.

Contents

Chapter 1—As Good as a Dog

The Letter Discussed

Attorney Mark Zimmer questions the defendant, Kristen Hall.

Zimmer: Are you aware of some letters that your father wrote to this court?

Kristen: Yes.

Zimmer: And do you think those are the letters of a loving person?

Kristen: Those are letters of the truth. These are things that happened. My father was angry. Everyone is entitled to be angry sometimes. That doesn't meant he doesn't love Harry.

Zimmer: He stated in one of his letters that he—if only Harry was.

Ms. Dautrich, Kristen's attorney: I'm objecting to quoting from a letter. I don't think this is evidence.

The Court: Overruled.

Ms. Dautrich: Nor do I think it was proffered as an exhibit when exhibits were due.

The Court: Overruled.

Zimmer: I can show it to her if you prefer. Your Honor, and ask her to read it.

The Court: You can read it. If there's an issue with your accuracy we can get into that. Just read it.

Zimmer: Okay. It states here, if only Harry was as good as a dog.

The court should have read the whole letter. They would have understood, with a little help, why I wrote that statement. The statement was part of the conclusion. Preceding that statement, I wrote that I asked Bryce what he liked best about his father. Bryce said, "The dog." I followed with that simple hyperbole. My daughter said when my letter was read in a pre-trial hearing she heard laughter coming from inside the room. She asked her lawyer what that was all about. Her lawyer said, "Oh! That was when we read your dad's letter where it said if only Harry was as good as a dog." As I am typing this chapter, I am looking at a quote by Andy Rooney in a collection of "dog quotes." The quote, "The average dog is a nicer person than the average person." Harry is not that nice. What did I mean by my quote? Much of my letter talked about Harry's lies "at sundry times and in divers manners." My meaning was that a dog can lie about someone but not lie about someone.

It was August 26, 2008, the date of our 41st wedding anniversary. The custody trial was scheduled for 9:00 am to noon. We, my wife and I, were going to finally have a chance to have our voices heard in testimony in court. We had been waiting for two years. We had to be sequestered along with Matt who was also to testify on Kristen's behalf. Harry would witness in behalf of himself. A few minutes later Kristen came out of the courtroom to tell us that Harry's lawyer had requested an hour and a half. We would be limited to an hour and a half. In no way would that be enough time to testify to all that had transpired in those two years.

Two hours later Kristen came to us outside in the hallway of the courtroom. Harry had finally finished. What do we do? It was decided that we start with Matt's testimony, then Mary Lynne's testimony, and finish with Kristen's. Kristen's lawyer was reluctant in letting me testify. Why? I could have testified first.

It was Tuesday. I had already started teaching my two College Algebra classes as an adjunct professor at Penn State Berks Campus held on Monday, Wednesday, and Friday. This was to be my first day of class as a teacher at RACC, Reading Area Community College. That class was to start at noon and follow with math lab hours as an assistant from 2 to 6. I told those around me that I would run to First Presbyterian Church and try to find out the progress of the suit against the church. The courthouse is on Court Street between 6th and 7th

Streets, the church on 5th Street, and RACC on 2nd Street. It was not a long run to the church. I asked the secretary if I could speak with the pastor, Dr. Keevil. She said he was not there. I asked if she knew anything of the suit. She said she could not say anything. Before the trial, she had been with the pastor, a representative from the Law Office of John Roland, and me when I was suspended without pay. Over those months, I left several messages with the church to have the pastor call me about the progress of the suit. There were no return calls. It had been four months since I resigned from my position as Children's Ministry Director because of the intended suit of the church and subsequent suspension.

I ran back to the courthouse and looked up. There was not enough time to go up all those floors, come down, and run to RACC. A lady was sitting on a bench nearby with a cell phone. I asked, "May I use your cell phone? It's a matter of grave importance." I might as well have said, "Life or death." To my surprise, she gave me the phone. I got my wife, Mary Lynne, and told her I was unable to find out anything about the suit. She told me that they learned that the suit had not been further pursued. However, she did not tell me at that time that my letter had been brought up in testimony on the witness stand. I ran to the RACC parking lot to pick up my teaching materials. I had parked there and walked to the courthouse earlier that morning. I ran up to the 5th floor in time to start my first class, Algebra I.

I finished teaching my class and went across the hall to start my job as math lab assistant. I was only working a few minutes when my wife came into the math lab. She tells me that Kristen finally got on the witness stand that afternoon and is still there. Better yet, they will allow me to testify. My math lab supervisor tells me to go. It was 2:30. I ran down the steps, dropped my teaching supplies in my car on the parking lot, and proceeded to run up Court Street to the courthouse, and took the elevator to the 5th floor. This time I didn't use the stairway. It was getting close to 3:00 and my daughter was still on the witness stand.

I did not realize that while I was waiting to take the witness stand my letter to the judge was being discussed again. The discussion was between both attorneys and the court. They knew more about the intended suit than I knew. The ultimate conclusion was that the suit was not carried out because the church knew nothing about my letter.

That was my intention. I had real facts about the case that I wanted to present.

What follows are the last discussions before I would take the stand:

Ms. Dautrich: On cross examination of my client, she asked about the letter that her father wrote, something about Mr. Hall and a dog. I think really what would be brought out was that one of the children said that they, you know, love being with their father, that they love the dog. And the next comment was something about Mr. Hall, if only he was—

The Court: In one of the letters?

Ms. Dautrich:—as good as a dog or something.

The Court: There was only one letter that came to me that I'm aware of.

Ms. Dautich: Exactly.

The Court: I didn't even—at the time, I didn't even know who sent it, whose side it was on. Because as soon as I saw it was a church matter, you know, solicitation from a church or something, I stopped reading it, sent it to counsel.

Zimmer: There were actually two, Your Honor, The second was sent to you on the fourth of June.

The Court: There was a second one?

Zimmer: June 4th, 2008.

Ms. Dautrich: I thought that was the only one.

Zimmer: I could be wrong. I thought there was a second. Maybe I'm wrong.

It was 4:00. Kristen and her lawyer came out of the courtroom. They told me I would be given only few minutes on the stand. I could not be asked anything that already been discussed. Also, I could not talk about Kristen's character because Judge Lash said, "all grandparents say that their child is a good parent." I had two suggestions. First, I would tell of catching Harry with the lie in the courthouse stairwell and the directive by his lawyer to all parties at that time. Next, I would tell that Bryce said in the first expungement hearing that "mommy did not hit me, Trey did." Judge Lash would not allow me to testify about my knowledge of what Bryce said at that hearing.

On the witness stand I got to tell of Harry's lie, but not the directive. Kristen's lawyer forgot to ask me about the directive. I thought this would be the most important testimony of the trial. When she said there were no more questions, I looked over to her and said, "What happened after that?" Judge Lash exclaims, "You cannot ask questions!"

Harry's lawyer starts with his cross examination of my testimony.

Zimmer: You're testifying today for your daughter, correct?
Myself: What?
Zimmer: You're testifying today for your daughter?
Myself: I'm testifying for the truth.
Zimmer: What is the truth?
Myself: What I know, what I've seen, what I've observed.
Zimmer: You think Harry is a liar?
Myself: Yes.
Zimmer: And your daughter tells the truth?
Myself: No, not always.
Zimmer: But you do?
Myself: But what?
Zimmer: But you do?
Myself: But I tell the truth? I have to here on the stand, here, yes.
Zimmer: So your daughter may lie on the stand, Mr. Hall may lie on the stand, but you—
Myself: I did not say my daughter would lie on the stand. I said but—
The Court: That's correct. You didn't phrase it that way. You said lies. You didn't say anything about on the stand.

Zimmer goes on to ask more questions about my letter. None of those questions were really pertinent to the case against Kristen. They were simply an example of his using the "fallacy of characterization" against me. He would go on to state that I wrote the second letter to the court. I did not. Judge Lash agreed that he did not receive that second letter.

Zimmer: And there were some fairly hurtful statements in the second correspondence, wouldn't you suggest, I mean statements made about Mr. Hall's deceased father?

Myself: That was not part of the letterhead paper.

Zimmer: It was not in the correspondence on church letterhead. But it was in your private correspondence, the one, the one sent to me?

Mr. Zimmer goes on to state that the "hurtful" thing I said was that Harry's father was an "alcoholic." I said it was the truth that his father was an alcoholic. But I did not write that in either my letter to the judge or Mark. Mr. Zimmer lies. What was "hurtful" is what Harry and Mr. Zimmer had said about Kristen all that morning. What follows is my letter addressed to Attorney, Mark Zimmer. It was addressed Dear Mark.

I want to first thank you for being Harry Hall's lawyer. I have tried for twenty months to have a conversation with Harry to no avail. He would not listen to a word. It is apparent he has listened by reading my letter to the judge. I can say, however, I was surprised to get that much of a reaction. I can understand why he would try to sue me, but why the church?

My purpose in using the letterhead was simply to verify my position in the church as Children's Ministry Director. I believe that I was told at in-service programs in school that a professional working with children must report child abuse even those not within that professional setting. I did not tell the pastor or ask permission to use the letterhead because I did not want anyone in church to know of it. Unfortunately, now many will learn of its contents.

The letterhead was also used as a justification for my statement in the second paragraph for "seeking justice." I did have the wrong title. It is <u>THE BOOK OF ORDER</u>. It is, however, the Constitution of the Presbyterian Church (U.S.A.). The section was called, "Reconciliation: Justice and Peace." It is section

W-7.4000. The church has reacted quickly. I have been suspended without pay. As a result, my witness to the children has been compromised. I have resigned from that position.

I do, however, stand by the content of the letter. Truth is not defamation of character. I will use my new found time to write support statements of the letter. You will be the first to get them. Thank you for communicating these words to Harry.

My letter was written without formality on purpose. It was meant to be a "friendly" letter. It had six purposes. First, it was written to inform those involved that the church was not aware of the situation and should not be involved in a suit. Second, I was informing him that I had resigned from my position at the church. Third, it was hoped that a dialogue could be opened with Mark being the mediator for both parties. Harry would not give the true reasons for this whole affair. Harry would say in court that we did not try to communicate with him. I thought this letter was communication. Fourth, I wanted Mark to know the truth of what Harry had done to Kristen the previous twenty months. Mark was Harry's third lawyer. He had only been Harry's lawyer for the four months prior to my writing the letter. Surely, Harry had only told him the lies he told everyone else. Fifth, I wanted to inform him that I would be writing articles concerning the case from the beginning to its final result. Sixth, we wanted to get rid of the secrecy of what each parent is doing with the children. Harry tells the children not to say what goes on when they are with him. They don't. Both parents should inform the other of what goes on so that both can be on the same page. That was a main part of the family counseling which apparently Harry does not agree to. In a letter I had informed Harry that I only taught Bryce how to ride the bicycle without training wheels because he asked. I told Harry I was intending to let him help Bryce, but that was not happening. I thought that was a good example of worthwhile communication.

I ceased sending my articles to Harry and his lawyer because I got nothing in return. Apparently, there would be no dialogue, no communication.

Chapter 2—Therapy

Put it in a Book

One fact to which I wanted to testify was that I, along with my wife and daughter, heard Bryce say in the expungement hearing, "mommy did not hit me, Trey did." Judge Lash would not allow that testimony. He would say if you want that testimony, it would have to be from the child live. I find that interesting. Most of Harry's testimony that morning was Harry saying what someone else had said. One of those was Bryce. Why was Harry's testimony of what Bryce supposedly said allowed, but my testimony of what I heard Bryce say disallowed? Why does Judge Lash say that testimony was part of "another case?" Earlier in the trial, Judge Lash allowed the testimony of Harry saying what Bryce said to the doctor.

The Court: And if you turn it around, if someone on his behalf had sent a letter putting whatever it is, saying whether it's truth or lies, you wouldn't want me to consider that, would you? These things I cannot consider. The only thing I can consider is what's in open court.

Myself: Is testimony.

The Court: Even to the point where testimony in another case, such as your grandchild testifying in another case, I can't—

Myself: Right.

The Court:—accept that either. It has to be here so I can examine it for myself that is the basis for justice. Do you understand that?

Myself: Yes.

The Court: So if there is impropriety, it was in you sending that letter.

Eight of the fourteen pages of my testimony were concerning my letter, suspension by the church, and attempted suit of the church. Most of that testimony was lecturing from Judge Lash. I was simply asked to affirm what he had to say. I did not consider that as giving testimony. Mark Zimmer wanted to discuss with me the meaning of truth and who was telling the truth. Actually, I thought the basis for justice was truth. Looking at my answer of "yes" to Judge Lash, I wonder what I was thinking at the time. I am also wondering if any of that testimony was pertinent to the case. I was accused, by Mark Zimmer, of writing something that was not in either letter. And, that was the only mention of content of either my letter to the judge or to Mark. Was that also a waste of testimony time?

Before I entered the courtroom for testimony, Judge Lash told both counsels that no items previously discussed should be repeated. I did not know when I took the witness stand that my letter had been discussed previously. I did not want it discussed. I only wanted to testify to facts I thought were really pertinent to the case. Why did Judge Lash allow discussion of my letter when Mark Zimmer brought it up with Kristen on the witness stand? Even more so, why did he allow Mr. Zimmer to bring it up again while I was on the witness stand? So, if there was impropriety, it was in Judge Lash allowing my letter to be brought up. Anyway, Judge Lash continues. Once again, notice my great testimony. Sarcasm intended.

The Court: Mr. Rathman, we're going to end this right now.

Myself: Okay.

The Court: All right. I don't know what hard feelings you have with Mr. Hall and yourself on other issues. But on this particular issue, you sent a letter to the Court. That's improper.

Myself: Yeah.

The Court: And you say you're seeking justice. The reason that's improper is a judge can't know whether—what you put in that letter are truth or lies.

Why does the court not know what hard feelings I have with Mr. Hall? What was Judge Lash listening to all morning and afternoon? The man is trying to destroy my daughter. That is one of my issues. The man is trying to alienate two young boys from a loving, nurturing mother. That is another issue. How does Judge Lash determine whether what Harry said on the witness stand was truth or lies? Hmm, that could be a third issue.

Why did Judge Lash say it was improper that I sent a letter? I heard one judge on TV state that you should send information to a judge. He said they need all the information they can get. Others recommended directly to me that I send a letter to the judge.

Upon studying the trial transcript, I learned that Judge Lash had asked pertinent questions of other witnesses. Why could he not ask me something pertinent? I did not have to be lectured on what was proper or improper. My few minutes on the stand were two valuable. I was told before taking the stand that I would have only three minutes. Judge Lash's lectures lasted twice that long. I was there to testify live. The way he said he wanted testimony. I was a witness of child abuse by Harry Hall. I am a witness to the facts of the case. Why was he stating it was improper for me to seek justice?

What might be considered amazing is that between Mr. Zimmer's and Judge Lash's questioning, they could convince me that Harry did not try to sue the church. Mr. Zimmer would take all the credit. My last statement on the witness stand was, "I am not blaming Harry for losing the job, no." What I did not get to say was that I blame attorney, Mark Zimmer, and the Honorable Judge, Scott Lash, for losing my job. Mark sent my letter to my church. Judge Lash had given my letter to Mark Zimmer. So, why did Mark Zimmer try to sue the church? Why does Judge Lash think it such a bad thing to write him a letter, but have no opinion of someone suing a church?

Earlier in my testimony, under the questioning of Mr. Zimmer, I said that I had written a bigger series of letters now to explain all the things that had happened.

Zimmer: So do you intend to send more letters?

Myself: No, I was told it doesn't do any good in court anyway, so I stopped it. I just wrote them for myself.

Zimmer: Okay.

Myself: Therapy.

I did not need all the lecturing from the judge. All I need is the next step in my therapy. It would not be to send letters to Mark Zimmer, Harry, or Judge Lash. My next step would be to write more letters and articles, and send them to others. Then, I will take that bigger series of letters and articles and put them in a book.

CHAPTER 3—EXTRA-ORDINARY LOVE

Character Reference for Kristen

Ms. Dautrich: Your Honor, my client had asked about her father testifying. He wasn't available this morning. He is available this afternoon. Most of what he would testify to would be repetitive. She had indicated it was important for her father to be able to talk.

Wrong, Jamie. I was available in the morning. I had to work in the afternoon. I was in the courtroom until we were sequestered in the hallway during Harry's testimony. I wanted to testify in the morning. Weeks before the trial I had written a "battle plan" which I wanted Kristen to give to Jamie her lawyer. It had been weeks since Jamie had seen Kristen. She got to meet with Kristen the day before the trial. She had not been given my plan. I believe she did not want me to take the stand because she was not prepared for me to be a witness. She had been working "pro bono" since Kristen's initial payment two years before the trial. It is true that some of my testimony may have been repetitive. But, I thought that would have been good to demonstrate corroborating testimony. There were, however, many facts of the case that I wanted to testify of which I was privy. The two things I did not want to talk about were my letter and the intended suit of the church. Below is the pronouncement of Judge Lash before I came into the courtroom to testify.

The Court: It's your call. If there's something germane, I'll hear it. But I don't want to hear repetition or she's a good parent. Every grandparent says that about their child.

That is wrong Your Honor. Harry and Kristen received Bryce as a foster child when he was only six months old because a grandparent said that the parents were not being good parents. I am sure they are not the only grandparents to have done that.

Only a week after writing my letter to the judge, I wrote an article concerning the character and experience of my daughter. The following is that article entitled, "A Matter of Character: Extra-Ordinary Love."

Kristen does not smoke, drink, or use illegal drugs. Nor do her parents. She does not use the language of the Hall's or beat her children. The words I would use to describe her character are accepting, trusting, forgiving, loving, and competitive. Those are her good traits. Her bad traits are that she will carry these to the extreme. She can be too accepting, too trusting, too forgiving, too loving, and too competitive. She is willing to accept a person wherever she finds that person. She was willing to accept Harry even after finding out about his family history. She should have run the opposite direction. She takes people at their word trusting that they are telling the truth. Even with all the lies Harry has told, she still accepts new information from him as the truth. She is too forgiving in that she gives too many second chances when she has been wronged by an individual. Kristen tries to be loving to all. At her receptionist job she has a smile for everyone, not a bone of prejudice. She has had offers for lunch at here job from people who were waiting for a friend or relative to have a procedure done at the hospital. If they were green and weighed 400 pounds, she would accept that offer just to be friendly. At least one evil man, evil according to Harry, she met through one of those offers. So being too friendly and too accepting may get you into trouble.

Having the traits above the custody evaluator would describe as being "naïve." Kristen does not like to lose, especially in relationships. She would not want it said of her that it was her fault for not making a relationship work. That is her competitive nature at work. This can be a problem. In dealing with people in the real world, carrying all these traits above to the extreme is a problem. However, having these traits what makes a mother special to their child. They are traits I would use to describe the unconditional love given by a mother.

Thru her elementary, Jr. and Sr. high, and college years, Kristen was a helper and later a teacher for me in the summers for the Bible and Sports Schools I directed. She was always a great encourager to the children. She loved the children as they loved her. Her classmates in high school recognized her genuineness in her kindness to others by voting her Homecoming Queen. Usually someone from the band is not chosen for that honor. She did not wish to be nominated. Her home room teacher urged her to accept the nomination. At one time she thought of becoming an early elementary school teacher. She opted, instead, to enroll in Millersville University to major in Social Work. She would receive a degree in that major and also minor in Criminal Justice. She believed she could help those who had been mistreated or even wrongly accused. Her college internship dealt with the abuse of children.

Her first job after graduation was working in a daycare. She did it faithfully, lovingly, and conscientiously, down to the changing of the diapers. She needed better pay, her pay only slightly above minimum wage, and something more appropriate for the use of her college degree. So she took a job with a firm that provided daycare for adults. Her first client was retarded middle aged man and the second an elderly gentleman. Again, she was liked and loved by both clients.

Finally, she was able to get a position as a Juvenile Corrections Officer and Counselor at the Berks County Juvenile Detention Center. After working there three years she resigned. Her resignation was not due to problems in working with the juveniles. She resigned because she did not like some of the methods that workers were encouraged to use in working with the juveniles. Some of those workers said she was too kind to the juveniles and she should use harsher language with them. She could not. But now, she is being accused by Harry of using "bad language" with a four year old. Using her methods at the detention center for three years, she never had to physically restrain a juvenile. Some of the workers were jealous of the respect she gained with the juveniles with her loving approach. A few weeks after she left, the supervisor of the facility was removed from the position because of tactics he used with the juveniles.

Her next job was working as a Conference Officer with Berks County Domestic Relations. She calculated and established child support orders and conducted child support conferences. After four years she resigned from that position. By that time she was married to Harry Hall and had planned to soon have children. She did not like the pressure of having to tell parents the amount of money they would have to pay for support. She felt it was unfair that the ones that paid the most support got to see the children the least. Maybe, that is why in the beginning of this custody battle she only wanted to go for 50/50 custody with Harry. She only wanted to be fair. Harry did not.

So next, she took a job as a County Clerk in the Berks County Prothonotary Office. It would be a pay cut, but there would be less emotional pressure. Harry and Kristen became Foster parents of Bryce in September of 2002. Harry and Kristen had been in Foster training for only a few weeks when Bryce came to them at six months old. Not long after getting Bryce, Kristen would become that stay at home mom that was discussed before the marriage. There would be no daycare. Harry and Kristen had been trying, without success to have a child before entering the Foster Parent program. They would continue as Foster parents until Bryce was adopted in 2004.

Kristen would not take a job again until January of 2006. Harry was getting less hours of work and told Kristen it was necessary that she find part time work. She was able to find a position with Concern, an agency that provides adoption services. It is the same agency through whom Harry and Kristen adopted Bryce. Her job was to prepare Foster parents and their foster child for adoption. She made portfolios for the children. She used the money earned for the family daily living expenses. It was this part time job that Kristen would eventually have to give up when Harry filed that first PFA, Protection from Abuse, charge. Harry destroyed the computer she used to do her work and the child abuse accusation made her legally unable to work with children. That job had paid twenty dollars per hour. Her receptionist job at the hospital pays less than ten dollars per hour.

Kristen had been accused of not loving Bryce, of treating him differently than Trey. "Not loving" is not what Kristen does. She demonstrated love to those babies and children at the daycare center brought their by mothers on welfare. She showed love to the retarded man and elderly man. She showed love to those juveniles in the detention center who only a mother could love. She treated with kindness and with respect those with whom she dealt with in Domestic Relations. How could she not show love to Bryce. To show love to her birth son is a given, but that is ordinary love. The love she has shown to Bryce has been extra-ordinary.

She gave up her job when receiving Bryce. For the next twelve months Bryce had all of her attention as the only child. Then, Trey was born. Attention had to be shared. It would not be 50/50. Bryce was only 18 months old when Trey was born. At that age Bryce was very mobile, into everything, and only content when he was. So, who got most of the time, love, and attention from Kristen? Bryce did, 80/20. The only way for her to give special attention to Trey was for her to have help with Bryce. Unfortunately, little help was to come from Harry instead, it came from my wife and I. Many times I would take Bryce aside and play with him, or go on special excursions to places like "Roadside America" or "Cabella's." Those excursions were interesting. Bryce loved playing "hide and seek" in those places. Of course, I was always the seeker.

The several months before the adoption would be crucial. By the time of the adoption, Bryce would be a few months past two years old. Kristen was realizing already that Bryce was a little different from the normal child. She also needed more help from Harry. What did Harry do at this time? He took a job which required him to work more than ten hours a day for seven days a week. In addition there was two hours of commuting time as the job was near Philadelphia. Harry would leave home before the boys would get up and get home after they went to bed. But Harry would make a lot of money. The pay rate was higher than that in Reading. Harry is all about a lot of money. At one point Kristen pleaded with Harry to take a day off to spend with the family. He would not. This would be the falling out of love period. She had put up with Harry's condescending attitude and other traits, but this was a breaking point.

Seeing she was to get no help from Harry, only criticism, she was having doubts about proceeding with the adoption. She had worked in the Juvenile Detention Center and realized a lot of the juveniles there were from parents who have been involved in crimes. Bryce was from two such parents. She expressed concern to Harry. He would not listen. Bryce would be adopted. Trey would have his brother. Kristen would go through with the adoption. Why? It was not because of Harry's insistence. It was because Kristen thought Bryce would get more love from her than anyone else, and she would have the help of her parents.

After the hearing on the first PFA, Kristen was allowed to go home and babysit for free for Harry. She did it willingly because of her love for her children. Often, during that time, my wife and I had to pick up Kristen from Harry's when he got home. She was borrowing one of our two cars and some days we needed both. Harry always made a scene during those pickups as she said her good-bye to her pleading children. Even today, the children dread the time when they have to be taken back to Harry. At least, the dog is there.

When Harry wanted Kristen to sign the house over to him, she did it willingly. She did not do it because Harry filed the second PFA against Kristen accusing her of abusing him. That was a ridiculous charge. She signed it over to him because she wanted the boys to have the house they knew. One they could grew up in. She did it because of her love for the boys. After these past two years, I do not believe they have any good memories left of the family being together in that house. Trey was only three and Bryce four and a half when Harry filed that first PFA.

For the eight months after the first PFA, Harry had temporary primary custody mostly because he had possession of the marital residence. Kristen found a job at St. Joseph's Medical Center. Any job she accepted would have to be with the children's best interests in mind. She needed the job to give her the chance to earn 50/50 custody. It had already been three months of Harry's temporary primary custody when she took the job. She did not expect it to be many more months of that custody arrangement.

After going through the evaluation process, Kristen finally received 50/50 custody. Upon receiving that recommendation, Harry would start looking for things of which he could accuse Kristen of child abuse. Thus the two bumps on the head accusations filed as PSR's against Kristen, neither of which she caused. The biggest bump on the head of Bryce I felt was the one Bryce received at Harry's house. It was between the times of the bumps used as accusations by Harry. Bryce got the bump when he got up quickly from sitting on the lawn tractor under the deck at Harry' house. Harry called Kristen about the bump. He did not have to call. She would not have accused Harry of child abuse. She never has. She was willing to give him 50/50.

In all that Kristen has done it has been in the best interest of the boys. She is fighting for custody because of her love for both them. She has shown love, extra ordinary love.

Your Honor, is there anything in this article you would like to have known before awarding primary custody to Harry Hall?

CHAPTER 4—ABUSE OF CHRISTIANITY

A Letter Not Sent

In my letter to Judge Lash I wrote that I would be giving information to substantiate my claims in that letter. In my letter to Mark Zimmer I wrote that I will use my new found time to write the supporting statements of that same letter to the judge. In court I said that I had written more letters and articles substantiating my claims of Harry's abuses. My letter to Judge Lash contained the statement, "He has abused Christianity." A few weeks after writing my letter to Judge Lash, I wrote an article with the title, "Abuse of Christianity." I wrote it in the form of a letter to Harry. I did not intend to actually send the letter to Harry. I do not think that I did. It was written to substantiate my statement in the letter. You could say I wrote it for myself. Does that make me self indulgent? I did not know when writing it that it was part of my therapy.

> Thank you, Harry, for proving my points. I do not know the specifics about the suit of my church. I do not know if it is still being pursued. I don't see how it could be when the church did not know about my letter. You, however, have proved my major point. That is, you are all about revenge and financial gain. I should have included that you don't care what you have to do

to achieve the above or who you are adversely affecting with your revenge.

You have succeeded in defaming my character and forcing me to resign from my position as Children's Ministry Director. Of course it will be difficult for me to find a part time job like this for $20,000 plus. This sounds like grounds for a suit – defamation of character and loss of income. It also means I will not have that money to spend on my grandsons and daughter. But you have not considered that, or have you?

The church had been looking for a Children's Ministry Director for a year. It is difficult to find someone of quality and experience for a part time position. I worked closely with the children at FPC. For the three young Hispanic children from the neighborhood I had at least become a grandfather figure. We had a Bible and Sports School and a Christmas program that the children enjoyed. I did not miss one Sunday with the children in the ten months I was their CMD and teacher. Would you please tell the children the reason they no longer have their teacher? Would you like to explain to your own children how you sued a church and caused their grandfather to lose his job? Did you ever explain to your children why their mother can not take them to Sunday school? In all you have done have you considered the legacy you are leaving Harry III? Knowing the history of Harry I and Harry II, would he want to be known as Harry III?

A Christian would defend the honor of his daughter when knowing the truth of how she was wrongly accused. That is what I must do. A Christian must fight for justice when there is injustice. I do not know what you are asking from the church. If it is money, it proves my point that you are doing it for financial gain.

I know the little game you are playing in going to church now, or at least since filing that first PFA. A Christian is not simply one who attends a Christian church. A Christian is a part of one body of all believers. If you are a Christian, you are suing yourself. A Christian would have believed his wife, not the lies of a stranger. If something did happen, a Christian would seek reconciliation, not revenge. We are to be ministers of reconciliation.

You would think after 20 months of attending church that you would have picked up on something of what it means to be a Christian. What does your pastor think of your suing a church? Are your "fruits" those of the "flesh" or those of the "spirit?" Or, do you think I am just a "nut?" Do you remember our one talk two days after you filed the first PFA? I explained how the husband is to be head of the marriage as Christ is the head of the church. The husband is to love his wife as Christ loves His Church. I talked of Christ dying for his bride, the Church. I spoke that He forgives those in His Church. You got it wrong. You have not died for your bride. Instead, you have crucified your bride. If you call yourself a Christian, you defame the name of Christ. You are an abuser of Christianity.

Before the PFA, Harry seldom attended church. It was his day to recuperate. When he did attend he appeared uncomfortable. When the children came into the family, his excuse was that he did not want to put them into the nursery. He barely tolerated Kristen's playing in the bell choir or with BRASS IN PRAISE. After filing the PFA, he started attending church regularly with the boys. He attended the church where his sister attended. Of course, it was all for show. He would be able to impress others that he was the more religious parent. He would even impress the custody evaluator and the judge. Kristen, on the other hand, did not take the boys to church on Sunday mornings when in her custody. For the most of the two years since the first PFA, she only had the boys for four mornings a month. Two of those were Sunday mornings. When she worked during the week, she left home each morning before the boys woke up. Those Sunday mornings with the boys were too precious to give the boys to others. Keep in mind that for most of those two years Kristen was under a "founded" record for indicated child abuse. She would not have been allowed to go with the boys into a class with other children. She was not able to bring her own children to my activities I had for the entire time I was Children's Ministry Director for First Presbyterian Church. Once Harry won primary custody in the custody trial of 2008, he ceased taking his children to church.

Chapter 5—Warning Signs

The Time before the First PFA

Does your spouse handle all the finances for your family? Do you have a separate checking account, savings account, and credit card? Do you sign the bottom line of the tax forms your husband puts in front of you without looking at the other pages? Do you vote in favor of the bill without actually reading it? Sorry, wrong story. Do you know how much your husband earns weekly, monthly, or yearly? Does your husband pay all the bills? Do you know your assets? Does your husband give you an allowance? Do you know how much money is in your joint checking account? Are you "happy" that your husband handles all the finances? Kristen was "deliriously happy" that Harry would handle all the finances. She would also give the wrong answers to the other questions.

Kristen's first marriage with Tim lasted about a year. One important reason for the divorce was that Kristen wanted children. He did not. Perhaps, that should have been discussed before they got married. A second reason dealt with finances. Her husband tried to start a business selling cleaning products for the home. He needed thousands of dollars to buy the products needed to start the business. It was his plan that eventually he would become a distributor with others under him. She allowed him to use her credit card with the stipulation that she would not have to do the selling. They ended up with enough cleaning products for several life times. Kristen paid the three hundred dollars for the divorce. A few months after her divorce, she filed for bankruptcy. Hopefully, she had learned two warning signs. First, before agreeing to marriage, ask your spouse about children. The second should have been that you learn about how your spouse will deal with finances.

Kristen met Harry at the allergist's office. They were both there to get shots. They both "snickered" as a parent was having trouble with their child. They got to talking. They agreed to meet and talk some more. Harry was not married. Kristen was separated and filing for a divorce. Kristen wanted children and so did Harry. Harry said he wanted the mother of his children to be a stay at home mom. Kristen saw possibilities. Kristen met his family. Kristen was impressed by what Harry rose above. She should have seen the warning sign. Instead, they were married on July 28, 2000. Even the wedding plans should have been a warning sign. Kristen would have been satisfied getting married at the Justice of the Peace with only a small reception if any. Harry insisted on the more expensive wedding and reception. There was another warning sign given to Kristen on that special day. One of Harry's sisters, Kristen thought jokingly at the time, said, "Harry surprised us telling us he was getting married. We thought he was gay." Harry was over thirty. He had never talked to Kristen of any former romances. Again, Harry had said on a number of occasions that two men living together can really make out well financially. What was he suggesting? Maybe Kristen missed more warning signs.

Kristen had been impressed that Harry saved thousands of dollars over his life. She was also impressed by his story of moving out on his own shortly after high school. She was impressed how he eventually had completed an apprenticeship program to become a member of the pipe fitter's union. He also served as an unofficial guardian, on separate occasions, of two of his nephews when he was not much older than them. All this was accomplished before having met Kristen. But there was a warning sign. Both nephews would eventually wind up in trouble with the law. Apparently, Harry's good traits were not transferrable to his nephews.

Harry and Kristen, working together, were able to save more money, enough to buy land and build a house. Harry did a lot of work in building the house. He was able to install the radiant heating system. I, along with others, helped with that project. He also installed a different kind of cooling system. It never worked. But Harry was able to get all his money back from that failed project. Family from both sides helped in painting the inside and doing the other projects. Kristen had actually helped Harry in the design plans for the house. Harry built a huge deck in back of the house. He would pay a contractor to build the railing for the deck. Harry said he did not like the way the corners were done. So he paid the contractor only for the materials and not for labor. He would brag about withholding that money. In my letter to the judge I would write, "He abused those with whom he did business." I consider this a warning sign.

Before receiving Bryce as a Foster child, Kristen had worked for more than eight years for the County of Berks. She was owed retirement money. On receiving that money, she would not put that away for retirement. Partially on Harry's urging and thinking it the fair thing to do, she used that money to pay off her college loans. They would not have that monthly payment. Harry would not have to help in paying off her student loans. Maybe, that was a warning sign. Kristen would not have that money for herself for an emergency. She would have no other savings.

Four months after getting Bryce as a Foster child, Kristen got pregnant. It was shortly after Harry got the needed operation. Kristen had gone through a number of tests to find out why she could not get pregnant. It was not her problem. It was Harry's. It was not long after the birth of Trey that Harry took a job with a lot of overtime. The job was located in the Philadelphia area with a higher pay scale then local. He would make a lot of money. Kristen would not learn how much. He would work more than ten hours a day and have a two hour commute. It would be for seven days a week and last six months. Kristen could not get Harry to take one day off to be with the family and help with the boys. That was a warning sign.

There was something that really bothered me when Harry and Kristen first got Bryce as a Foster child. Taking in a Foster child, they were allowed to get free milk from a program called WICA. Harry would be angry with Kristen if she did not take advantage of the program. It seemed to me that it cost as much to drive into the city as the free milk was worth. When anything was supposedly free, there was Harry. When Kristen had Trey, she really needed help with the two boys. Many times, Mary Lynne or the both of us would drive Kristen into town with the boys to receive the free milk. Knowing the amount of money Harry made, we felt "creepy" going into town to receive free milk with other "welfare mothers" who received the same. Of course Harry made out well on those days because he did not have to pay for the gas. Besides, Harry would drink some of that milk. Kristen is lactate intolerant. Now that was a warning sign.

There were some things about Harry that bothered my wife that didn't occur to me. She told me that Kristen had told her that Harry told her that he was jealous of Kristen when she was pregnant. He said he wished that he was having the baby. I say, "go for it Harry." I saw what Mary Lynne meant about two years after Kristen gave birth to Trey. Harry and Kristen were going on a vacation that required them to stay three nights. We would babysit for both boys. It would be the first time that Harry and Kristen would not have the boys overnight. After pulling into the driveway as they returned, Harry jumps out of the Durango to run into the house to be the first to hug and kiss the boys. Kristen can probably run faster than Harry. She just did not realize there was going to be a race. I give Mary Lynne credit for seeing that warning sign.

In January of 2006, Harry explained to Kristen that he needed help with the family finances. He was not getting overtime like he had in the past. At least he was getting home earlier and could help with the boys. So Kristen looked and found a part time job with Concern. It was the same organization through whom they received Bryce as a Foster child and eventually adopted him. She would help in preparing Foster children for adoption. Some of the work could be done on the computer at home. When visiting the foster child and parent, she could have her parents or Harry babysit the boys. When she started work the allowance from Harry for running the household stopped. Now she would use only her money to run the household. She also started receiving three hundred dollars a month for Bryce because she worked to get him diagnosed with special needs. That money was also used by Kristen to run the household. It should have been a warning sign when Harry stopped the allowance.

In March of 2006, Harry took out a home equity loan. He told Kristen he would be able to pay off other loans including the one for the Dodge Durango. They had gotten that as the family vehicle with the trade in of Kristen's Cavalier. Harry still had his Chevy pick up truck with close to three hundred thousand miles. We did not understand at the time of the equity loan that it was a warning sign. Kristen never learned the amount of equity in the home at the time or the amount of the loan.

Something else vitally important to the understanding of this issue of warning signs happened that same month. Harry was told that his father had five months to live. His father had a disease of the liver. Harry, eight months later to the custody evaluator, would describe his father as having been a "verbally abusive alcoholic." Harry had told Kristen, before they were married, that he (not his father) had gone to psychotherapy for ten years. He told the evaluator that he went to psychotherapy to help to overcome the verbal abuse from his father. Harry said that his father was especially verbally abusive to his mother. He said he left his home as soon as he could afford it so that he could get away from his father. That might have been a warning sign.

With the announcement of his father's impending death, an extreme change in Harry's attitude and actions towards his father occurred. Before, he would rarely take the boys and Kristen to see his father. Now, he would take the boys to see him as often as he could. It appeared he no longer hated his father. Now he seemed to hate the fact that his father was dying. Harry could not simply hate a fact. He had to direct his hate at something or someone. To whom would he direct his hate and revenge? How should I know? I am a math teacher. Where is a psychiatrist when I need one? What was Harry's psychotherapist doing with Harry at this time? I do not hate Harry? I believe I know why he is angry. I believe Harry needs help. Does anyone see a warning sign?

Harry was now willing to carry out his father's wishes for the last months of his life. His father wished for a pre-death party. I am not sure which came first, the home equity loan or the knowledge of his father's impending death. Either way, Harry had the money for the party. The party was to be held at the American Legion in Birdsboro. That is where Harry's father spent most of his life. He had not held a job during most of his son's life as he was on disability all those years. Now his family and friends could enjoy the place he enjoyed the most. Actually, we sort of enjoyed the party. I am not kidding! This was not a warning sign.

It was July 4, 2006. Harry, Kristen, and the boys were to join us to watch one of the most amazing parades in America, the Wyomissing 4th of July parade. It is a made for movie parade without being made for a movie. All that is needed is seventy-six trombones. It was a great parade as usual. There were lots of flags, lots of stars, and lots of stripes. Kristen had the boys looking sharp. Their shirts had white stars, one being red with blue trim and the other the reverse. Across the street I noticed a person taking pictures. I thought the pictures were of the parade. After the parade the photographer came across the street toward us. She asked for permission to use one of the pictures of the boys for the Reading Eagle. Harry and Kristen signed a paper to allow a photograph to be used for the newspaper. The next day there was a picture of Trey in the Reading Eagle. It was a good picture. To our surprise, Harry was upset with the picture. He was upset that the picture was not one with both boys. That's the way it goes Harry. What was it that was really bothering Harry? We missed a warning sign.

I give one more warning sign, maybe two. Beware when things have the appearance of getting better, while the circumstances dictate they would get worse.

A few days after the parade, my wife and I were with Kristen's family at their house. The phone rang and Harry went to answer it. It must have been a strange call. It was. We would learn that it was a message from an irate woman saying that her boyfriend was having an affair with Kristen. She said Kristen's phone number, along with others, was one of the numbers on his phone. We also learned that Harry went to meet this woman at a bar. There, the woman would tell Harry that her boyfriend said he had the affair with Kristen when she was working at the courthouse. Kristen told us that the phone caller's boyfriend did have an affair with someone working at Domestic Relations. It was not Kristen. Kristen, only a year later, would learn that Danny did tell the lie about having an affair with Kristen to his girl friend. Kristen last worked at the courthouse four years before the phone call. Kristen first met Danny several years before that time. Danny was her social work project. On occasion, she would meet him at lunch outside the courthouse. She would try to teach him how he should treat women.

She was trying to rehabilitate him. He was wearing orange clothing when she first met him. He was serving time for abusing the woman who made that phone call. This was not a warning sign. The warning signs follow.

To Kristen's surprise, Harry did not dwell on that phone call. Yes, we did learn he went to talk to that woman. Perhaps, he recognized the fact that she could not be having an affair. Kristen was with the boys 24-7. The only time she was not with them was when her parents babysat while she went grocery shopping. What followed, Kristen describes as some the best weeks she had with Harry. There was a reunion with my side of the family. Two weeks later, we had a reunion with Mary Lynne's side of the family. Things seemed to be going well with Kristen and Harry. That was a warning sign. On the last day of July Harry gave Kristen a dozen roses. That was a first. That was another warning sign.

Chapter 6—The Stoning Incident

Filing the First PFA

It was almost two weeks after the roses. Mother was in the kitchen. The boys were outside. I don't know where Harry was, but I believe he was waiting for something to happen. Something happened. Kristen heard a cry from Trey. She sprang outside to see "what was the matter." The boys were standing in the stone driveway. Bryce had just clunked Trey on the back of the head with a small stone from the driveway. Kristen picked up a stone to use as an object lesson. She would go on to say something like, "do you know what it would feel like to be hit by this stone?" Harry arrives and takes Bryce away for a spanking. Kristen lets Harry do the spanking. She discovered early on that with Bryce spanking does not really work. With Bryce, you simply try to keep him from hurting himself and others. Kristen didn't know it then, but this would be the last time that Harry would see Kristen in some way discipline or instruct either of the boys. At that time, Bryce was only four and a half and Trey would soon turn three.

The commotion was over in a minute. Kristen would proceed to the basement to do work on the computer while Harry took control of the boys. Kristen had part time employment with an organization called Concern. It was the same organization through whom they acquired Bryce as a Foster child and later aided in his adoption. She was now helping other children to be adopted. It was difficult getting work done when home alone with the boys. By themselves the boys could get into trouble. Together, the boys could get into trouble exponentially. She would have to make good use of this time with Harry watching them.

She had been working about two hours when she started wondering how Harry and the boys could be so quiet. The doorbell rang and then she heard knocking on the door. She proceeded up the stairs to the front door. She opened the door and was greeted by two policemen from the Oley Police Department. Her immediate thought was not what would be told. They told her that she would have to vacate the premises. She looked around. Harry and the boys were nowhere to be seen. They told Kristen that Harry filed an emergency 24 hour PFA, that is, a Protection from Abuse petition against Kristen. Kristen had worked for the Berks County in Domestic Relations. She knew about PFA's. She was apologetic to the police. She understood they were just doing their job. They let Kristen gather up a few items. She left the home using Harry's pickup. She would go to her parent's home and live there the next three months.

Of what was Kristen accused? The findings of fact as stated by Judge Scott Lash in his report for the Custody trial of August 26, 2008 are as follows:

> The parties separated pursuant to a Protection from Abuse Petition filed by Father on August 11, 2006. Father's allegations related Mother being menacing, including threatening to throw a stone at Bryce. A Temporary Protection from Abuse Order was entered on August 11, 2006 awarding Father temporary custody of the Minor Children, with Mother to have no contact with the Minor Children. On August 25, 2006, at the time scheduled for the hearing on the Protection from Abuse Petition, Father agreed to withdraw his Petition, and the Temporary Order was vacated.

The attempted stoning was described above. What was meant by "menacing?" Some of that was that it was claimed she used bad language against Bryce. Harry wrote, on the PFA, the language of the "Hall family", not Kristen's. Other lies of menacing, as described by Harry, can be seen from the dialogue in the custody trial of 2008. Keep in mind his testimony in that trial could only be of events that occurred before August 11, 2006. Harry had no chance to be an eyewitness of such events after that date. Yet, in the custody trial and prior custody evaluations he would testify with many accusations against Kristen. None of those could he have observed. Harry attributed his knowledge of all those accusations to others. The following dialogue is from the trial.

Zimmer: Is there any disparity of the way the mother treats the two children?

Harry: Yes.

Zimmer: Could you go into some detail?

Harry: There's always been a disparity between the kids. Bryce would get disciplined severely for his things he would do wrong, and Trey would—our youngest child would just get a, oh, sweetie, you know, a little pat on the back, don't do that kind of a thing.

Zimmer: Is the disparity of treatment obvious enough that it would be obvious to the children?

Harry: Yes.

Zimmer: Does she discipline the children differently? (Harry just answered that, Zimmer.)

Harry: Yes.

Zimmer: How so? (I didn't know you knew Chinese. Sorry for the sarcasm.)

Harry: Like I said, Bryce would get more severe. He would—he would get physically twisted or—terrorized, would get the scream close to the face, you know, while he was being held, those kinds of things,—

Again, this had to be going on before Trey had turned three and Bryce was four and a half. Do you discipline those ages differently? Anyway, Harry's testimony was all lies. I do, however, have some questions for Harry. What were you doing while Kristen was disciplining Bryce? If she was terrorizing Bryce, why did you not stop her? When Bryce was doing wrong, why did you not take care of the discipline or instruction? I think we need to make distinctions between the words discipline, instruction, and punishment. Why did you allow your lawyer to lead you down this path of self-incriminating testimony?

Later in the trial Harry said that Kristen would call Bryce "every name under the sun." I don't even know "every name under the sun." I believe Harry must have sat around a table with his family one day and tried to think what names Harry could use in that first PFA. Harry's oldest sister was adept at filing PFA's. The names in the first PFA were as Harry said. I cannot write them here. I would never have thought of them. Kristen would not use them. Kristen does admit to calling Bryce "fatty" when he was about a year old. It was said "lovingly" and "sweetly." He was "chubby" at six months old when he was first given to Harry and Kristen as a Foster child. Sorry!

What did Harry achieve in having Judge Lash sign that first PFA? Filing a PFA, as Harry did, is a marriage killer. It also had the effect of murdering her husband. How so? She lost her means of financial support as a stay-at-home mom. She lost the person who was supposed to be giving her emotional support. She lost the person who was supposed to be the one to help her with the boys. Harry was mostly absent to help her with the boys before the PFA. Now he was guaranteeing that he would not be that helpmate.

She lost employment opportunities. Not only would they be lost for the immediate time, they would be lost for her future. The abuse charge meant that she could not visit the child she was preparing for adoption. Because she had to leave the family home for two weeks, she could not do the paper work on the family computer. When allowed back in the home two weeks later, the computer was gone. Harry, however, had gotten a new computer for himself. Kristen would have to use her parent's computer. She had to buy the necessary software to finish the report on the last client she had with Concern.

She lost her house and most of what was in it. Some would argue she didn't legally lose her house at that time, but effectually that was what happened. There would be only two more nights that she would spend in that house. It would be three months until she was able to acquire an apartment. It was then she was able to take some items from the house. The only items she would take were those she had purchased before her marriage or those that were her parent's and were given to help furnish the marital residence. When Harry would say in the custody trial he gave her everything 50/50, he was referring to those two classes of items. Everything that was his before or that was purchased since the marriage he claimed as his own, including the Durango and the dog. Many personal items belonging to Kristen were still in that house at the time of the trial.

She lost her motherhood, at least for those first two weeks after filing the PFA. It was as if the boys were "kidnapped." She did not see nor hear from the boys. Neither would the boys see or hear from Kristen. I call that "alienation" from the mother. I call that "child abuse." What did Harry say to the boys concerning their mother during those two weeks? How did he explain the absence of their mother? I have no clue. I believe Judge Lash has no clue. Does he care? Harry Hall II, what did you tell the boys?

She lost her respect and honor as a person. When this happens based on lies, I believe it is called defamation of character. What was the ultimate result of Judge Lash signing that first PFA? Kristen was pronounced guilty and sentenced without trial or even a chance to speak on her own behalf. I had always thought a citizen was presumed innocent. I asked Kristen why the judge signed the PFA in the first place. Kristen had worked in Domestic Relations and understood. She said that judges have to sign the PHA's in order to protect them selves. From what must they protect them selves? I still do not understand. I am seeing more and more that judges do not seem to be accountable to anyone.

Kristen's attorney, upon reading the PFA, said that the accusations would not hold up. They did not constitute the requirements for a PFA to be upheld even if they were true. It would be easy to have the PFA dismissed. They were, two weeks later, because Harry withdrew the charges. In Judge Lash's trial report, he commends Harry for dropping the charges. What he does not report was that Harry dropped the charges because Kristen signed a paper that would give Harry the temporary primary custody he wanted. Judge Lash did not report that Harry threatened he would not drop the charges until she signed the paper. Kristen knew from her experience in Domestic Relations that if she did not sign the papers then, she would not see her children until there would be a custody hearing. She knew that would take many months. In her case, it did take eight months for a decision to be made that she would receive 50/50 custody. It may have taken that long before she would have seen her boys. In addition, Kristen knew, under her circumstances at that time, that Harry would have received temporary primary custody because he had physical control of the marital residence. He gained that control with that emergency 24 hour PFA on August 10 when the Oley Police had Kristen removed from her home. Judge Lash fails to mention that fact in his finding of the facts of his custody trial report. Harry accomplished a lot with those first lies in that first PFA, more than we first thought. How many others have had a similar experience in family court? I know there was at least one too many.

CHAPTER 7- MULTITASKER

Preparations and Accomplishments

Harry Hall had made many preparations in the weeks before the first PFA. He was able to accomplish much in the days before, the day of, and the days immediately after filing that PFA. He accomplished so much that I must give him credit for being a multitasker. According to my "spell check", I invented a new word. So be it. Harry was a man with a lot of money to spend. He was also a man with a relationship to mend, and one to tear apart. I am talking about his father and his wife. As mentioned, Harry must have spent a good amount of money on that pre-death party. The amount of food, drink, and people at the American Legion was substantial. It had to take time and energy in planning that event. Harry was mending his relationship with his father. Harry would also spend money on Kristen that month. It was for a beautiful Mother's Day card. The sentiments, that is, the words, were surprisingly appropriate. So much so, that Kristen saved that card. So it seemed Harry was also seeking to improve his relationship with Kristen.

Kristen had earlier been asked to be in an attendant in her cousins wedding in June. The wedding would be held in Charleston, South Carolina. Kristen said that she would save the family the money by going there by herself. Harry said he would pay for the whole family to go to Charleston. The trip would cost a lot of money for someone as frugal as Harry. She had already been surprised that Harry would let her spend money for the dress. We learned in court, more than two years later, Harry spent a lot more that June. That was the same June Harry would claim he hired a lawyer. The purpose for the lawyer was to help him obtain primary custody of the boys thru the use of child abuse accusations. Harry was multitasking.

In the month of July, Harry would do more spending of both money and time on Kristen. Remember the phone call from the accuser of the affair? Harry may have started his electronic surveillance of Kristen after that call. Danny was Kristen's social work project at the time she was working for the County. When she became a stay-at-home mom she no longer had time for such a project. Her project had become three boys, including Harry. It had been a long time since Kristen and Danny had seen each other. By chance, they would see each other across a parking lot of a mini mall on route 12 where Danny was working on construction. Several days later, much to Kristen's surprise and dismay, Danny appeared at her home. He had found out her address and arrived there on motorcycle. He knocked on the door. She told him he should not have come there. He said he wanted to talk. She said she would give him her phone number, but he must leave immediately. He left putting her phone number on his cell phone. Danny's girlfriend would call all the numbers on his cell phone. She got Harry. Also, she would erase all Danny's phone numbers. Danny would have to go back to Kristen's house again. If there was an affair, why did Danny not know Kristen's phone number? The simple answer was that there was no affair between Kristen and Danny.

Kristen is in the bathroom. She hears a motorcycle outside. She hears a doorbell. Bryce lets Danny inside. Kristen asks why he came back despite her warning. He says he needs her phone number again. But now Kristen needs to talk to him about Allison's phone call. She gives him her phone number again so he will leave quickly. She would talk to him on the phone another day. Danny told Kristen that Allison was saying that he had an affair with Kristen when Kristen worked for Domestic Relations more than six years ago. Kristen knew Danny did have an affair with someone in Domestic Relations at that time. It wasn't with Kristen. Kristen had listened to his problems those many years ago. Now Kristen would tell Danny her problem. That would be a big mistake. Harry had her under electronic surveillance.

Kristen would tell Danny of Harry's condescending attitude. She told how she had gotten little help from him with the boys the past years. He was more interested in making money. She told Danny things had been different since Harry learned that his father had been given a death sentence due to his years of drinking. Harry was now taking more time with the boys, taking them to visit his dying father. Kristen told Danny that she was somewhat fearful for Trey, not yet three at the time. Bryce, a little over four, had yet to learn fear in what he may do to himself or others. Recently, Bryce had hit Trey with an object not understanding the consequences of what he was doing.

Danny told Kristen he was moving out of the state. He forgot to mention the little fact that Allison was filing charges against him again. Do you know those little "white lies" you may tell when greeting someone or say good-bye? When asked, "How are you today?" You say, "Great." However, you really are not feeling that great. It's like saying as you leave, "It was great to see you today." You wished, however, you had not seen them at all. For Kristen this would be one of those moments. She would say her good-bye by trying to make Danny feel important. She said to Danny, "I should just leave Harry, take Trey, and go with you." She lied. Two years later on the witness stand I would tell the court that Kristen does lie. This is the lie I thought about at that moment. Unfortunately, this was the lie Harry would obtain thru his electronic surveillance. She had no intention on leaving Harry or Bryce. She is not the type of person that would want to be blamed for a relationship not working. She was committed to her marriage.

The date of the stoning was Thursday, August 10, 2006. Shortly after the stoning of Trey by Bryce, Harry took the boys and went to the District Judge's office to file the emergency 24 hour Protection from Abuse Petition. Thru that petition he was able to use the Oley Police to force Kristen to vacate the house. When they came to the house they were quite apologetic about what they had to do. They said it would probably only last the 24 hours and she should not worry. Apparently, they realized how bogus the charge sounded. Kristen did not leave kicking and screaming. She was apologetic to the officers expressing that she understood that it was just a job they had to do. She did say, however, she did not believe this would be the last thing Harry would do to her.

That night Kristen called Harry from her parent's house. She told him she would be willing to go to counseling if he would not file a regular PFA. He said he would not file that PFA if she would admit to having an affair. Kristen said she could not admit to an affair. There was no affair. The next day Harry filed the PFA with Judge Lash. From what we would learn in the following years, we would come to understand that Harry would not have dropped the PFA if she did admit to an affair. He would have used that confession to his advantage against her. I consider filing two PFA's in two days to be multitasking.

Harry had a lawyer. Kristen did not. The next morning, Friday, August 11, we would drive into Reading. We had gone less than a mile when Kristen told us she thought we were being followed. She continued to bop up and down peering out the rear window all the way to Reading. All the while she was checking if we were being followed. We were. She first went into "Women in Crisis" to see if she could obtain counsel at that time. No one was available at the moment. She checked with the courthouse to see if Harry followed through in filing a PFA. He did. We went to the Berks County Bar Association on Court Street. They gave us the name of an attorney, Jamie Dautrich. Having worked in Domestic Relations and in the family law system of the court, Kristen had known Jamie's mother who was also a lawyer. We would be able to meet with Jamie in a few hours. Her office was in the same block and on the same side of the street as the Bar Association. We had time for a walk. We went to Pauline's Soup Café at 5th and Penn Street. I had eaten there many times in the past three years. At the time I worked across the street above the McDonald's. The second floor was the location of the classes for YOP, an alternative education program for students sponsored by the YMCA. I had taught there for those three years and would be starting my fourth year in a few weeks. I taught math and science. Pat, the other certified teacher, taught everything else. I digress, sorry. Again we felt like we were being followed. We went into the café and sat down. Our follower walked by outside the café. We ate some of their good baked goods. I said we should cross the street and go into my school. Barry was there. He was packing. He said we would be starting classes in a nicer facility across the street. It would be on the third floor of the building one building removed from Pauline's. Months later, I would get a visit to that third floor from a pastor looking for a Children's Ministry Director. We told Barry we were trying to shake a private eye. An hour or so later we would get to see Jamie. We would go to see her again on Monday.

That weekend we noticed a car parked on the lot above and behind our house. Mary Lynne and I decided to take a walk with a purpose. We started walking up the hill. Looking down the street, we could see that there was someone in the car on the ridge above and behind our house. We turned down the street and walked directly behind the car. Mary Lynne pulled out her pad and pencil. She wrote down the license plate number. The private eye escapade brought some levity to our otherwise stressful situation. That afternoon we went to see Jamie again. She agreed to be Kristen's lawyer and required only an initial fee. After that, she would work "pro bono." We told her of our escapades of being followed. We gave her the license plate number to check out. As she was doing that we looked out the front window unto Court Street. A policeman was talking to a man double parked on the street. It looked like the policeman was giving the man a ticket. The vehicle was not the same that followed us into Reading days before. However, the man looked liked the one who had followed us on Friday when we walked the streets of Reading. Jamie received the results of her phone number search. It was for a private eye. She acquired a phone number and called. The party answering said not to worry. In court, Harry would admit to hiring a private eye one time. He said he thought it was for a day. So, not only was Harry able to hire a lawyer and set up electronic surveillance, he found time to hire a private eye. Harry was a multitasker spending a lot of money.

On the day we were in Reading hiring our lawyer, Harry's father died. Harry's father was alive long enough to see his son initiate his plan for obtaining primary custody of the boys. Harry already had the plans made for the death of his father. Both his parents had been living the past several months with his sister Eileen's family. Also living there at the time were her husband, daughter, son, a nephew and his friend, four dogs, and some cats. Jeff was one of the two nephews who had lived previously with Harry at sometime. We believe that Jeff was on parole at the time. We also believe that Billy, the other nephew who had lived with Harry at sometime, was in prison at the time. I believe it had something to do with a "meth" lab. Harry was there with the boys, Bryce and Trey, as his father died. I give his family credit for being there together for that time. The boys got to see how a dead body is removed from a house. Harry got to teach them about death at an early age. Harry called us to tell us that his father died. Mary Lynne and I volunteered to take care of the boys while he made the necessary arrangements. He said, "No thanks." Of course, Kristen could not attend the festivities due to the PFA conditions. Harry had already made and paid for all the funeral arrangements and the post death meal. Harry is an extra ordinary multitasker.

There were still some loose ends Harry had to deal with. Kristen needed clothing. When Harry had called about his father's death, we were able to talk to Harry about Kristen's need. Harry told me to come to his house in two hours. I did. On the front porch of Harry's house were most of Kristen's clothes, accumulated over a period of fifteen years. She had not gained weight over those years and had not parted with any of her clothing. Kristen was now living in one of two bedrooms of our manufactured rancher placed in a fifty-five and over community. It was to be our retirement home. I had to remove my clothing from the closet of that not really spare bedroom. She was able to fill that closet with half her clothing. That is a lot of clothing for a size four. To me, getting rid of all that clothing in the manner that Harry did says, "I am not really looking to reconcile." Harry would say to the custody evaluator, four months later, one of the three things he wanted was to reconcile with Kristen. Harry lied to the evaluator when he said he wanted reconciliation. Harry would also get rid of the computer Kristen needed for her work with Concern. That would eliminate another need for her to come back to the house. In addition, it might also cause her to lose her job. Speaking of money, a check for three hundred dollars would be arriving in the mail. It would be written payable to Kristen Hall. It was a check received from the state because of Bryce's special needs. Kristen had done all the work to acquire the money. Therefore, it was in her name. In all the chaos of that week, it is amazing that Harry thought about that check. It is money. Harry is all about money. Harry called the necessary authorities saying that the check was lost. He told them to write the replacement check in his name because he now was primary custodian of Bryce. Of course, custody had not yet been determined when Harry accomplished the switch. After more than four years, Harry still receives that check. That is truly the work of a multitasker.

There were two items that Harry did miss during those two weeks Kristen was not allowed to see or hear from her boys. She would not have missed those two items. One was an important appointment for an evaluation of Bryce for which it had taken six months to schedule. Another was a doctor appointment for Bryce. Even the multitasker, as good as Harry, could not think of everything that was needed to be done.

CHAPTER 8 – ABUSER BE MY BABYSITTER

The Time of Babysitting for Free

The following is from the custody trial on August 26, 2008. Harry is on the witness stand first on behalf of himself. Harry would have no other witness speaking on his behalf that day.

Zimmer: Now, during that time period, what was the custody arrangement, if you recall?

Harry: I had primary—temporary primary custody.

Zimmer: Was there an order to that effect, if you know?

Harry: Yes.

Zimmer: And how did the order take place? By agreement or by hearing?

Harry: At the PFA hearing, the—after two weeks, we were in here for a hearing. And we agreed to that in lieu of a hearing.

Zimmer: Okay. Was Miss Hall working at that time?

Harry: No.

Harry lies. How could Harry not remember that Kristen was working on the computer doing her work for her job with Concern when he "kidnapped" the boys from the home and went to file the 24 hour emergency PFA? How can Harry not remember that he trashed and removed the computer during the two weeks to make it difficult for her to complete her work? How can he not remember she could not meet with her client with Concern, a child, because of the PFA which included an accusation of child abuse? How can he not remember the people she was working for were the same people through whom they received Bryce as a Foster child and secured his adoption? I would like to ask Judge Lash why he believes Harry is a credible witness.

It was August 25, 2006, the day of the hearing concerning the attempted stoning. Kristen and her attorney, Jamie Dautrich, had already had their discussions. Kristen was going to sign the papers to give temporary primary to Harry. Jamie said it would be easy to win the case. What Harry wrote in his PFA would not have held up in court as child abuse. Jamie, learning of Kristen's financial situation, had said she would work "pro bono." It would be easy to eventually win 50/50. Kristen could not wait the many months it would take for the court to schedule a trial to make the decision. She needed to see her children, and they needed to see their mother. Two years later, Judge Lash would commend Harry for dropping that first PFA. There was no need for a commendation. Harry was planning to drop the PFA all along. Harry did not have to threaten Kristen with, sign or else. Besides, Harry needed a babysitter.

The hearings started at 9:00 am. Mary Lynne and I did not know what to expect. Kristen did. There were many cases to be heard. Kristen and Harry were called about 11:00 am. Mary Lynne and I had gone to the hearing to support Kristen. Harry had two people in the courtroom for support. One was his sister, Eileen Mohn. The other was Nancy Unger, the mother of a bicycling friend of Harry from the past. I don't believe any of the supporters knew that it basically meant nothing to be there in the court at that time. We would not be asked to provide any testimony. The discussions to arrive at an outcome or order would be done outside the courtroom. It was interesting that when Kristen and Harry first went before Judge Lash the he recognized Kristen. Also, there were other lawyers in and out of the courtroom throughout the morning that recognized her. Imagine their surprise to learn she was the defendant having been served a PFA for child abuse. She was respected by all those that knew her work in Domestic Relations. There was another person surprised to see Kristen in court. That was Harry's attorney, Jill Koestel. She was also acquainted with Kristen. Harry had asked Kristen at one time who she thought was one of the best family court lawyers. Kristen answered, "Jill Koestel."

It was at Eileen's house that Harry's and her father had died less than two weeks before this time. We believe she participated in the writing of Harry's PFA. After the order was given by the court, all parties left the courtroom. Eileen came over to offer few words. She would say, in an unloving way, "do you know what your daughter did?" She did not say if she was talking about the supposed child abuse or the supposed affair. We never did learn what she was talking about. We said nothing. It was too awkward to offer condolences for her dead father. I presume she thought Harry was justified in his actions. What had Harry told her?

As a young man, Harry had stayed for several months at the Unger's home. It was an escape for Harry from the verbal abuse of his alcoholic father. Approximately nine months after this courtroom scene, Ms. Unger would write a character reference letter to attest to this fact. She would say, in that letter, how it was so wonderful that Harry was able to rise above the situation he was in as a youth to become such a great person and father. I did not know that her letter became an exhibit for the custody trial held two years after this hearing. She was not a witness in the trial, but her letter, accusing Harry's father of being an alcoholic was an exhibit. My character was defamed in that trial because it was claimed I wrote in a letter that Harry's father was an alcoholic. No, it was Harry's and attorney Mark Zimmer's exhibit that stated Harry's deceased father had been an alcoholic.

The hearing was completed. The two weeks were over. Kristen would see her children. The boys would see their mother.

In the custody trial, Mr. Zimmer questions Harry.

Zimmer: When you and Miss Hall separated, who removed themselves from the marital residence?

Harry: The initial separation was a PFA was presented to Kristen to vacate the premises. And after that, after the PFA was over, she was—she had access to the house, full access, to the house for some period of months.

Zimmer: Was there a point in time when she moved—removed herself permanently from the home?

Harry: Yeah. I don't remember the exact date. But in that time she had full access to the house, she didn't stay there frequently, just a couple of times. And then she went to live with her parents.

Zimmer: And when did that take place?

Harry: I'd have say a month—well, she actually left and went with them immediately upon leaving the house. And as I said, she came back and stayed a few nights but then stayed at her parent's house.

Zimmer: Okay, how long had she resided at her parent's home after that?

Harry: Off and on for maybe two months or so, three months I guess, until she got an apartment. I don't remember the exact time.

It was three months, Harry. You knew that was the maximum amount of time we could have a guest in our home in the adult fifty-five and over community. Kristen never removed herself from the marital residence permanently. Harry accomplished that with another PFA based on lies. What was the point of this questioning? I failed to see the point in much of Mr. Zimmer's questioning. Maybe the point was to waste time so that there would be little time left for the defense. Harry, however, was able to take the time to get in more of his lies. And Harry, what about the children?

In the cross of Harry in the custody trial, Kristen's attorney begins.

Ms. Dautrich: And then after there was an agreement entered that you would have temporary primary and Kristen would come and take care of the children while you were at work, you indicated she had full access to the house?

Harry: Oh, there was a master closet. I did put a lock on that. I had some personal things in there. And I asked my attorney at the time if I could do that. She said, yeah, you can do that. So that's what I did. And I may have—I did lock the master bedroom, but she just popped it with a pin and got in anyway. It didn't really matter. You can use a toothpick and unlock those.

Ms. Dautrich: So you locked the master bedroom and closet? (She should have included master bathroom.)

Harry: Yes.

Ms. Dautrich: Did you change any other locks in the house.

Zimmer: I'm going to object. This is not an equitable distribution hearing. I'm not sure where we're going here.

The Court: Yeah. What's the point?

Ms. Dautrich: Well, Mr. Hall indicated she had full access to the house. And I believe that his statements were incorrect, that it was something he testified to based on Mr. Zimmer's questions. But I'll move on.

The Court: All right.

Ms. Dautrich: You indicated she wasn't working at that time when the two of you split up. But isn't it true she was working with children with Concern?

Harry: Oh, that's correct. She did have a part-time evening position, yes.

That's correct Harry. You were just caught in more-lies in court. Is that perjury? It was not necessarily an evening position. She worked on the computer during the day at home to complete forms and produce portfolios. Anyway, that was just a minor point. Harry was truthful when he stated that she only stayed a couple of nights during that three month period. The week following the hearing, Kristen started the babysitting for free period of time. Either she drove herself to Harry's in the morning, or we, her parents, drove her there. After two weeks of coming back to our house after babysitting she learned from Jamie that legally she was allowed to remain in her house overnight. It was still her residence as much as Harry's. She tried. She could not sleep on the sofa due to being too allergic to the dog hair. She tried to sleep on the floor in one of the boy's bedrooms, but that did not solve the allergy problem. The real allergy, however, was not the dog. It was Harry Hall. He was just too condescending. She could not stand to let the children see how their father treated their mother. It was better that she leave immediately after Harry came home.

I said that we drove Kristen to and from Harry's on occasion. It was not by choice. Kristen came to us the afternoon she was made to vacate her home with Harry's pickup truck. The Chevy had logged approximately 300,000 miles. When she came to us with the pickup, she said it was driving "funny." It was. I drove it back to Harry's that same night. To keep the brake pedal and truck from shaking, I had to drive it with one foot on the gas and the other on the brake. I was glad it was an automatic. I left it at the bottom of the hill of the culdesac at Harry's house. Harry would get the brakes repaired weeks later. Kristen would get back the truck a few weeks later and have an accident. She was able to drive it home. Somehow, Harry was able to get forty-three hundred dollars from the insurance as they declared it totaled. Harry bought it back for two hundred dollars from the junkyard. Harry can wheel and deal. He would give Kristen that check in exchange for him keeping the Durango worth more that twice that much. That is what Harry calls 50/50. Harry in the custody trial would state, "I gave her everything 50/50." After all, the check amount was 50 percent of the worth of the Durango. Months later, after paying off our car with a credit card, we would sell it to Kristen for a dollar. She would need the money from the check for car insurance and other expenses.

What was it like babysitting for free? In some ways it was different than before the PFA. Before the PFA, she had a little help with the boys from Harry. Now she would have no help from him for the time she was at the home. As soon as Harry got home from work, Kristen would leave. Before the PFA, the boys did not understand how Harry was being condescending to their mother. Now it was clear in the way she was being treated. Imagine, even mommy is locked out of daddy's private rooms. Harry said in court that Kristen was able to get into those rooms. If that was true, then why did she still have many of her personal items in the home at the time of the custody trial? Before the PFA, she paid for groceries with the money she earned through her job with Concern and the check for Bryce. She lost both of those sources of income. She could not earn money while babysitting for free. Some babysitters are provided with lunch. Kristen had to provide her own lunch unless there was enough left over after the boys ate their lunch provided by Harry.

Harry would go on to state in court that during this time Kristen would put him down in front of the boys. That was a lie. Kristen could not stand to be in his presence any longer than necessary. However, there was something to which Mary Lynne and I, as eye witnesses, could testify. When we picked Kristen up from babysitting, Bryce would always come running after Kristen begging her not to leave. Harry could never stop Bryce. Harry would yell at Kristen to leave quickly. In court, Harry would state that Kristen always made a scene when she left from babysitting. So, who is the real abuser?

CHAPTER 9 - THE TAPE RECORDER INCIDENT

The PFA for Abusing Harry

Judge Scott Lash writes the following in his Decision and Order for the custody trial of 2008:

> On November 8, 2006, Father filed a second Protection from Abuse Petition alleging Mother was acting in an aggressive and harassing manner. A Temporary Order was entered at that time. The matter was continued several times. Ultimately, by agreement of the parties, the Petition was withdrawn and the Temporary Order was vacated on March 6, 2007.

In the 2008 custody trial, Ms. Dautrich continues the cross.

Ms. Dautrich: Mr. Hall, you testified that there were multiple times you called the police on Kristen and once on her father. Is that correct?

Harry: Never said that.

Ms. Dautrich: Okay, so how many times did you call the police on something Kristen did?

51

Harry: Let me see here. Three, maybe four times total. I don't know the exact number. It would take awhile.

Ms. Dautrich: And the children were there all the times, correct?

Harry: At least two. Now, when you say there, they were in the home. They weren't listening to the conversation. I always remove myself from my children when I discuss adult matters.

Ms. Dautrich: And were the police—did they come to the home while the children were there?

Harry: One time, they came to the home. I believe it was one.

So what event led to Harry filing that Kristen was being aggressive to and harassing Harry? Kristen had not seen the boys the day before when she was supposed to see them. She called Harry on the phone, but he would not answer. She drove to Harry's house to see if he and the boys were there. When Harry has the boys alone, he usually takes them to his sister Eileen's home so he can have help with the boys. This time Harry was home alone with the boys. He was outside the home when Kristen pulled up in the car. She got out and proceeded towards Harry. She wanted to ask him why he had not answered his phone. Harry holds an electronic device above his head and says, "I am going to record you."

Kristen goes over to Harry to try to knock the device out of his hand. She is five feet four inches tall, and he is six feet two inches tall. Not being the state high jump champion, she misses the device and hits Harry on the arm. Harry says, "I am going to dial 9-1-1." Kristen backs off and goes into the house. Kristen proceeds to the kitchen. Legally, the house was still the marital residence. She had every right to be there. Kristen started washing the dishes. Harry went to the bathroom.

Several minutes pass. There are knocks on the rear and front doors of the house. In the doors storm two state policemen. Harry had dialed 9-1-1 from the safety of the bathroom. Now Harry comes out of the bathroom. The state police had a discussion with Kristen and Harry. Before leaving the residence, they tell Harry to never call again. Harry was becoming a master teacher of the children. First, they saw how a dead body was removed from a residence by ambulance personnel. Now, they got to witness, first hand, how the state police respond to a frantic 9-1-1 call involving domestic violence. Thus, Harry would make a trip to file the PFA against Kristen. He claimed she was causing him great physical and emotional harm.

What would be the result of the filing of that PFA? It meant that Kristen could no longer be in the presence of Harry except when needed in order to facilitate a transition of the children. It meant that Kristen could not enter the marital residence when Harry was there. Kristen had just gotten a job that week as a receptionist at St. Joseph's Medical Center. She would no longer be able to babysit for Harry when he went to work. Harry was anxious to keep Kristen from coming to the house since she could no longer be his babysitter. Harry would tell Kristen that he would give her $10,000 for an apartment in exchange for exclusive rights to the house. Kristen would agree. She knew she would have to have a place in order to have the boys. That agreement was the main reason Harry was willing to withdraw the PFA against Kristen. So Kristen gets $10,000 for rent of an apartment for a year, and Harry gets the house valued at the time as worth $275,000. Harry says, "I gave her everything 50/50." Harry had the $10,000. He must have gotten a lot of money from that home equity loan.

One of the articles, which I wrote shortly after my letter to Judge Lash, contained my thoughts about the first PFA's filed by Harry against my daughter; the first abusing Bryce, and the second abusing Harry. At the time of writing the article, it seemed they were part of a grand scheme. My article described a six step plan.

> Step one. File a PFA saying your wife is abusing the children. It does not matter if it is true or false. Either way, you will succeed in getting your wife removed from the home and away from the children. You will be awarded temporary primary custody since your wife has no place to live or care for the children. To seal the deal, you say you can provide babysitting.
>
> Step two. Make sure your wife has no means of support. This can be done easily when your wife's job involves working with children you filed a PFA that is declaring her to be a child abuser. Just to make sure she loses the job, remove or destroy the computer that contains the files she needs to do the work.

Step three. Have your wife to sign the house over to you. You steal the home. Phase one in this operation is to use up all the equity in the home. Fifty percent of zero is zero. Harry did this. Where did all the money go?

Step four. Start compiling miserable memories in the home so that your wife does not even want to look at it because it reminds her of what her husband did to her there. Harry succeeded in doing this during the babysitting for free period. Of course, he did much in the few years before this whole affair to contribute to the misery.

Step five. File a PFA saying your wife is abusing you. This will result in making it that your wife can not come to the house because she must stay away from you. You will also have to arrange to do transitions of the children away from the marital residence.

Step six. Say that you will drop the PFA if she would sign the papers giving exclusive rights to the marital residence to yourself.

I learned in the many months, even years, after writing the above that indeed there was a grand scheme. It was far grander than my little six step plan described above. It was far grander than I could have imagined. It would take a book to describe the scheme.

Kristen did sign the papers for the exclusive rights. More than a year after the above event she would sign the house over to Harry for no additional money. It was at the time of the divorce settlement. She did not do it because of any scheme by Harry although another scheme was involved. She signed the papers for the boy's sake. She did it because of her love for them.

Harry's attorney at the time of this incident was Jill Koestel. She had represented Harry at the first PFA hearing in August. However, she was not part of the filing of the first PFA by Harry. Harry filed the second PFA without her knowledge. Six days after its filing, she would resign as Harry's attorney. Did she understand something about Harry that Judge Lash does not? Three days after her resignation, Harry acquires

Jeffrey Karver esquire as his new attorney. Harry must have gotten a lot of money from that equity loan.

Before moving on, I must admit to being puzzled. Harry said in court that he hired a lawyer in June, before he filed the first PFA in August. Was he referring to Jill as that lawyer hired first? If so, would she have agreed to what Harry pulled with that first PFA? It seems that she did not agree with what Harry pulled with the second PFA. Was Jeff his second or third lawyer? When did Harry hire Jill? Maybe, Harry will give me the answers when he reads this book.

Chapter 10 - 50/50 Easy

Preparing for the Evaluation

Kristen's lawyer had said it would be easy to obtain 50/50 custody. That would be easy for her to say, but it would be Kristen that would have to prove she was worthy of 50/50. In mid October, she was informed that the custody evaluation would take place November 22, 2006. The cost for that evaluation would be $2200. Kristen was to pay $400 and Harry $1800. The costs are prorated according to income. That is a good thing done by the courts. However, Kristen was babysitting for free for most of the four months before the evaluation. Perhaps, Harry should have paid the entire fee. The fees had to be paid before the evaluation could take place. Kristen had to use plastic to pay her fee. Harry had a lot of money from the equity loan. Kristen knew the importance of the custody evaluator's report. She knew from her experience working in Domestic Relations that judges rarely waver or deviate from the custody evaluator's recommendations. Kristen knew there was a lot she had to accomplish to earn 50/50. Once she found out the date, there was a little more than a month left to prepare for that evaluation.

The first order of business was to find a job. She knew she could not continue with Concern as it was only part time and she would need a full time job with benefits. She completed the work with her final client in September. She would also need a job with hours that would enable her to care for her children once she earned 50/50. While searching for that perfect job, she applied for work through MACK, a temporary employment service. She discovered that MACK was in charge of finding temporary jobs for St. Joe's Hospital that was opening a new facility in November. She applied for a position at the new hospital. Her mother went with her to apply also. They both got receptionist's positions. The days would be Monday thru Friday. That would be good for the present because she only had her children two weekends a month. The hours would be 5:30 am to 11:30 am. She would be able to continue working a few hours a week for Concern. She liked the idea of the hours because she could tell the evaluator that she would have more active time to offer the boys. She was always thinking, "what is best for the boys?" There were slight problems with the job. The pay was less than ten dollars an hour. The job did not include benefits. Kristen and Harry were not divorced so she was still under Harry's health plan. At that time, she believed that she would be able to obtain alimony and child support from Harry. The job would not add to her resume for someone who had a degree in Social Work with a Criminal Justice minor. It would at least put her in a better light with the evaluator then she was when babysitting for free only weeks before the evaluation.

Second, she had to demonstrate that she had appropriate housing for the boys. As mentioned, for those first three months after the filing of the first PFA, Kristen lived with her parents in a two bedroom, two bath rancher in a fifty-five and over community. She was counted as a guest. She would exhaust her 90 day limit early in November. After the initial two week "kidnapping," she was allowed to have the children with her every other weekend. Kristen and the boys had to share the second bedroom, which they were happy to do. Kristen had two weeks to find housing. That housing had to include a separate bedroom for the boys. So Kristen needed a two bedroom apartment.

Only a mile down the hill from her parent's house in Summit Crest, the name of the adult community, was Maiden Creek Villages, a complex of two and three bedroom apartments. The location was great. A creek, a playground, and the township park with basketball hoops were less than a minute run away for grandpop. There were, however, problems in acquiring the rental. The rental fee was just under $900 per month. The renter or renters were required to have an annual income of at least $40,000. We were given a way to get around that obstacle. The way would be to have someone cosign for the lease and pay for enough months in advance. Kristen's plastic would not have been enough. My plastic was. We signed the lease having faith that Kristen would someday receive something in settlement from Harry. A few weeks after moving in to the apartment, Kristen would get the $10,000 from Harry. She would receive little more from Harry. But, early in November of 2006, Kristen had adequate housing.

It was not a furnished apartment. An empty apartment will not impress the evaluator or other authorities that would have to determine if Kristen had adequate facilities for the children. Harry would again surprise us with his generosity. He would allow her to take a number of the items from the marital residence that Kristen had owned prior to their marriage and those that had been Kristen's parents previously. Anything that Harry owned prior to their marriage or had been purchased during their marriage would remain in the marital residence. There would not be much to move from the marital residence to Kristen's apartment. For the kitchen and dining room area Kristen had the small round pub table, two accompanying tall chairs, and her parent's hutch. Her parent's table and six chairs would remain with Harry. For her living area, Kristen would have her sofa and coffee table which had been spending time in Harry's basement. From the three bedrooms of the marital residence, Kristen would get to take her queen size box spring and mattress. That's it. The boy's bedrooms at Harry's would remain intact. Harry would keep the dressing table her parent's had purchased and Kristen's shelf in the boys room that she had purchased many years before unfinished and had painstakingly finished. The boy's bedroom at the apartment would have been empty if it were not for my wife's cousin. Darlene completely furnished the boys bedrooms with new furniture. Kristen's laundry apartment had its own laundry room. It included everything except a washer and dryer. Harry had a washer and dryer, but this little mommy had none. But Harry says, "I gave her everything 50/50."

The only thing left for which to prepare was the evaluation itself. She needed no further preparation. She had the truth and would get to tell it. Harry had only his lies on the two PFA's. She had no previous record of child abuse. He had no eyewitnesses of child abuse or her abusing him. She had no affair. Harry's private eye found out nothing, but he was found out. There was nothing for the private eye to find. She had been a stay-at-home mom and nurturing parent. What could Harry say to the evaluator? It would be easy to get 50/50 custody.

Chapter 11 - It is Paramount

The First Custody Evaluation

The following paragraph is the last of the 24-page, PSYCHOLOGICAL EVALUATION FOR CHLD CUSTODY, written for the evaluation held on November 22, 2006 by Dr. Peter Thomas.

> Again it is of paramount importance for Mr. Hall to terminate his aggressive effort to convince people about mother's failures and faults. Whatever the court recommends, it is critical for Mr. Hall to accept this outcome and to work within that framework to simply provide the best experience for Trey and Bryce.

We knew Harry filed the two PFA's. Going in to the evaluation, Kristen thought she only had to prepare for the accusations offered in those PFA's. She did not know that Harry also submitted a package of writings to Dr. Thomas two days before the evaluation. One writing described the total transformation program/parental support program Harry claimed he was using. He enclosed materials suggesting that he had filed for relief from abuse from Kristen. He talked at length about Kristen calling Bryce "dumb, stupid, retard, and fatso." Those first three words apply more appropriately to the accuser. Kristen would never have used those words to describe Bryce. He was quite the opposite.

He started saying words early and was always curious about how things worked. His intelligence and curiosity would get him into trouble. He had to be watched constantly. He learned video games quickly. Mr. Hall included a letter he had written to Judge Lash on August 25, 2006. The same Judge Lash told me in the custody trial that my letter to him was inappropriate. In that trial Harry's lawyer, Mark Zimmer, asked me on the stand, "Do you think it was appropriate that you sent your letter to Judge Lash?" Why was Harry's letter appropriate? Harry also sent records from Reading Pediatrics that indicated that Bryce was treated for an arm injury in October of 2006. That "babysitter's elbow" incident occurred during the babysitting for free period. If Kristen would have let go, Bryce would have had a real bump on the head. Additional materials were reviewed. Harry was very busy before the custody evaluation.

Dr. Thomas' report was not submitted immediately after the evaluation. We did not know that Harry was continuing his attacks on Kristen after the evaluation interviews. On December 13, 2006, Harry forwarded a letter to Dr. Thomas that he had written to a psychiatrist, Claire Malfero, who had worked with Bryce. Harry wrote that Bryce's anger displays had greatly dissipated because his PFA had reduced the conflict between the parents. What? Harry would state that his being off from work, he took off from work for the rest of 2006 following the evaluation, allowed him to work with Bryce with positive effects. Harry applied for unemployment the last two months of that year. With that arrangement, Harry ended up with more money than when he was working. He did not have to pay for daycare. Also, I believe he may have been working part time during that time. Anyway, Harry had turned from being "super liar" to "super dad." At least that was what Harry was attesting to be. I am sure Dr. Thomas was impressed by all the information Harry had given him.

Maybe Dr. Thomas was not that impressed. Dr. Thomas called the psychiatrist. One of her-responses was that she was distressed the father "wanted to villainize Mom." She expressed the belief that father would almost set mother up to fail and then criticize her. Harry had his psychotherapist, Sandra Lamma, send a letter to Dr. Thomas which he received on January 10, 2007. She wrote that she had observed Mr. Hall in some interactions with both boys and described him as a loving, patient but firm individual with both boys. Further she wrote, "Mr. Hall was overly active in gathering 'evidence' (Dr. Thomas' term) to show how intolerable the situation with his wife had become." Is it a wonder that in his evaluation report Dr. Thomas would include the following paragraph?

> Mr. Hall approaches very aggressively, can be very intense, even invasive. His therapist, Sandra Lamma, stated that Mr. Hall essentially overdid it in his approach to her, trying to convince her about mother's failures and faults when those were not even the issues of the therapy. Claire Malfero made exactly the same statements. In his approach to this evaluation, Mr. Hall was extreme in the amount of paperwork and writings that he submitted focused on establishing Kristen Hall's problems. These are also of concern.

Harry was still not finished with his giving information to Dr. Thomas. A fax was received by Dr. Thomas from Harry Hall on January 11, 2007. It was a six page letter of Harry's continuing communication of previously communicated themes. He said that Kristen cannot handle Bryce, Kristen does not want to be with Bryce at times, and Kristen says negative things about Bryce. Keep in mind that at the time of this fax, Kristen only got to have the boys four days a month. Also, Harry had no idea of how she felt about Bryce or what was going on with her and the boys. He was not there to observe any event. Before filing the first PFA, we, my wife and I, were with Kristen to observe her interactions with the boys more than Harry.

We three, Kristen, her mother, and I, did not know of these writings given to Dr. Thomas by Harry Hall before his final recommendation for custody was announced. We never saw them. Kristen had been given the full 24-page report by Dr. Thomas. She was mostly interested in the final verdict by Dr. Thomas. Would she get 50/50? She was made aware of the lies Harry had told to Dr. Thomas during the evaluation interviews. As Dr. Thomas told Kristen item after item of Harry's claims, he said Kristen had become angry. Some might say she became emotional. Dr. Thomas did. When I read the report of what Harry accused Kristen of doing and saying, I became angry. I call it "righteous indignation." It was and still is difficult for me to read the report and even more difficult to write about what was written in the report. Kristen had every right to become emotional and angry. Kristen could not and did not read the report in its entirety. It made her too angry.

Dr. Thomas concludes in his report that Bryce Hall presents with evidence of dysfunction. He states that there are extensive records from the Berks County Intermediate Unit. He stated that mother was involved with Bryce through evaluations and childcare programs at the BCIU. Mother could talk in a knowledgeable way about interventions that could be used with Bryce. He should have added that all these were obtained through Kristen's efforts. He did say that Harry had been less involved with the BCIU and, in general, his ability to describe Bryce's dysfunctions and procedures for that was modestly weaker than that of mother. In truth, Harry always blamed Bryce's poor behavior on Kristen's inability to parent. Harry said Bryce was normal. Dr. Thomas would admit in his report that Kristen was the primary caretaker up until Harry's filing the first PFA. He would go on to say that Bryce has been described as having ADD, attention defiant disorder that is also, at times, questioned. He has been described as having oppositional defiant disorder. He is a difficult child to manage. Later, months after that report, Bryce was more correctly labeled to have "Asperger's syndrome." My point is that Kristen, with our help and none from Harry, was able to cope with Bryce's condition. She would admit there is stress, but she did not take it out with anger towards Bryce as Harry claimed. Harry makes us angry.

Dr. Thomas stated that Harry said mother is out of control with her anger. He states that she is overwhelmed by her emotions at this time and acts in very destructive ways toward the children. Dr. Thomas would go on to say that Kristen adamantly denies these remarks altogether. Dr. Thomas concluded that paragraph stating that there are no other sources of information about these behaviors contributed to Kristen other than Harry himself. He states it is difficult to be confident in a conclusion on this issue. The anger Dr. Thomas saw from Kristen in the evaluation that day was all brought on by Harry's lies. Is that what Harry sought to achieve?

Dr. Thomas talked about sources of information in that evaluation. There was a statement Harry made to Dr. Thomas that Harry tried to use a source other than his own testimony. Harry complained to Dr. Thomas about "loud berating phone calls from Kristen. I can hear the kids in the background." Dr. Thomas expressed concern that the children are exposed to these types of messages the mother leaves on father's phone. Harry made these claims in court during the custody trial. The following is from the court transcript.

Zimmer: Your Honor, I'd like to play a section of a tape. How would you like me to do that?

Ms. Dautrich: I have never heard this tape, nor did I know that Mr. Zimmer has any tape he intended to offer. I don't—it wasn't provided to me as an exhibit.

Zimmer: We can—I can play it in the hall for Miss Dautrich.

Ms. Dautrich: I don't have any idea—

Zimmer: I'd be more than happy to play it in the hall for Ms. Dautrich before we play it in here.

The Court: Did you put it in your exhibits?

Zimmer: I did not. I received it recently from Mr. Hall. It is a voice mail left by Miss Hall.

The Court: All right. We'll take a recess, and Miss Hall can hear it also so counsel knows whether it's accurate and complete.

Zimmer: Sure. Where would you like to do that?

The Court: Just go out in the hall. Don't disturb anyone. I assume it's a short tape.

Zimmer: Very.

The Court: All right.

I arrived in that hallway just as Kristen, Harry, and both lawyers came out into the hall to listen to the tape. They would go back into the courtroom to finish the rest of Kristen's testimony on the stand that afternoon. The tape would not be heard in the courtroom. There was no way of telling if the children would have been listening as Kristen sent the voice mail. But the real reason it would not be played was because what Kristen said on the tape incriminated Harry, not Kristen. Mr. Zimmer would not allow it to be played in court. For some unknown reason, Judge Lash, after the recess, would not allow it to be played.

Dr. Thomas continues his assessments of Harry Hall. He states that Harry Hall appears to be a fairly bright individual. He has been hard working and committed to his work over a long period of time. Mr. Hall presents with some emotional intensity. There is a rigid quality to some of his positions. Mr. Hall can be invasive, taking an intense approach. Mr. Hall communicates a sense that he would be a difficult guy to reason with or approach to take a different point of view once he has made up his mind. Mother complains that father can be controlling. Dr. Thomas did say that Harry at times was very tearful and upset during his interview. I wonder if Harry was using the "fallacy of emotion" then as he did during his testimony in the custody trial almost two years later. He goes on to state that at times Harry sounded regretful about the marriage. At times he communicated more a sense of anger and bitterness toward Ms. Hall. Dr. Thomas concludes that he believes Harry is having difficulty dealing with these intense emotions and, consequently, may be more erratic in the emotional states that he experiences. I believe Harry's testimony with Dr. Thomas was a well rehearsed act.

Dr. Thomas would correctly state there was no history of physical mistreatment of the children by mother. He said mother's abilities as a nurturer are good. He did not state that about father. He said in a discussion during the evaluation, Kristen appropriately recognized an instance in which nurturance would be an appropriate response to her son. He said father did not recognize this in the same discussion with father. He goes on to state that by personality structure, she has the assets of a nurturing individual. Even though her relationship with Bryce has been significantly troubled, she remains a very important individual in his life. Her relationship with Trey is more consistently positive. Mother continues to struggle with her relationship with Bryce. Who says she struggles with her relationship with Bryce? It is not the relationship with Bryce that she struggles. She loves Bryce. That is why she adopted him even with his problems. There is a strain due to his dysfunction, but no struggle. The struggle is with Harry Hall.

Harry would also have something to say about therapy to the custody evaluator. He told the evaluator that he had gone to therapy for many years. He said he wanted therapy for Kristen. He stated he wanted to do therapy and parenting classes. So why did Harry refuse to drop the first PFA when Kristen said she would go with him to counseling if he did? He said to the evaluator he wanted reconciliation. How did Harry demonstrate that he wanted reconciliation? Harry continued by saying that if his only concern was money or having primary custody, he would have dropped the evaluation. He states that Kristen made him a very generous offer. He states that she offered for the children to be with him four days and with her for three days and that would financially it would be very good. For whom would it be good? Kristen never made such an offer. Harry lied again. He stated that the only "hang-up" was that Kristen would not go to therapy—"That's why we're here." Just think, Harry is a product of more than ten years of therapy.

Dr. Thomas says it is discouraging that this family was not able to accomplish an agreement on their own. Kristen Hall states she wants evenly shared custodial time. Harry Hall states that he proposed evenly shared custodial time except that the children would be with mother one night less than half-time. Of what is it less than half-time? Is it, a week, a month, or a year? Does anyone not get what Harry means? One night less than half-time means that Harry would be considered primary custodian and he would not have to pay Kristen support for the children. She would have to pay him support. He would get the maximum in free babysitting from Kristen and her family. And he would get child support money. So Harry, it is all about the money.

What was Dr. Thomas' recommendation? He states, "It is recommended that Bryce and Trey Hall share residential time with both parents on an equal basis." Sorry Harry. Do not forget. It is paramount.

Chapter 12 - Trash Talker

Harry Trashes His Family

Mr. Zimmer continues to cross examine my testimony in the custody trial. His intent is to demonstrate that I had trash talked Harry's father in my letter to him.

Zimmer: And there were some fairly hurtful statements in the second correspondence, wouldn't you suggest, I mean statements made about Mr. Hall's deceased father?

Myself: That was not part of the letterhead paper.

Zimmer: No, it was—

Myself: Okay. Yes, that was—

Zimmer: It was not in the correspondence on church letterhead. But it was in you private correspondence, the one sent to me?

Myself: Well it was the truth. Yes, it was the truth.

Zimmer: The statements said about Mr. Hall's—

Myself: Yes.

Zimmer:—were the truth?

Myself: Uh-huh.

Zimmer: So did you think it would comfort him to make vile statements about his dead father? Pretty easy question.

I don't know why some of the testimony and conversation was removed from this section of the transcript. The conversation removed dealt with Harry's father's alcoholism. When I said, "yes", I was referring to the alcoholism. I was not saying "yes" to having written that in either my letter to Judge Lash or my personal letter to Mark Zimmer. Harry's father was mentioned in neither. I am not the trash talker of Harry Hall's father or his family. The trash talker of Harry Hall, Sr. was Harry Hall, Jr. The following excerpts are from the custody evaluation with Dr. Peter Thomas from November of 2006.

> Mr. Hall gave the following family of origin history. He states that his father died very recently. He states that his mother remains living. He states that his father was disabled due to back issues and never held a job during Harry Hall, Junior's lifetime. Mr. Hall states that he has three sisters, he being the youngest. Mr. Hall states that his father was an alcoholic. When asked to describe the family, he stated, "It wasn't good. My dad was a verbally violent alcoholic. We were terrorized." He states that there would be outbursts from father perhaps four out of every seven days. He states that most outbursts were at his mother but that they all were terrified at those times. Further, he states that "in turn, each of us got more verbal abuse" as they got older. He states family life was chaotic. Mr. Hall states that he really was not disciplined. He states that he had an enormous amount of freedom for a child. Essentially he describes both parents as being absent and focused elsewhere. He states that anger was the only emotion from father. He describes his mother as "emotionally unavailable" due to not being around. Mr. Hall describes his home life as "dark and scary." Mr. Hall states that he was not ever physically or sexually abused in his family or elsewhere. He states that his mother never had any problems with drugs or alcohol in his lifetime. He states that his parents did not have mental health issues.

Mr. Hall tearfully stated, "My dad was an alcoholic. I did therapy in ACOA groups." He states that he does not want his children to be mistreated or go through the types of childhood experiences he went through.

I would like to ask Mr. Zimmer if he would consider any of the above statements about Harry Hall, Junior's father as "hurtful." Would it be hurtful to have your children around a person who you consider as being a "verbally abusive alcoholic?" When Harry found out his father had only months to live he started to visit his father often. He had not done that before the revelation of his father's impending death. Not only did Harry visit his father, he took Bryce age four and Trey not yet three with himself. It was during this time that Bryce picked up on the "f-words." A few weeks after the death of his father that language from Bryce ceased. Harry told Dr. Peter Thomas in the evaluation that Kristen used the words "f-a-h" (Sorry, I have trouble typing those words) to Harry, and that Bryce learned that language from Kristen. Harry lied. His father was the master of "f-words."

I would like to ask Dr. Thomas if he believes there are no mental health issues in Harry's family. Why did he not give some psychiatric opinion or gobbledygook concerning Harry's family history testimony? If there were no mental issues, why did Harry think he needed more than ten years of psychotherapy? Would Dr. Thomas consider Harry's words to be "trash talk" of his own family? What does Dr. Thomas think of Harry naming his younger son, Harry Hall, III? Perhaps I should ask Harry the question.

Did Harry Hall, Jr. rise above the level of his father? He is not an alcoholic like his father. Junior was earning a good salary, while his father earned none for many years. His father verbally abused his mother. How does that compare to what Junior has done to his wife, the mother of his children? Which is worse, being abused, or being accused? It is one thing accusing someone of something using the truth. It is quite another thing accusing someone using deception and lies. Being abused is done mostly in private. Being accused is done before the world. Two out of three isn't bad, or is it?

In the evaluation, Dr. Thomas asked Harry about the PFA. Harry stated that mother picked up a rock to hit Bryce. He said he got between them. She should have thrown the rock then. He said that Kristen has been verbally abusive toward Bryce. He said she called him stupid, a retard, and fatso. He said that she threatened to take Bryce out of the home and leave him at Children and Youth Services. Keep in mind that Bryce was less than five at the time of this evaluation. Actually, it would be Harry who would take Bryce to CYS, but not to leave him there. The purpose would be to have Bryce testify against his mother. He stated there were three times when Kristen would pick up Bryce and put him down hard and pin him down. That was the only instance of physical abuse Harry could come up with. Was she awarded three points for the pin? I have to admit to doing that many times. It was necessary to get Bryce dressed. Many times Bryce would escape while I tried to get him dressed. He would run laughing all the way. I was thankful we did not have diapers that required real pins. I would have drawn blood many times. Harry stated that Ms. Hall told Bryce about having two strikes and that he would be out of the home after the third strike. Harry states that when she got to the second strike, he went to see a lawyer. He states this was in June of 2006. Apparently, Harry knows wrestling, baseball, and paranoia. Harry states that mother said things to Bryce such as, "I'll beat you to a bloody pulp." Bryce hit Trey with a pole in July for the third strike. Maybe, Bryce was trying to find out what a "bloody pulp" looked like. Bryce hit Trey with a stone for his fourth strike in August. Bryce was not thrown out. Kristen was. Harry would state that Kristen had transferred her anger to Bryce because she had an abusive relationship with a boyfriend of Italian descent while in college. I guess Harry was qualified to make psychiatric diagnoses because of his ten plus years in psychotherapy. Dr. Thomas offers no opinion of Harry's testimony to the accusations. My opinion is they were well rehearsed and completely insane.

Harry said his mother was mostly not there for him. Now, he has made it so that his own children do not a have their mother who had been there for them. So, Harry is only two out of four better that his father. That only puts him even with his father, not above.

That is enough trash talking. Harry said to the evaluator, "I don't want the boys to be taken from their mother. The point is to get help for Kristen." Harry would also say, "I don't ever want to take them from her (Kristen's) parents. Her parents are really good people, great people."

Mr. Hall stated that he did not want his children to be around the man with whom she had the supposed relationship. Does he mean the supposed relationship she had with Harry himself? I could agree with that. Harry would go on to state, "Where would my boys be if she had primary custody? Who would they be around? Who would be in their lives? I have an answer for Harry. It would be the ones he described as being good and great.

Chapter 13 - The Blue Bowl Incident

The Hall Caught Lying in the Hall

During the custody trial held on August 26, 2008, Mark Zimmer questions Harry Hall.

Zimmer: At some point did Berks County Children and Youth get involved with you and the children?

Harry: Yes, they did.

Zimmer: Do you know when that occurred?

Harry: March of '07, I believe was the first time they were involved.

Zimmer: Do you know what incidents caused their involvement?

Harry: Yeah. Bryce had come home with—he had—I found a sore spot on his head, and he said mommy hit him in the head with a bowl. That was the first time they became involved in our situation.

Zimmer: Did you call CYS or someone else?

Harry: I think I called CYS, and they instructed me to take him to a doctor.

Zimmer: Did you do that?

Harry: I did?

Zimmer: Which doctor did you take the children to?

Harry: Reading Pediatrics. That doctor, I don't recall her name. We have a document that says that.

Zimmer: May I approach, Your Honor.

The Court: Yes.

Zimmer: Do you want this marked? It's marked as Exhibit 2 in our proposed.

The Court: Mark it.

Zimmer: Mr. Hall, are you familiar with the document that I just handed to you?

Harry: Yes.

Zimmer: What is that?

Harry: This was actually for the second time he was hit on the head. This isn't the first one. There's another one in there that is the one we were discussing. This is later.

So, who's on first? Attorney, Mark Zimmer, and his client, Harry Hall, had a comedy routine going on that morning. They did not get many laughs, but they sure wasted a lot of time. Maybe that was the point of it all. Harry says he thinks he called CYS. He was the one that filed the PSR, Petition for Special Relief, with CYS. Harry's own attorney asks him the name of the doctor and he doesn't know. There was no document in the exhibits from the doctor who examined Bryce concerning the bump on the head with a bowl. There was, however, a document from CYS written by caseworker, William Clemons, on March 13, 2007, that concerned this bump. It was an exhibit for the trial presented by Kristen and had been addressed to her. It stated, "This letter is to inform you that the report of suspected child abuse on Bryce Hall received by this agency on March 4, 2007 is unfounded."

Harry did not know the doctor's name and his attorney did not even have the right document. It was Dr. Sergi from Reading Pedes. Harry had given the note the doctor wrote to Dr. Peter Thomas to use in his second custody evaluation held more than a year after this incident. That is why Harry did not have it as an exhibit for the custody trial. The doctor wrote on the note, "when asked what happened, Bryce said that his mother hit him on the side of the head with a bowl." The note was undated. Dr. Thomas says that father again brought Bryce to a doctor with concerns about physical abuse. It could not have been again. The "blue bowl" incident was the first of Harry's use of doctors and BCCYS together for his plan accusing Kristen of child abuse. Three important points should be made as to significance of this small part of the evaluators report. First, it shows that Kristen was not able to tell Dr. Sergi the cause of the bump. She did not cause the bump. Second, why was it not considered important that the doctor ask why mother hit Bryce on the head? Third, Harry did not tell Dr. Thomas that Dr. Sergi deemed the bump "unfounded" because it was not significant enough to require an investigation. Why did Harry think it was significant?

What really happened on that day in early March of 2007? Kristen had just finished giving the boys their bath, and as is her practice, immediately began wiping out the tub. The boys went into the adjacent bedroom. There was a thud. The boys had turned one of the beds into a "sliding board" by taking the mattress partially off the bed. A trick learned at daddy's house. Other things leaned and encouraged by father include such things as jumping off beds and other furniture, running around the house pushing toys, wrestling, and other types of rough housing. These are all recipes for little disasters. These activities may be okay at daddy's house; however, they can be inconvenient in a second floor apartment with an older couple on the first floor. Anyway, Bryce slid down the makeshift sliding board and hit his head on the leg of the chest of drawers. A slight bump on the head is usually not a big deal. For Harry Hall, it became an opportunity. Harry reported the incident to CYS. He had not called or asked Kristen how the bump occurred before going to CYS or the doctor.

Eventually, we would be told that Bryce had said to a doctor, "mommy hit me on the head with a blue bowl." Kristen has no blue bowl. Bryce liked that story better than the real truth about the "sliding board." Bryce likes to make up stories. He still does. He is endearing and convincing when he tells them. Some, however, might call these stories lies. Bryce has told many such stories since then "at sundry times and in divers manners" (See Hebrews 1:1 KJV and a dictionary) to different people, including doctors, caseworkers, teachers, friends, Romans, countrymen, Kristen, Harry, Mary Lynne and myself. When Bryce tells his stories he sounds just like Harry, using the same inflection, tone of voice. That is when we know that Bryce is lying.

From where did Bryce get the idea of stating he was hit with a blue bowl? The morning of the day of the "blue bowl" incident Bryce helped his grandmother, Mary Lynne, make chocolate chip cookies. They mixed the batter in a huge "blue bowl." Bryce was impressed by the size of that "blue bowl." Being hit with a ceramic bowl of that size would bring any man down. Daddy would like that story better than a sliding board story. Bryce, by adding the thought that "mommy hit me," would be assured he had a good story for daddy.

Later that week, Kristen was to learn from Bill Clemons, a caseworker for CYS, that the case was going to be called "unfounded." That result was not determined by allowing Kristen to speak and explain how Bryce received the bump. It was determined by the doctor that the bump was simply not severe enough to be called abuse. It bothered me that Kristen never got to talk to the doctor. It also bothered me that no one asked what Kristen's motive was if indeed she did hit Bryce on the head with an object. Bryce never gave a motive. Harry to CYS, to the evaluator, and to the court in the custody trial, never gave a motive for the supposed crime. Neither Judge Lash nor Harry's attorney questioned about a motive. No one ever attempted to determine if indeed Kristen was the perpetrator of the bump. There was something else that bothered me when Kristen informed us of the meeting with Mr. Clemons. He told her that even if the bump would have been called "founded", an indicated verdict of abuse, then she would have still been able to see the boys. He said that she could sign a paper agreeing to "24 hour supervised visitation" which would allow her to see the boys. Why did he tell her that when he knew it was going to be called "unfounded?" Anyway, she was told the matter would be cleared up in the hearing that Friday, and she should not worry.

Mary Lynne and I did not hear about the bump on the head until we heard that Harry had filed the PSR against Kristen. She told us Bryce bumped his head Sunday evening by sliding down the makeshift sliding board. She told us Bryce said to Harry, a doctor, and CYS, "mommy hit me on the head with a blue bowl." We knew immediately Bryce had lied. Kristen did not have the "blue bowl." We did. Mary Lynne and I decided to get the truth to Harry's family. We also needed to see how the boys were doing. So we took the "blue bowl" and headed to Harry's sister's house. Harry' mother answered the door and allowed us inside to see the boys. Bryce would not talk. He looked like someone who just ate the cat. Somehow, Trey was sleeping on the sofa. We explained to Harry's mother that this was the "blue bow" and it was not in the possession of Kristen. She did not hit Bryce on the head with the bowl. Harry's mother did not want to talk. She would only say that it was between Harry and Kristen. I thought it was about the boys. We left with the knowledge of why Trey and Kristen came back with allergy symptoms after visiting that house.

A result of our trip to that house was another trip by Harry to BCCYS. It was on Saturday. Harry had persuaded the woman on duty to make a "threatening" phone call to us. My wife answered the call. She was approached by the caller in an unprofessional and rude manner. We were told to not interfere with the investigation. The problem in all these incidents is that we were never given the chance to tell what we knew as the facts. Outside the parents, we had been the caretakers of the boys. In response to the phone call, we went to Children's Service's to voice our concerns with Harry about the situation. We also complained about how Mary Lynne was treated with the phone message. The interviewer agreed that the worker should not have handled things in the manner that she did. We understood that the caller was just following Harry's directions. The interviewer said that they would get back to us. We called several more times and they said they would get back to us. They did not.

In that one meeting with BCCYS we were able to voice some concerns and give information. We told what we knew concerning the "stoning" and "blue bowl" incidents. We told our concern that Harry might be wanting out of the marriage because he was "gay." We also believed Harry was lying with these accusations because he was seeking primary custody for financial reasons. We said that Harry and Kristen had recently received word the custody evaluator was recommending 50/50 custody. Harry was not happy with that recommendation. Harry had taken a new job most of the last two months of the year of 2006. Actually, he was collecting unemployment and only worked for his new boss sporadically. The unusual part of his relationship with this new boss was that Harry and the boys spent the weekends with this man. Trey said that he slept between his father and this man when they stayed at his house overnight. Trey had an interesting observation at that time, and he was only three and a half. He said, "Mommy has her man, and daddy has his man." The difference is that Kristen only shares her bed with Trey.

Friday of the hearing on the "blue bowl" incident, I received permission to leave my job at the YMCA to walk across the street to the courthouse to be with Kristen. In the courthouse I decided to use the stairs to go to the fifth floor where the hearing would be held. Reaching that floor, there in the secluded stairwell was Harry threatening Kristen. He had told her that the caseworker had told him the bump on the head was going to be called "founded," that is, an indicated case of child abuse. He said she would lose the children unless he would speak in her behalf. He said that if she signed the papers he was waving at her, he would have the accusation dropped. I got there in time to tell her not to sign anything. We knew Harry was lying. I told her to go to her lawyer now and tell her how Harry had just threatened her. Kristen left the stairwell and went to her lawyer to tell of Harry's threat.

All parties left the courthouse to cross over to the Berks County Service's Building. I followed. I was outside the area where they met. Not long afterwards, the parties came out into the hallway where I was standing. Harry's lawyer, Jeffrey Karver, would make an important directive to all parties. Present in the hallway, besides myself, were Kristen and her attorney, Harry and his attorney, and Mr. Clemons, the caseworker for CYS. Mr. Clemons had just verified to everyone that indeed Harry had just lied to Kristen in the hallway of the stairwell. The verdict was going to be that the doctor had declared the abuse accusation "unfounded." Harry had not known that Kristen was informed of that fact earlier in the week. The Hall had been caught in the hall with a lie.

There in another hallway, Jeffrey Karver would say, "If a parent notices a bump or bruise on one of the children, that parent should question the other about their knowledge of how it occurred before taking the child to an authority." Harry was admonished for lying and not having asked Kristen how the bump occurred. At the time it seemed like a very reasonable request of both parties. A few weeks after this incident, Bryce got a much larger bump than the one gotten at Kristen's apartment. He was at his father's house sitting on the lawn tractor parked under the deck. He got up quickly and hit his head on the deck. Harry called Kristen about the bump. He would not have had to call. Kristen knows things like that happen with Bryce. She would not have filed a PFA or PSR. She would not have gone against the directive by Harry's lawyer.

Catching Harry in the hallway of the stairs was the one event of which I was able to testify in the custody trial. I told of hearing Harry's lie to Kristen. The other part of that event to which I wanted to testify was the knowledge of the directive given by Harry's lawyer in the other hallway. I had considered that to be the most important item to which I could testify. It would be a directive that Harry would not follow. After Jamie completed her questioning of me, I looked across the courtroom and said rather forcefully, "What happened next?" Judge Lash exclaims, "You cannot ask questions!" I was not talking to Judge Lash.

Chapter 14 – Super Nanny Granny

Testimony of Maternal Grandmother

It was April of 2007. Kristen had survived Harry's first PSR. The verdict for the "blue bowl" incident was "unfounded." Kristen and Mary Lynne received the news that St. Joseph's Medical Center was going to hire two full time employees to replace the four part time employees that had shared the receptionist positions since the new hospital had opened. Kristen and Mary Lynne were two of the part timers. Kristen took one of the full time positions. She had not found any other positions for which she could use her past experience and college degree. Replacing the part time with the full time position meant that she would now get benefits. Her starting time would remain as 5:15 am. Her ending time would be 2:15 pm. She also knew at that time that she would shortly be receiving 50/50 custody. She would need a babysitter. Of course that babysitter would be Mary Lynne. Mary Lynne would not apply for the other full time position.

Mary Lynne and Kristen had been riding together for the past five months. Mary Lynne's wake up time would remain nearly the same. On the days Kristen had custody of the boys Mary Lynne would be up and ready to get to the apartment before Kristen left for work at 5:00 am. Kristen would be making more money. Mary Lynne would be making none. Mary Lynne had resigned from her dental assistant job shortly after Kristen had Trey. She did that to be available to help Kristen with the boys. She took the part time receptionist job with Kristen to help her with finances. To the boys she was "grandma." Now she would also be "nanny."

Harry was asked by the custody evaluator, "who will take care of the boys while you work?" Harry said he a "nanny" who was a friend of the family and well qualified. He also had a criminal record clearance done on the individual. I find the statement "hilarious." He is admitting if they are a friend his family they should be checked for criminal clearance. I believe, at most, his "nanny" lasted two days. She could not handle both children at the same time. That was something Kristen was able to do successfully, with the occasional help from grandma, for four years. Harry would go on unemployment for the last months of 2006. It was not because he could not find work. I believe there were two reasons, maybe three, for Harry not working full time those months. He would not have to pay for daycare. Harry those two months would have the boys at those impressionable ages to train in the way he would want them to go. During that time, Kristen had the boys for only four days a month. Harry did say to Dr. Thomas that he was using a special training method. Anyway, Harry would put the boys in daycare once he took full time employment. This whole nanny affair is typical Harry's actions. He says one thing and does another. Was the nanny affair just another part of Harry's plan of deception? I believe Harry did exactly what he planned to do.

Grandma needed no criminal clearance. She had prior experience as a grandmother and mother. She also had a lot of experience working with other people's children. The week before we were married—our wedding date was August 26, 1967 – she was a counselor for young girls at Greenview Bible Camp. She was with the girls for six days and nights. The next day she was with the man. The year she was pregnant with our first child, we served together as volunteer youth leaders for our church. We were only six years older than some of our youth. She became a Sunday School teacher and worker with Brownies. She helped me for many years with the VBS and Bible and Sports Schools that I directed. She also had experience in the medical field. Harry's lawyer and Judge Lash were taken back by her knowledge of Bryce's condition. She obviously knew more than them. She was well equipped for the job of "nanny." Harry was not well equipped for the job of "nanny." As

Kristen received the fought for 50/50, April of 2007, her mother and I became even more involved with the upbringing of the boys. Mary Lynne, sixteen months later, would get to testify about some of those experiences.

Ms. Dautrich: And what types of things did you and your husband do with the boys when you're assisting with the children to care for them?

Mary Lynne: Well, since they learned how to ride bikes, we've definitely gone over to the park.—And so every morning before Dave leaves for work, he takes the bike and they bike ride. I walk over and assist if one goes one direction and one goes the other because they normally do.

Ms. Dautrich: Who taught them how to ride bikes.

Mary Lynne: My husband.

Ms. Dautrich: What other kinds of things do you and your husband do with the kids?

Mary Lynne: Oh, well, we—when I bring them over to my house, Bryce is a very compulsive child and is always interested in how things work and what adults use. And he likes to trim.—

Ms. Dautrich: When you indicated trim, you mean trim the grass?

Mary Lynne: Trim grass. Oh, yes. He loves that.

Ms. Dautrich: And what kinds of things does Trey like to do?

Mary Lynne: Trey has a big imagination, so he is able to content himself with cars and other Fisher-Price toys that I have. He is—he has—he can content himself, whereas Bryce is constantly moving, constantly doing. Its totally different with the two of them.

Mary Lynne would go on in her testimony giving knowledge of how the boys interacted. She would give knowledge of how the boys and their mother reacted to each other. She would tell how often I took Bryce aside to do things that he alone wanted to do.

Ms. Dautrich: So it's easier when there are two people there for the children?

Mary Lynne: Oh, yes, definitely easier with two people. But I managed through the summer, it has gone fairly well. I am very proud because it's been ten days a month I've had them by myself.

Mary Lynne had turned from being just "grandma" into being "super nanny granny." In addition, she is qualified as someone to deal with Bryce's special needs. Experience is the best teacher. By the time of the custody trial, she already had six years experience with Bryce. None of Bryce's caseworkers could have dealt with Bryce as well as she.

Ms. Dautrich: And what kinds of things did you do to educate yourself about Asperger's and Bryce's condition?

Mary Lynne: Well, getting on the Internet was one of them. I worked with a girl who had an autistic son. I don't work with her anymore, but I learned a lot from her because she was way ahead of the average bear in getting help for her son. And so I learned what autism was through my friend and on the internet.—

Mary Lynne:—Bryce is oppositional defiant. That is one of the diagnoses that he has—Hyperactive, ADHD, Asperger's. So the child is totally different than a regular child is. On the day I met him at six months, I knew he was special. He was very special and is. He's very intelligent.

Ms. Dautrich: Do you feel that children with special needs, particularly Bryce here, need to be treated specially or differently from other children?

Mary Lynne: Oh, they definitely have to be treated differently.

It is amazing how Harry and the court are always talking about Bryce in the proceedings, but neglecting Trey. Many birth siblings have difficulties because of problems created from those associated with Bryce's condition. Trey had a problem with daycare. When 50/50 custody started, Harry, under his watch, put both boys in daycare from 6:30 am to 4:30 pm. Bryce had to do that for only the first four of those sixteen months. After those four months, Bryce got to start full day kindergarten and could leave after two hours each day at daycare. He would return to daycare after school. Trey, however, was left in daycare for the entire ten hours.

Ms. Dautrich: Has Trey ever talked to you about the daycare he goes to when he's in Harry's care?

Mary Lynne: Yes, very much.

Ms. Dautrich: And what has he told you about that?

Mary Lynne: He hates it. I hate daycare. I don't want to go there.

Ms. Dautrich: Not that he doesn't want to hurt his dad, but that he doesn't want to go to that daycare.

Mary Lynne: Well, he—the days—the second day that I have him, he will say to me from time to time, this is a daddy day (meaning he will have to go to daddy that evening). And I said, "yes it is." And he's not happy about that. He's not happy if it's a daddy day. Sorry.

Mr. Zimmer cross examines. He asks Mary Lynne several times, "Do you encourage the relationship between the children and Mr. Hall?" He asks, "How about your husband? Does your husband speak of Mr. Hall in a positive light in front of the children? Does he talk about Mr. Hall, period? How does he feel about Mr. Hall?" Mary Lynne would answer, "You'd have to ask him." Good answer, Mary Lynne. Besides, what does "feel about" mean? The cross examination continues.

Zimmer: How do you feel about Mr. Hall?

Mary Lynne: I feel like he's a liar.

Zimmer: You don't like him very much, do you?

Mary Lynne: Because of his actions.

Zimmer: Such as bringing this custody case today?

Mary Lynne: Of all the lies he has used in two years?

Zimmer: And you don't like the fact he testified against your daughter when he was subpoenaed by Berks County Children and Youth Service's, do you?

Before we continue with Zimmer's cross of grandma, I must interject a thought. Zimmer is talking here about the expungement hearing with the administrative law judge. This is the hearing that Judge Lash would not allow me to testify about near the end of the trial. Here Judge Lash allows Mark Zimmer to discuss that hearing.

Mary Lynne: Why would a mother want that?

Zimmer: Are you angry with Mr. Hall for doing that?

Mary Lynne: Angry? It is sad.

Zimmer: It's sad that he testified for Berks County Children and Youth Services?

Mary Lynne: Yes. Because it was a lie.

Zimmer: It was a lie?

Mary Lynne: A lie.

Zimmer: You understand that he was subpoenaed to testify; he didn't do it under his own will?

Mary Lynne: Fine. It's still a lie.

Zimmer: But he lied?

Mary Lynne: Yes.

Zimmer: Okay. But despite the fact he lied, you understand that your daughter was indicated as a perpetrator of child abuse?

Mary Lynne: Could still be a lie.

Zimmer: So you think he made this up?

Mary Lynne: I think he premeditated this whole two-year experience.

Zimmer: So you think he conjured this whole thing up to bring us where we are today?

Mary Lynne: To bring us where we are today? No. No. I'm sure he hoped it would be over before today.

This "super nanny granny" would not be intimidated. Mr. Zimmer would try again.

Zimmer: Okay. So you're testifying today to prevent Mr. Hall from getting revenge on your daughter?

Mary Lynne: I am testifying to the truth. He is lying.

Zimmer: So although you didn't hear him testify today, you're going to assume everything he said was a lie?

The questioning and testimony starts to deteriorate. Help is needed from Kristen's lawyer and the Court. In my short testimony at the end of the day, I said, "I am testifying to the truth." Great minds think alike. Our testimonies were corroborating. It was not planned. It just happened. Maybe it was inspired.

> Mary Lynne: I have read all the so-called documents, yes.
> Zimmer: I wrote those documents. Am I a liar, too?
> Mary Lynne: You didn't write—
> Ms. Dautrich: I object. I don't know what documents—
> Mary Lynne: I don't either.
> Ms. Dautrich:—Mr. Zimmer's indicating.
> The Court: That's an improper question. Sustained.
> Mary Lynne: By the way, I know—
> The Court: Wait for a question.
> Mary Lynne: Okay.
> Zimmer: Would it surprise you that Mr. Hall testified to the fact that he doesn't have to use passive restraint to discipline the children?

The truth is no one knows what Harry does to discipline. No one else lives with Harry. I do not know of any positive things that he has taught them. I will not embarrass them to say of the negatives that I believe he has taught them. Maybe they learned those things at daycare. The boys tell us they are not supposed to say what goes on at his house, and they don't. I am anxious to hear how Mary Lynne responded to that last question. Of course, I would never be surprised at what Harry would say about anything. I take that back. I am surprised when he says the truth. One thing that surprised me about Mr. Zimmer's question was his lack of knowledge of the use of passive restraint. It is not a discipline technique. It is used to remove a person safely from a dangerous situation. Discipline is used after the situation has ceased. Kristen would explain the use of passive restraint when she took the witness stand later in the trial. Hopefully, Mr. Zimmer would listen and learn.

Mary Lynne: Well as long as you allow Bryce to have free reign of acreage and just run and do your thing, you wouldn't have to use passive restraint as long as he is doing what Mr. Bryce wants to do.

Zimmer: What Mr. Hall wants him to do?

Mary Lynne: No. What Mr. Bryce—I'm talking about—Bryce is so intelligent that he is a mister. And he wants to do his thing. And if you allow him to do his thing, he's happy; and you wouldn't have to use passive restraint. If you give him any restrictions, then that's when the problem would arise.

Zimmer: Okay. No further questions.

Mary Lynne has said that I haven't tried to teach her any math. Obviously, I do not have to teach her logic. She ended her cross-examination testimony with a very nice conditional statement. Apparently, Mr. Zimmer was still not convinced or content. He would ask for a re-cross examination.

Zimmer: You stated you do have the children—you do encourage the children to have a good relationship with their father? You said yes to that?

Mary Lynne: Yes.

Zimmer: Yes. Why did you roll your eyes?

Mary Lynne: I don't encourage—I don't—I don't verbally say, now, you must be good to your daddy and have fun and blah, blah, blah. No, I don't do that.

Zimmer: No?

Mary Lynne: I just go on to the next activity if they say, you know, this is a daddy day and he's upset about it. And I can tell by his body language that he is.

Zimmer: Nothing further.

The Court: Hold on I may have some questions here.

Mary Lynne: Okay. Oh, I didn't know you did that. Sorry. Go ahead.

The Court: Regarding Trey, what would your schedule be between these two parents?

Mary Lynne: I think Trey needs to be with his mother most of the time.

The Court: All right. And what about Bryce?

Mary Lynne: I think Bryce needs to be in a family with two people that are on the same page. Harry does not—he does not cooperate, and then they have a special needs child. You have to be on the same page. You have to cooperate together if you're going to be separate parents working with a child like this. He does not cooperate. He does not talk to my daughter about anything about the children.

The Court: What do you mean separate?

Mary Lynne: I think Bryce, if you—if he needs to be place with Harry, that's who he's placed with. Kristen would have Trey.

The Court: So you would have one child with one parent and one child with the other parent?

Mary Lynne: Right. Bryce is not a brother to Trey. He isn't in any shape or form.

The Court: What does that mean?

Mary Lynne: He doesn't relate to him on that level. He truly doesn't. He knows the term brother, yes. He does not interact with him very much. He—he is domineering. He is just—

The Court: Well now, Bryce is not your blood. And Bryce has issues, from what I'm hearing.

Mary Lynne: Uh-huh.

The Court: Do you consider Bryce your grandchild the same as you consider Trey?

Mary Lynne: I do. I feel all children, even my own children, I always felt were God's not mine. And I loved every child the same.

I had hoped Judge Lash would demonstrate discernment in recognizing "truthful" and "meaningful" testimony. If the boys would be together as brothers, they should be with two parents. If each parent remains single, then it would be better that the boys lived separately. Bryce requires one parent for himself. He has to do his own thing. If either parent married, then the two parent system with the married couple having the brothers would work. If both parents remain single and the boys must be kept together, then both parents have to cooperate. "Super nanny granny" has spoken. "Super nanny granny" has discernment. Does Judge Lash? Perhaps, "super nanny granny" should be the judge.

Chapter 15 - An Excellent Prospect

An Autobiography of the Author

I am reading an article written by Dr. Phillip Keevil for the Ivy Tower, the monthly newsletter of the First Presbyterian Church in Reading, Pennsylvania. The month is March of 2007. The title of the article is "Growing the Church into the Future." Dr. Keevil writes, "At the time of writing this article an excellent prospect has emerged for the director of children's ministry. I believe God has brought us someone who will enable us to develop an educational program marked by excellence in every aspect of spiritual and intellectual nurture." What would make someone an excellent prospect?

By June of 2003 I had survived thirty –six years of teaching, all but one of those for the Berks Career and Technology Center. Many times before retiring I would be asked, "So, when are you planning to retire?" I would say, "Why should I retire now? I am just getting good at it." I meant that sincerely. In 1968, I was hired to teach Algebra, Geometry, and Trigonometry to students for senior high Vo-tech students in the trade areas that required academic math as part of their curriculum. Also, there were students who requested those math courses because they had aspirations of furthering their education. An obvious question students would inevitably ask was, "when will I ever use this math?" I was never threatened by that question. Teaching at the Vo-tech, I would discover many answers. Only six of the sixteen trade areas required academic math. I would talk to teachers from the other trade areas. They would tell me of their student's weaknesses in math. We agreed that these students needed to take more math courses. A few years later it was decided by the Vo-tech board that a career math program should be offered. I was intrigued by the prospect of developing that math curriculum. I volunteered to teach Career Mathematics. I developed a lot of curriculum, but needed a better method of delivering it to the students. The career math students only had math class twice a week. I gave the students pretests and post tests on the fundamentals. In one of the units, the scores increased from 30% to 60%. Sixty percent does not cut it, that is, the piece of wood to the correct length. It makes a lot of waste.

The method used by teachers of the trades was called CBVE – Competency Based Vocational Education. Each trade had a list of competencies for the student to complete. The student would have to complete the competency to a level described as industry standards. The student would test and retest until that level of competence was met. Many students in a particular class would be working on different competencies at the same time. In some ways it was like a one room school house with eight different grade levels. I did, however, like the idea that a student in a CBVE math program might have to test and retest until they score at a high level, even 100%, in order to pass a particular math competency. It sounded like a nice concept, but at the time I did not think it was possible to set up a course in which that criteria could be met. I would not be given the choice of determining the possibility. I was told by the curriculum coordinator to write the Career Math course using the competency based format. I did. Eventually I would design the curriculum for the academic courses to be competency based. The first year I taught math with a competency based format was the 1979-80 school year. On the day of the custody trial, August 26, 2008, I started teaching a Competency Based Algebra I course I had just designed for RACC, Reading Area Community College. In the years between, I designed many competency based math courses, not only for BCTC, Berks Career and Technology Center, but for a number of industries, and an alternative education program, YOP. I also gave seminars to teachers on using the competency based method.

In February of 1981, my second year of teaching by the competency based method, the principal of my school made some observations concerning the teaching methods and techniques. He stated the CBVE math was working fine. He said what was accomplished was greater that what was expected. He observed there to be a significant difference of learning between CBVE and the traditional method. In May of 2002, another principal made the following observation: "The students in this class were extremely respectful of the educational process and seriously on task. It is obvious that Mr. Rathman sets standards this class responds nicely to them." I have to admit that one of the reasons I retired in 2003 was that higher authorities were saying we could no longer teach in the competency based mode. For the next school year we would have had to use recommended textbooks and the traditional methods of teaching.

For my seminars for teaching I wrote an article entitled, "Overcoming Math Anxiety." The article expresses some of my philosophies, not only for teaching, but for life. One section speaks of giving "second chances."

In athletic competition there are many examples of getting a second chance. In baseball it takes "three strikes" to get you out. A coach does not take a basketball player out of a game after missing one shot. Randall Cunningham was not required to complete 100% of his passes. Imagine the "anxiety" created if the batter gets only one strike, a basketball player is taken out of the game after missing one shot, or the quarterback benched for not completing his first pass. I am sure batting averages, shooting and passing percentages would all go down. It would not be because of decreased ability, but it would be caused by the anxiety created from the knowledge of not getting a second chance.

In life we often make "wrong choices." We are told to "learn from our mistakes." Often in academic classes in general, students are not given the opportunity to "learn from their mistakes." Using the competency based teaching approach gives that "second chance." If the student fails a test, they are given the opportunity to retest until the passing score is attained. Knowing they have this opportunity helps in overcoming "math anxiety."

Yes, I know I said previously (Chapter 4) that my daughter gives too many "second chances." She must have taken this out of context. It is true there is a point of diminishing returns. There is a point where we have to tell the person that they might not be cut out for being a brain surgeon. Did I just use "cut" and "surgeon" in the same sentence?

"As for me, to live is Christ, and to die is gain." The apostle Paul wrote this to say how he could overcome anxiety in living a Christian life. He was describing a "no lose situation." That is what is needed to overcome "math anxiety." The fear of failure is one of the greatest causes of "math anxiety." This is because of the consequences of failure. Failing a test in mathematics, or any academic course, is always met with a negative response. The grade is lowered. Enough failures in tests results in failure of the course. The problem is that the anxiety caused by the fear of the consequences of failure may also be the cause of the failure.

The competence based approach takes away the anxiety by eliminating the fear of failure. When a student fails a test that grade is not counted into their test average. Only passing scores are used. The student is given attitude points for effort. The only thing not rewarded is lack of effort. It is a "no lose situation." If the student passes the test, they know they have mastered that competency to a high level of competence. If they failed, they still receive some credit, but more importantly they receive the help they need to try again. Fear of failure gained from personal experience has created "math anxiety." Students who have taken a competency based math course have spread the word, which is, "If you try, you will get by." For the school year 1993-94, all math courses at BCTC will be competency based. "Math anxiety" has been overcome.

For my retirement jobs in the fall of 2003, I signed on for one College Algebra class at Penn State Berks Campus and two math courses at Reading Area Community College. I would enjoy the lecturing, but I missed the one on one contact I had when teaching my competency based math courses the previous twenty plus years. Upon seeing their test and quiz results, I would think, "if only." In November of 2003, I attended my fortieth high school class reunion. I talked with Pat. She said she was teaching for an alternative education program in Reading. She informed me that their math and science teacher had quit a month ago. She taught all the other courses. They had a maximum of 30 students in the school at a time. She asked, "What do you think?"

The next week I showed up on the second floor at the corner of 5th and Penn Streets above the McDonald's Restaurant. I talked to the supervisor of the Youth Outreach Program, Barry Jackson. He asked when I could start. I was intrigued by the prospects. They did not have a required text. They would be happy about any math I could teach. I could choose the curriculum. I could use some of the 2000 plus competency based tests I had written over the past twenty years. Even the prospect of teaching science was a plus. Many of the competency tests for the Vo-tech I had written were application competencies involving scientific principles. I had taken Physics and Chemistry as electives in college. One of my brothers has a Doctorate in Chemistry and the other in Physics. Perhaps, I have some aptitude in science. My daughter was successful with the same types of youth when she was a Correctional Counselor from 1994-97 at the Berks County Juvenile Detention Center. I asked if I could start part time by squeezing between the times of my math classes at Berks Campus and RACC. Barry said, "Yes." I came in to start math class the next day.

There was one other thing that solidified my accepting the position. On Friday mornings, the youth walked the several blocks to the gymnasium in the YMCA to play basketball. One of my reasons for going into the teaching profession was to have an influence on the lives of young people. Besides teaching, I wanted to be a basketball coach. My first year of teaching was at Downingtown Senior High School. The only coaching position available was as an assistant junior high track coach. I took that coaching position. Oddly enough, the sport I participated in at college was track. BCTC had no sports program.

Our students were from sixteen school districts and they participated in sports at their home schools. I did, however, one of those years, have the opportunity to coach junior varsity basketball for one of those home schools. YOP had a basketball team. They played against three other alternative education schools in the county. The previous year YOP was the champions of the four team league. It sounds like a league of its own. Fortunately, the whole schedule was only six games and a championship game. Unfortunately, I had to referee those games. It was much more fun the days we had no games. On those days I got to play with my students. They laughed the first day I came out on the court. I was picked last. That was the last day I would be picked last. I knew this job would be fun. I did not have to worry about "fouling out" as I did in most of my games in high school. You could say I was given many "second chances."

I've taught in many different situations. My best experience was those four years teaching for YOP. I blame that on my Barry, my supervisor. At the time I was hired, he already had thirty years of experience working with problem students. Half of the players my first year at YOP were black. The rest of the players were Hispanic. I believe it was not the fact that Barry was black that he was successful with that type of student. He disciplined them as a loving father would in order to give them a chance for success. Imagine, as a teacher, what it would be like to have the father in your classroom making sure their son would make the most out of their education. I worried not about discipline. There was no absentee father. Their father was there. I worried about teaching them as much as I possibly could. And I did. For my second year of teaching math at YOP, I used the same Competency Based Geometry course I taught my last year of teaching at BCTC. Seven of seventy students at BCTC made the "100 Club." At YOP, four of the thirty students who attended most of the year made the "100 Club." One of those students was listed as being in eighth grade. To make the "100 Club," the student most complete all 100 competencies listed for the course to a level of 100 percent.

In early November of 2006, the Berks County Children and Youth Service's Quality Assurance Unit conducted a site review of the Youth Outreach Program. They stated that YOP accepts students who have exhibited defiant behaviors in their home schools. They would describe my math and science programs.

> Each student within the program has a binder filled with academic goals they must complete. The student must complete lessons and have an understanding of each academic concept before they are able to complete a test. This method of learning allows the program to be individualized and continue to meet the student's academic needs. The Quality Assurance Unit observed the materials to include concepts of calculus, trigonometry, geology, biology, chemistry, etc.

For those who have some knowledge of calculus, the last math competency I would teach at YOP was, "determine the area under the curve using integration." By integration, I mean the inverse of differentiation not segregation. They would go on to say that four students were interviewed.

> The students were able to compare experiences with other alternative educational programs. They reported feeling they were "learning more at the YOP." One student reported liking the one-on-one interaction between themselves and the teachers. All four students reported feeling respected by the staff. Another student reported the staff will work with the students until they got it compared to night school where, "I was given a piece of paper and told to figure it out on my own." One should keep in mind that this targeted population has a history of lack of commitment to the school system, and to observe their ability to leave the building and return in a timely manner shows a positive improvement in attitude about school and learning.
>
> The Quality Assurance Unit recommends that funding continue for the Youth Outreach Program. This program was observed to meet the needs of one of the toughest populations faced by the school system.

This program welcomes children pushed aside by other school systems and keeps them off the streets, which benefits the community, and society as a whole. The YOP is an alternative education program that has succeeded in encouraging it students, who have previously been relegated to programs that have been less successful, to become successful.

By January of 2007, the handwriting was beginning to appear on the wall. No, the students were not writing on the wall. We knew there was a good possibility that the Reading School District would no longer send students to YOP. I should start looking for another job. It was possible that my hours could start to be cut at anytime. That same January, I heard from the pulpit that First Presbyterian was looking for a part time person as Children's Ministry Director. In February, I would send an application for that position to FPC. Perhaps, I could do part time YOP for the YMCA and part time CMD at FPC concurrently. They were only several blocks apart.

But, does my teaching experience qualify me to be a Children's Ministry Director? No. A high school math teacher does not necessarily teach math for 12 months of the year. There are summers and weekends. I did have another life. Most of my summers were filled with children's ministry work. My Sundays were filled with Christian music and Christian education. Most of these experiences were done on a volunteer basis.

I taught my first Sunday school lesson when I was nineteen. It was for an adult class. I was never a full time teacher, but often, when I did teach, it was a lesson or series of lessons that I had written. The first time I designed my own curriculum of teaching the Bible to children was in Junior Church for children aged four to seven. I started doing that when my son had turned four. One of my lessons for Junior Church was about the covenants. One family, upon visiting the church, had their child come to Junior Church when I was teaching one of those lessons. The parents were impressed when their child came back to them with the knowledge of the difference between a conditional and unconditional covenant. They returned and became members of the church. At that church I would become the Assistant and later the Sunday School Superintendent.

Children's ministry for the summertime means VBS. I taught in VBS for the first time in 1972. The next year I would be the Vacation Bible School Director. The following year I would be the director again. This time I would write the curriculum. The theme song I wrote for that curriculum was, "I See God." In 1977, I would design a Bible and Sports School. I held what I thought would be my last Bible and Sports School in 2001. Over those years I directed 45 such schools in ten different churches. The most schools I held in any summer was five. The following paragraph contains some statements from an article entitled, "A Different type of Bible School." It appeared in a Reading Eagle newspaper article in the summer of 1991.

> Bible schools are held at many Berks County churches on various weeks throughout the summer, but there's one that is different from all the others. It's a Bible and Sports School, offered annually late in the summer at West Lawn United Methodist Church, in addition to the traditional one in June. He developed the Bible/sports theme after he noticed dwindling participation in the regular Bible School he directed for the church he attended in the 1970's. "I also wanted a program I thought my own children would enjoy as they were growing up," he said. The first one was held when his son, Todd, had completed second grade and his daughter Kristen, kindergarten. Both since have gone on to college. Todd and Kristen had been helpers in many of those schools.

The article would go on to describe the program in detail. It was a school, in that students earned points in a taking a quiz on the Bible lesson, completing a working sheet by looking up scripture, and memorizing Bible verses. They also earned points by doing four individual sports activities each day. Students earned small ribbons for sports skills and seals for Bible skills all these to be placed on a certificate. Top point getters earned the special gold, silver, and bronze medals. Music was also an important teaching tool. I decided on music that fit the theme and wrote several of the theme songs. I developed ten themes over those years. I wrote all the curriculum materials.

In 1980, I directed my first music camp at Greenview Bible Camp. My son had just completed grade 5 and two years on the trumpet. I could not afford to send my children to camp so I volunteered to hold camp so that my children could go for free. For those camps I served as music director which included arranging all the music. I also wrote the Bible curriculum. I arranged the scheduling for the week which included time for sports activities. The camp took care of archery, horseback riding, boating, eating, etc. We held music camps for five additional summers. Other summers, I served as a Bible teacher and helped with other activities, including overnight sleep in counselor.

There were other summers that I served as VBS teacher where I was not the director. For the summers from 2001 to 2006, I volunteered for one or more weeks each summer with Child Evangelism Fellowship at Rosedale Campground just outside the City of Reading.

My Christian ministry projects were not the only situations in which I worked with children. My son, Todd, played soccer on a team when he was six. The next seven years I was the coach of his soccer teams as he proceeded thru different age groups from age seven to fourteen. I played soccer in high school. I started teaching Todd trumpet and Kristen the French horn before each of them started playing in school in four grade. As a private instructor, I started other children on brass instruments. Some of those would become members of the youth orchestra at my church. Some would also become part of my Bible and Sports School's orchestra and event helpers with the sports activities. All I am saying is that I had previous experience working with children.

On March 29, 2007 I received a letter. The first paragraph would read: "It is with great pleasure and enthusiasm that I offer you the position of Director of Children's Ministry at First Presbyterian Church, Reading. This is a part-time position starting June 1, 2007 with an annual salary of $20,000. The weekly commitment is 20-25 hours. Rev. Dr. Keevil believes that you have a strong call to serve our congregation and lead our children." My salary for teaching full time with YOP had been $26,000. Throw in teaching some college courses as an adjunct and I would increase my salary for the next year even while losing the YOP job. I would need to help my daughter financially.

This letter came only two weeks after my daughter had received a letter. Her letter said that the child abuse accusation with the "blue bowl" was called "unfounded." Many people were surprised that I kept doing the "Bible and Sports Schools" after my children had gone their own ways and were no longer participants or helpers. I kept doing them because to stop would have been "sin." One aspect of "sin" is not doing what you believe you should. I call the opposite, "living by faith. Without faith it is impossible to please Him." It's simply doing what you believe is right. I always, however, had in mind something I wanted to do. I wanted to continue doing the Bible and Sports Schools until I would be able to have my grandchildren participate. I saw that was not going to happen with my son's daughters as they attended another church. It did not seem that it was going to happen with my daughter's children either. At the time I stopped doing the schools my daughter was thirty and did not have children. Taking this job, I could make that happen for Kristen's boys. I should know better than to say, "I."

The following article would appear in the Ivy Tower newsletter for May, 2007. It had a long title, "David Rathman to Join Staff as Director of Children's Ministry."

> The Search Committee for the Director of the Children's Ministry is delighted to report that David Rathman has been hired for that position. He will officially begin in that capacity the first of June, but he has already been participating in meetings of the Children's Ministry Team. We are blessed to have Dave as part of the staff; he brings a wealth of experience and gifts to the position, as well as enthusiasm and a deep faith in the Lord.
>
> David Rathman's background includes an MS in Secondary Education from Kutztown and extensive teaching experience in public schools and colleges; he also has many years of experience as a Sunday School teacher, Sunday School Superintendent, and Vacation

Bible School director in local churches. Rathman is currently teaching in the Youth Outreach Program, an alternative education program for Junior and Senior High School Students.

In addition, he comes to us with a special giftedness in music! He was director of music at this year's Easter Dawn Service atop Mt. Penn. David is married to Mary Lynne and they live in Blandon.

Upon accepting and receiving the position I was given a book. It was titled, "BOOK OF ORDER: The Constitution of the Presbyterian Church (U.S.A.)." I would have to do some reading. The previous twenty years I had been in a Methodist church, the twenty years previous to that a non-sectarian (independent) church, and twenty years previous to that a church that was a split off from a Mennonite tradition. If asked my doctrine, I would say, "the Bible." I opened up the book. The page to which I turned contained a section called, "Reconciliation: Justice and Peace." Upon reading the words of that section, I knew I was in the right place. I attended several staff meetings in May before I took over the job as a paid employee in June. In one of those meetings I volunteered for the devotions. I read to those in attendance words from that section. I finish this chapter with some of those words. No further explanation is necessary.

The church in worship proclaims, receives, and enacts reconciliation in Jesus Christ and commits itself to strive for justice and peace in its own life and in the world. Justice is the order God sets in human life for fair and honest dealing and for giving rights to those who have no power to claim rights for themselves. The Biblical vision of justices calls for working for fair laws and just administration of the law and redressing wrongs against individuals. There is no peace without justice. Wherever there is brokenness, violence, and injustice the people of God are called to peacemaking. In prayer the faithful lift intercessions for all who experience

brokenness, violence, and injustice; give thanks to God
for reconciliation, peace, and justice in Jesus Christ;
commit themselves to be reconcilers seeking justice and
pursuing peace.

The important question is not whether I would be an excellent
prospect for the position of Director of Children's Ministry, but would I
be an excellent prospect for the position of minister of reconciliation.

Chapter 16 – The Squirty Bottle Incident

A "Founded" Verdict of Indicated Child Abuse

Harry had been on the witness stand talking about the "blue bowl" incident. The exhibit that his lawyer presented did not refer to that incident. It referred instead to the second bump on the head incident that Harry had reported to CYS (BCCYS).

Zimmer: Okay. Well, why don't you explain what that is?

Harry: Okay. This is—we went to see Dr. Reuben. Bruce came home with a bump on his head and said that mommy hit him on the head with a spray bottle. So I took him right to the doctor. And Reading Pedes, they evaluated him. And as we were in—getting evaluated, both children——

Zimmer: What did you understand the injuries to be as a result of this incident?

Harry: Bryce had a bump on his head, and it was painful when I found it. I just touched his head and he winced in pain. You know, he said mommy hit him in the head with a spray bottle. And Trey told the doctor that mommy hit him on the head with a cup.

Ms. Dautrich: Objection.

The Court: Overruled.

Zimmer: Did the doctor recommend any treatment as a result of this visit?

Harry: There was no treatment for the injury. He reported it to CYS.

The Court: He, being Dr. Reuben.

Harry: Correct, Dr. Reuben.

Three months after the event, I asked Trey how he knew that "mommy hit Bryce on the head with a squirty bottle." Trey said, "Daddy tells me that every day." I never heard of a cup or spray bottle until seeing the trial transcript and doctors report in December of 2008. I thought the only words used to describe the weapon were "squirty" and "bottle." What did the doctor say in his report? Read below.

> "Patient comes for evaluation of bruise on top of head. He and brother report that mother hit him with a cup yesterday. He states that this hurt him at the time and it continues to hurt. On exam shows a small bruise/hematoma on the top of the head. There is minimal bruising. This is approximately 2 cm in diameter and firm. Mildly tender to the touch. In discussion with father they are in divorce situation and there are custody issues. Apparently, mother has issues with physically disciplining/hitting the children in the past. Child states that he has not been hit with a cup like this before, no other evidence of bruising or trauma. Discussed with father, will report to BCCYS for further investigation since caused significant pain."

He did report to BCCYS. However, there was no further investigation with the good doctor. Also the good doctor never talked to Kristen. So where does the doctor say, "spray bottle?" Why does the doctor say hitting the children? Why did Harry go to the doctor without checking with Kristen first as he had been directed by his lawyer, Jeffrey Karver, three months before this incident? Why does Harry talk to the doctor as if she has a long record physical abuse? She had no record of abuse. How does "mildly tender to the touch" translate to "significant pain?" If Bryce had received a bump on the head that caused "significant pain" at Kristen's house she would have reported it to Harry because of the directive.

Harry would go on to say that CYS came to his home to interview himself and the children. He would say in court that when interviewed by CYS the bump had been caused by a spray bottle. There was no mention of a cup. I would discover a report in the custody evaluator's second evaluation another description of the weapon of mass destruction. It was from the Child Protective Services part of CYS. It stated, "Child grabbed mother's hair with his toy. Mother hit child in the head with a "squirt gun" causing a knot on top of child's head." The report indicates that the pediatrician saw the child for this and believed that the child was in severe pain. Notice that the person from CYS did not say that the child was in severe pain. Since when is "to believe" considered a definitive pronouncement?

Kristen, in the second evaluation, would talk about the incident. She stated that Reading Pediatrics reported that the weapon was a "squirty bottle." She had not seen or read the reports from different sources. She only knew of the term "squirty bottle" from the boys. That is the term Mary Lynne and I knew and we learned that because it was the term used by the boys. So, was it a cup, a spray bottle, a squirty bottle, a squirt gun, or none of the above? How would Kristen describe the incident?

Kristen would say to the evaluator the children were playing with some type of toy and that Trey hit Bryce on the head with this toy. We called the toy, "the claw." She states that she was in the bathroom cleaning up the tub as she does every time after the boys bathe. She stated that Bryce hit her on the head with his toy and pulled her hair with it. She stated she spanked Bryce and sent him to bed. She said, "I spanked him. I gave him ice for his head." Ms. Hall stated she did not hit Bryce on the head that occurred between Bryce and Trey. Ms. Hall states that Mr. Hall again called CYS. She stated that Reading Pediatrics indicated this as child abuse. She is now indicated as a perpetrator of child abuse. Ms. Hall is very upset about this. She states she is a social worker and cannot work with this type of record – "I have appealed it.

I have a hearing May 1, 2008. I need a child abuse clearance to have a job."

The second evaluation report was done on April 22, 2008. She used the term "squirty bottle" in that report. In the trial, August 26, 2008, she would use the term "spray bottle." Why did she change terminology? "Spray bottle" would be used in the second expungement hearing held in July of 2008 by CYS in describing the weapon as they defended their accusations against Kristen. I thought the doctor said it was a "cup."

That's enough about the weapon's issue, but what about the "significant pain" issue? There was none. If there was significant pain, then Kristen would have told Harry about the bump. She would have followed the directive of Harry's lawyer. She would have told her parents about the bump. The incident was no big deal. Besides, Harry was to speak to Kristen if he discovered a bump or something. There was someone else who testified about the incident in the custody trial. Will "super nanny granny" please give your testimony?

Ms. Dautrich: Now, you know your daughter was indicated as a perpetrator of abuse of Bryce. Were you with him, Bryce, the day after that alleged abuse occurred?

Mary Lynne: I was. That's what was so strange about the whole thing. Because I came over that morning at 4:30 am. And Bryce promptly got up at 6:30 (Kristen left for work at 5 am) and immediately went over to the bathtub to get into the bathtub. And at that time he was obsessed in loving baths. Every chance he got, he wanted a bath. So I didn't ask him if he had had a bath the night before. I just let him go in. He started the water up. He's always capable of everything he's doing.And he took his bath. I washed him. Believe it or not, I washed his head, poured water on it, used the plastic thing. But I doubt whether I went over the back of his head. (Kristen, Mary Lynne, and I thought the bump was the back of the head. That was the one Kristen described to us that was made by Trey with the claw toy. The bump Harry describes and the doctor is said to be on the top of the head. Was that bump administered by Harry?) I only dried him off and used the brush. Never winced, never made a sound.

My husband came over after he got up. And he said, "I'm gonna take Bryce over to our house—which is three minutes away—and let you get Trey ready and then you can come over and get Bryce and take him to day care, which he did. He didn't say anything to my husband either, nothing. He didn't act—sorry. He just didn't. There was no indication of any injury.

Ms. Dautrich: And this was all before he was even transferred to Harry's custody?

Mary Lynne: Right. He went to daycare. They observed him at daycare. He was fine. He was great. Went to his dad, and all of a sudden his father feels the need to have a lump checked, that he said he winced in pain.

Ms. Dautrich: And did Bryce ever make any statements to you that Kristen had hit him with anything?

Mary Lynne: No, not at all.

Ms. Dautrich: Did Trey ever tell you that Kristen hit Bryce with something?

Mary Lynne: No. No. Sorry.

Harry would go on in the custody trial to state that he had received a letter from CYS stating that the second bump would be considered indicated abuse. The letter was written by Mr. William Clemons, Caseworker for CYS. Mr. Clemons states, "This letter is to inform you that the report of suspected child abuse concerning Bryce Hall received by this agency on June 27, 2007 is indicated, and will remain on file in Harrisburg until the above-named child becomes 23 years of age." Wasn't that the William Clemons that verified that Harry Hall had been caught lying to Kristen in the hall of the stairwell in the courthouse? Wasn't that the same William Clemons that told Kristen that even if the "blue bowl" bump had been called "founded," she could still see her children if she agreed to sign for 24 hour supervised visitation? Harry had said in court that Kristen had been interview by CYS about the "squirty bottle" incident. She did not get to tell her story of how Bryce got the bump. She was only told that the incident was determined as "founded" as being an indicated case of child abuse. She was told by William Clemons that she had to sign for 24 hour supervised visitation in order to see her children.

The letter to Harry Hall from Mr. Clemons was Harry's exhibit #4. Exhibit #5 was written on December 17, 2007, and addressed to

Harry Hall. It was from the Office of Children, Youth, and Families, Harrisburg, PA. It was as below:

> We are writing to inform you that the person who abused the above named child has REQUESTED A HEARING to appeal the case.
>
> KRISTEN HALL has requested a hearing instead of an administrative review of the report. The request has been forwarded to the Bureau of Hearings and Appeals which will schedule a hearing.
>
> As a subject of the abuse report being appealed, you have the right to be informed of this action. You will not be permitted to take an active part in the hearing unless called upon as a witness. It may be several months until the hearing is scheduled. If you are interested, please contact the above named children and youth agency or the appellant to learn of scheduling arrangements.

The first expungement hearing would be held May 1, 2008. That would be almost a year after the incident. A result of the "founded" verdict for indicated child abuse would be that Kristen would not be able to be a helper for me at the Bible and Sports School I would hold the summer of 2007 at First Presbyterian Church. My grandsons would not be able to participate in the B & SS. Kristen would be able to help in 2022.

CHAPTER 17 - MISSION IMPOSSIBLE

Surviving 24 Hour Supervised Visitation

What had been done to Kristen this time with the PSR, Petition for Special Relief, would leave her with another mission impossible. Her mission statement would be simple. Find a way that she could survive and be a parent to her children. To survive, she knew she needed help financially. That was made much more difficult because criminal clearance was necessary for obtaining employment in many social work positions, mandatory with children. She was offered jobs that she could not accept those because of the required criminal clearance. For the time, she would remain with the receptionist job at St. Joseph's Medical Center. It seemed impossible for a single person to survive on her income considering that she had to be able to provide her own housing. Add to that she would have expenses created by caring for two young children fifty percent of the time. She needed help in raising the boys. She needed a man willing to be both husband to her and father to two boys not his own. Add to that one with special needs. It seemed impossible to find a man with moral character that would be willing to date a mother who was found to be indicated of child abuse.

Kristen received pending 50/50 custody in April of 2007 based on the custody evaluator's first evaluation and report. That was eight months since the first PFA and two months before the second PSR where the verdict was called "founded." We were surprised that the

50/50 custody recommendation was certified that July despite the verdict from the second PSR. The arrangements made for custody were for a two week rotating basis. She would have the boys Monday, Tuesday, Friday, Saturday, and Sunday on the first week. The second week she would have them on Wednesday and Thursday. She would need a lot more finances to take care of the boys. She needed more help for babysitting. The second problem was easier to address as her mother had resigned from her part-time receptionist job. That, however, did not help Kristen financially because her mother was no longer able to give her some of her earnings. Kristen knew from her work experience in determining support for others that Harry would eventually have to pay child support because of the 50/50 custody agreement. Harry did not give in to that without going to a hearing. It was not until August of 2007 that he would start paying child support. Kristen never received alimony.

Kristen had no time to think about long term survival goals. She had immediate survival issues. Her life and her family's lives were further complicated by the 24 hour supervised visitation conditions imposed upon her. Where were she and the boys going to live? Besides her mother and father, who would be supervisors when she had the boys? Would she have enough money? She was faced with a "mission impossible."

Kristen's paid up rent for her apartment was only good for two more weeks. Her income did not qualify her to live in those apartments. She was able to rent the apartment the first time because she paid for nine months in advance. She could not do that again. There was also another problem. Her neighbors below (Kristen lived on the second floor), had complained about the noised from Kristen's apartment above. Most of that was from Bryce running around pushing a toy truck. Bryce always wanted to be doing something requiring motion. Both boys enjoyed jumping off the bed and other furniture. These activities were greatly encouraged by their father. Bryce was five and Trey would be four in a few months. They needed someplace to live where they would not bother someone. It was not too much for the old people below when she had the boys only four days a month. In April, when it first became fifteen days a month, it became too much. Another thing she could not do again was move in with her parents in their two bedroom home in the adult community.

Naturally, Kristen's parents would be supervisors. Her mother was already the babysitter when Kristen worked. Her mother came to the apartment before 5 am so that Kristen would be able to get to work by 5:15. Kristen would get home by 2:30 pm to take over for her mother. Under the 24 hour supervised visitation conditions her mother would have to remain as a supervisor. Without other supervisors, Mary Lynne would have to be with the boys for 48 or 72 hours without a break. Kristen could not have the boys without having a supervisor. Kristen would get a break from the boys when she had custody, grandma would not. It was during this time that my work transitioned from working for YOP to working as Children's Ministry Director. I would be there to help with the boys after work. We would also share night time supervisory detail. Grandma would stay some days overnight. Kristen had a bedroom. The boys had a bedroom. We had the sofa in the living room of the apartment. The other fifteen days a month my wife and I could live together in our home. In some ways it was like a prison sentence. Kristen understood that. Did BCCYS and Mr. William Clemons understand that? Harry understood that. It was a mission impossible, but we took it on one day at a time.

Kristen realized she needed other supervisors to help her parents survive this time. It could last as long as six months. Kristen knew from experience that it was difficult for one person to watch these two boys for even a few hours. In school, a year later, teachers would be given an aide just to watch Bryce. Kristen needed to find a supervisor to help sometimes during the day. She also needed someone willing to be a supervisor for overnight. In addition, these supervisors would have to be willing to work for no pay. Finding supervisors is a mission impossible.

Before receiving 50/50 custody, Kristen did have free time during the week to date. She also had two free weekends a month to date. None were interested in the commitment Kristen would require. It was far more difficult to continue that quest once she received 50/50. Around the time of the "squirty bottle" incident, Kristen got an interesting phone call while at her receptionist station at work. The caller said his name was Matt. He said he noticed her sitting behind the desk at the hospital. He said he never did this before, but he was asking her for a date. Kristen said, "Yes." She had not noticed him at the hospital. He had not made himself known. She would learn he was tall and athletic looking. He worked for a restaurant supply company driving truck and delivering supplies. He said he had been in the marines in some kind of security position. They started dating. He worked most days to five or six. Kristen, being desperate, asked Matt if he would be willing to be a daytime supervisor. Matt said, "Yes." My wife and I were surprised, at the same time grateful, and then somewhat suspicious. We learned from Kristen that Matt's father was a retired policeman and now worked as a driver for CYS. We told Kristen of our suspicions. Goofy Kristen told Matt of our suspicions. Matt laughed. But Matt would supervise. Thank you, Matt. I liked Matt. One time we played basketball two-on-two against some youngsters. Our average age was 48, the other team 19. We lost in overtime 10 to 12, counting by ones. Matt was approved by CYS. Did his father have any influence? I have never been able to decide if Matt was animal or plant concerning his relationship with Kristen. If animal, then it was the normal boyfriend relationship. If a plant, then he was planted there by CYS. Maybe, Matt, over time, evolved from plant to animal.

Matt and I also got to sit on a bench together on another occasion. The bench was outside the courtroom. We were sequestered as we waited to testify in Kristen's custody trial. I had seen Matt earlier before going into the County Courthouse. He was standing outside the County Services building talking with his father and waiting to go into the adjoining County Courthouse. Two hours had gone by before my daughter came out from the courtroom to tell us that it was time for someone from our team to get off the bench and get into the game. In those two hours on the bench together, Matt let me do most of the talking. That was true most of the time when with Matt. Sometimes, to me he seemed like a body guard for a witness protection program. Anyway, it was time for Matt to take the witness stand to testify. I had no idea what his testimony would be. Kristen's lawyer questions Matt.

Ms. Dautrich: How do you know my client, Kristen Hall?
Matt: She's my friend.

Ms. Dautrich: And were you at some point in time required to supervise her and her children?

Matt: Yes.

Ms Dautrich: And about how long of a period do you think you spent supervising them?

Matt: Well, I've known her for six months. But I don't know if it went on for that long.

By the time of the custody trial, Matt had known Kristen for more than a year. He may have remembered the six month number because that was the proposed time for the supervised visitation to last. The supervised visitation time was dropped after four months. The caseworkers that visited her during that time said it was not necessary. Matt had followed through as supervisor for the entire period of 24 hour supervision. That was from July through November of 2007. Kristen would find a new boyfriend later in December. Matt still calls Kristen on occasion. Matt would testify to the amount of time he spent as supervisor. With his work schedule he could supervise some days after 5:00. It would give Mary Lynne and I a few hours break during the week. He was also available some weekends. His important testimony would be how he observed Kristen as a mother.

Ms. Dautrich: And you were able to observe her interacting with them and how she was parenting them?

Matt: Yes.

Ms. Dautrich: How would you describe the way that she disciplined Bryce and Trey?

Matt: Like any other mother.

Ms. Dautrich: So what kinds of things would she do if they misbehaved?

Matt: Say stop doin' that. I'll put you on time-out, that's not right.

Ms. Dautrich: Did she ever while you were there hit the children?

Matt: No.

Ms. Dautrich: Did she do anything that would cause you concern as the supervisor, concern for the children's behavior?

Matt: No.

Ms. Dautrich: I'm sorry, the children's safety?

Matt: What was that?

Ms. Dautrich: Were you concerned for the children's safety?

Matt: No.

Ms. Dautrich: And what kind of a bond do the kids seem to have with their mother?

Matt: They always—always call her, wanted her. They wouldn't want to do anything with me alone. The always wanted her around.

Ms. Dautrich: Did she appear to favor one child over the other?

Matt: Not that I saw.

Ms. Dautrich: Now, in order for you to be a supervisor, did you have to talk with Children and Youth Services of Berks County and be approved by them to supervise her?

Matt: Yes.

Matt did get to see Kristen interact with the boys in the time between the first PFA and the custody trial. Harry did not. Who would be the better witness concerning Kristen's interaction with the boys, Harry or Matt? Harry's lawyer would continue with the cross-examination. There would not be much information from Matt that could be used by Harry's team for their favor.

Zimmer: You were there all the time, correct?

Matt: When I could be.

Zimmer: But you weren't there 24 hours a day, correct?

Matt: Correct.

Zimmer: So it's possible that there were other individuals that you were not aware of, correct?

Matt: Just her roommate. That's all I know of.

He was not a roommate. He was a house mate. He was the other part of the solution to the problems involving housing and supervision. His name was Bern. He was the brother of Danny, the one with whom Kristen supposedly had an affair with years ago. Kristen had learned that his brother was interested in a finding a place to rent outside the city. She learned from Bern that Danny told his brother that he should look out for Kristen. Danny was shocked learning what was done to

Kristen by Harry because of their supposed affair. He thought surely Kristen and Harry had reconciled once Harry had learned there was no affair. Bern would tell his history and his relationship with Kristen during an interview by Dr. Thomas at the second custody evaluation held in April of 2008. Bern would be Kristen's night time supervisor and, more importantly, share the costs for the rental farm house from July 2001 to July 2008.

Bern stated that he had a problem when he was 18 or 19 years old. He states, "I burglarized gun stores and sold guns to people in Reading. It was stupid kid stuff." Mr. Harrison stated that he was incarcerated for over nine years. He stated he was released from prison at the age of 28 and at the present was 36 years old. He stated he was married in 2004, but was not officially divorced. He has a four year old daughter from that marriage, Shale. He has another child, a son born a year earlier. He stated that both children live with their respective mothers. He states he sees the children every weekend from Saturday evening to Sunday evening. He was a foreman of a crew that did plaster and stucco work. He had been working for the firm for almost 8 years.

Bern's working hours would avail him the opportunity to be night time supervisor. He just had to be approved by CYS. Bern went for an interview and he was approved, much to his surprise. Kristen was not as much surprised. She was the master at second chances and she thought he had earned it with his 8 year clean slate. He also had no record of child abuse. Of course, Kristen did not have that child abuse clearance. Apparently, that did not matter to Bern. I was impressed with Bern's intelligence and demeanor. Bern said to the evaluator that the highest grade he completed was tenth. He did say that he earned his degree while incarcerated. He said he did a lot of reading and studying. I would have some meaningful conversations with Bern, probably more so than with Kristen with her four year college degree.

The most important part of Bern's testimony to the evaluator would be his observations of Kristen's parenting. It is important because judges in custody cases rarely break from the custody evaluator's recommendation. Mr. Harrison was asked about his involvement with Bryce and Trey. He stated that his children love Ms. Hall's children. He states, "I'm like an uncle to Kristen's children basically." He states he plays with them and spends some time with them. Mr. Harrison states he might discipline his own children when they are all playing together. He states his discipline is limited to verbal interactions, reprimands, and redirection. Mr. Harrison states the Kristen Hall is always there and "she's 100% in charge." Bern should have added there were times when he left Kristen watching his children as well as her own. Bern trusted the "child abuser" with his children, but Kristen could not legally work with me with children in church. Bern should have added that he taught Bryce how to play video games with his play station. He would set up his old play station for Bryce on the third floor of the farm house. Dr. Thomas would not arrive at any negatives against Kristen concerning this arrangement with Bern. But, what would Harry say about Bern in court?

Zimmer: Are you concerned with regard to mother's judgment?

Harry: Yes. Her—she's had several men in her life in the last year or two that I don't want my kids around, long criminal records, serious, serious issues there.

Zimmer: Do you know of any of the other individuals—any of the individuals mother may have resided with?

Harry: Last name Harrison. I'm drawing a blank on his first name. The man she lived with. Bern. The kids called him Bern. Bernard Harrison.

Zimmer: Did you meet any of these individuals that mother resided with?

Harry: Yeah. I met him once or twice when he was with mom when I transitioned the kids. We never spoke. He was just there.

Zimmer lies. He says there were individuals that resided with Kristen. Bern was the only one and that was necessary because of the 24 hour supervised visitation brought about by Harry's insistence to CYS. In the trial no other individual would be brought up With—whom Kristen resided. Harry lies. He says there were several with long criminal records. Bern was the only one with a criminal record. And that was more than eight years ago. Harry's nephew's criminal records are more up to date. But CYS gave Bern the okay as a supervisor. Unlike Kristen, Harry is not a person to give someone a second chance. The Court should have recognized these lies of Zimmer and Harry. Harry never came up with any individual that was with Kristen that harmed the boys in any way. There would be those that gave time and other things including finances. I can come up with a name of one individual who was with Kristen and had harmed the boys in some way. The name is Harry Hall.

Ms. Dautrich: Now, the house that you lived in that you discussed in the country, was that the one where Bernard Harrison was the roommate?

Kristen: That was the roommate I found. That was the only person I knew that was, you know, looking for a place to live. Because at that point, he was living with his brother in a row home in the city. And he wanted his kids to have, a nice big yard, nice big home, a lot of room in which to play.

Ms. Dautrich: And did you ever live with anyone else other than your parents and Mr. Harrison form the day you and Harry split up?

Kristen: No.

Ms. Dautrich:—to today's date?

Kristen: No.

Ms. Dautrich: And when did you move out of that place?

Kristen: I moved out of the house in Oley, July 15th. That was my moving date.

Ms. Dautrich: This year, yes. I moved back to the apartment.

I wish Kristen and everyone else would stop saying that Bern was a roommate. Bern would tell her, a few months after sharing the house, that he would also like to share a room. They had separate bedrooms in the house. That was part of the deal. Years later I would explain to Kristen the connotation of the term "roommate." She would say, "Oh!" They would complete the year of the lease for the farm house. With the help of Matt and Bern, Kristen would survive the time of the 24 hour supervised visitation provision. At least, one of Kristen's "mission impossible" acts had been completed as of November in the year of 2007.

CHAPTER 18 - IN THE DRIVER'S SEAT

The Transition Lie

Harry, in the custody trial, describes an event that happened only a few days after Kristen was placed under the 24 hour supervisory visitation provision. We heard from Kristen that Harry had gone to the supervisor at CYS in charge of approving supervisors. She said that Harry had given his own list of those that he would approve as supervisors of Kristen. When we heard his list, we knew it would be impossible for any of them to do the job. That was no big deal. The big deal was that he wanted us, Mary Lynne and I, excluded as supervisors. He thought he was in the driver's seat in this whole affair. The CYS supervisor said to Harry that she would decide who would be approved. I give the supervisor credit for that decision. We were approved along with Matt and Bern. I needed to find a way to talk with Harry. I wanted to ask him one question. "Why did you try to have us eliminated as supervisors?" He knew that without our help Kristen would surely have to give up the fight and give him primary custody.

Overnight I formed a plan. The next day Kristen planned to transition the boys with Harry coming to drop off the boys at our home. While Harry would be handing over items for the boys, I would sneak around to the driver's side of the Durango. I would slip into the driver's seat and take the keys from the ignition. I would give the key back after I was able to ask my one question. I didn't even care if he gave an answer. At least, he would learn that we knew he tried to eliminate us as supervisors for Kristen. Harry would describe his version of that transition.

Zimmer: Was there ever an incident involving Miss Hall and her father?

Harry: Yeah. There was a time when—when Kristen had her apartment in Blandon, and we were still transitioning the kids at her apartment. I would always—I did all the moving, all the pick-ups and drop-offs, at her house. One day she asked me to come up to her parent's house—which was only another mile up the road—to drop the kids off, which I did. I didn't think of anything of it. And I got there, and we're transitioning the children. I'm on the passenger side of my vehicle talking to Kristen, handing over the book bags and whatever else we had to hand over. And I see my father-in-law go around my—the side of the truck. And he opens the door and he's leaning in trying to get the keys out of the ignition. Well, so I went around that side and got between him and the truck. And I got in my truck. It turns out the keys were in my pocket anyway. Again, so I close the door. I start the engine. I'm ready to leave because I don't like the drama in front of the kids. And then Kristen climbs in my car and starts screaming at me something about don't hurt my father or something like that. And I just wanted to leave, and I had to wait until she—and the kids were standing right there watching the whole thing. I had to wait until she got out of my truck so I could leave.

When I left, I went to the Turkey Hill. And I called the local police, and I filed a police report on that incident.

I would love to see that report. If it is as idiotic as his testimony, they had a good laugh. Why would Kristen get in the door to tell Harry not to hurt her father when he had already closed the car door and started the engine? Let me see, I was leaning to grab his keys in the ignition. Harry, at the same time, was able to squeeze into the driver's seat. How does he do that?

For what crime was I accused? It could have been the crime of getting into the driver's seat. But Harry did not admit that I got there first. He wants to be in the driver's seat. So again, Harry lied about an event. I had gotten into the driver's seat as Harry was handing over the items. As I originally planned, I would take the keys out of the ignition and run with them. I thought the boys would enjoy an adult game of cat and mouse. I wanted to see if the cool cat, Harry, could catch the mouse with the key, Mr. Ratman. It would have been funny. I would have given the keys back after I got to ask my simple question. But my plan was ruined. So I just sat in the driver's seat. Harry got in on the passenger's side. Good. I wanted to tell Harry to shut the door and talk. Instead, he was the one who would make a scene. He screamed, and it probably appeared that he was trying to shove me out of the driver's seat. At least, that was Kristen's impression. She really did not have to follow Harry into the passenger's side of the Durango. I got out of the driver's seat and went around to the passenger's side to get Kristen out of the passenger's seat. Besides, the seat was too small for Kristen and Harry to be beside each other. That was the closest they had been to each other in a year. Harry got out next and went back in on the driver's side. He sat in the driver's seat and drove off. At the time I did not know he went to file the police report. Maybe the whole scene was funny to the boys. It was like a game of musical chairs using truck seats. There were two seats and three people. I never did get to ask my question.

Harry has never described truthfully any event that I have observed. Nor, does he ever describe the context of any of those events. He was deceiving in other ways in much of his testimony. He said, in the testimony above, that he went out of his way to do all the transitioning by going to her place of residence. He is so magnanimous. The truth is that he only did that for a few months of the two years before the custody trial. After the event described in this chapter, which occurred a year before the trial, he required that they transition the boys at a neutral place. The other fact he failed to mention was that after the filing of the second PFA and the babysitting for free time, he would not allow Kristen to come to his house at all. If there was something still at the marital residence that we needed which was Kristen's or ours, I would have to go to the house to pick it up. One of those times is described by the event which occurred a few weeks after the above.

Describing someone as being "in the driver's seat" would seem to give the impression of someone who likes to feel he is in control. That is Harry. Harry likes to give the impression that he is always in control of his children. The truth is no one knows what goes on at Harry's house. The boys say Harry tells them not to say what goes on at his house. I found out one Saturday what went on that day. I remember the date well because it was only a week or two before the Bible School I was to hold at FPC in late July of 2007. I had hoped, when taking the job as Children's Ministry Director, that Kristen would be able to bring the boys. Because of the child abuse accusation and "founded" verdict of indicated child abuse, she could not accompany her children to the program. At their young age, they would not want to go there without her. In addition, Harry would have custody for some of those evenings. Anyway, I went to Harry's house to retrieve my barrel of balls that was in the basement. I had used the balls for my Bible and Sports School in past years.

It was a Saturday noon when I went up the steps to knock on the door. As said, Harry would not allow Kristen to come with me to the house. I knocked on the door and happened to look through the door window. The boys and Harry were all wearing only underpants. Trey came to the door immediately. Harry came a few seconds later as he had gone to put on shorts. Thank goodness! Bryce was running around the inside of the house pushing a small plastic truck. I noticed that Harry had the inside doors unlocked so the boys could pass through the hallway into the master bedroom and complete a nice circuit. Those doors were locked when Kristen had come back to the home after the first PFA to babysit for free. Harry seemed perturbed. I told him I needed my balls. I said they were in the basement. We, that is, Harry, Trey, and I, went into the basement. Bryce remained upstairs continually pushing his little plastic truck around and around. The barrel was empty and the balls were scattered about. Harry and Trey helped to gather up my balls. In the basement were "Nerf" balls of all sizes and shapes, three sizes of footballs, softballs, whiffle balls, soccer balls, a sport ball, basketball, golf balls, and one screw ball. I did not take the screw ball. I carried the barrel of balls up the stairs and outside the house. As I got into my car, I looked down the street. There was Bryce 200 feet away about ready to go down the hill out of sight in his underpants pushing that little plastic truck. Nice job, Harry. You have great control. It only took one distraction for Bryce to escape from Harry. You could say that Bryce was in the driver's seat. Why could not Harry at the least get him a better toy to push? He was five, not three. He was old enough to be used as the only witness to have his mother accused of child abuse. Excuse me, Harry did use Trey also who was less than four years old. As I left Harry told me to call in advance next time. I did not wish there to be a next time.

Maybe you could say that Bryce was really the one in control. He did tell us a story of something he did to Harry that he had also done to mommy when she was still living at the home with the boys. Harry is able to lock Bryce's bedroom door from the hallway. One day Bryce did that to daddy. He locked Harry in that bedroom. Bryce had done that to Kristen. To get out they both had to take the screen off and jump through the window to the ground. I don't know if that is called a "high" jump or a "low" jump. Bryce thinks it is a "funny" jump.

For several weeks the summer of 2007, Bryce would say when reprimanded, "I am going to tell that mommy hit me with a squirty bottle." That phrase seemed to gain Bryce a lot of attention that summer. He would also gain a lot of attention at daycare that summer. He was getting to be known as the little liar. Harry taught him well. Bryce felt like he was in the driver's seat.

Harry did not accomplish everything he had hoped with the second "bump on the head" PSR. He was able to make it more difficult for Kristen to get a better job. He was able to make it that Kristen could not participate at anytime with the boys in any of the children's programs under her father's tenure at FPC as CMD. He was able to force Kristen and us to live under 24 hour supervised visitation. However, he was not able to force Kristen to relinquish primary custody to Harry. It remained 50/50 custody through the next year, until the custody trial of 2008. Harry acted, however, that he was "in the driver's seat." After all, he had the marital residence. And, Kristen was convicted of child abuse.

Chapter 19 – Life on the Farm

The Best of Times

Harry was not happy with 50/50 custody. He wanted primary custody. What did he have to offer the boys the summer of 2007? Trey would turn 4 years old in three months, and Bryce would be five and a half when he started full time kindergarten. During the week both boys, when in Harry's custody, would get up at 5:30 am so that Harry could have them at day care when it opened at 6:30 am. They would be the first ones there. Bryce would have more variety once school started. Bryce could then leave daycare by 9:00 am, return to daycare at 3:30 pm, and be picked up by Harry at 4:30 pm. The boys would be tired enough with ten hours of day care and school to want to go to bed by 8:00 pm. We never learned what Harry did with the boys when he had them. The boys said Harry told them not to say what goes on at Harry's house.

On the farm with Kristen, her parents and other supervisors, the lives of the boys would be much different. For the first four months, which included the summer of 2007, Kristen was under the 24 hour supervised visitation provision. She also had to be visited by special caseworkers for Bryce because of his special needs and from BCCYS who had to observe Kristen to see if she could refrain from being abusive to Bryce. The supervision period was scheduled for six months, but it was shortened to four months for obvious reasons. In summary, there were many that would enjoy that farm in the Oley valley that summer.

The owner of the property neither farmed the property nor lived there. But it was a working farm in that many acres were planted in corn and soybeans by a local farmer. The huge barn was used for storage. It was a great place to enjoy the benefits of living on a farm without the burden of the work. Kristen and Bern could choose between two houses on the property to rent. The house closest to the creek was once part of a mill built in the 19th century. It was well restored with an added addition. It looked like a house that could have been built in the 20th century. The other house had a date stone that read 1741. The interior was completely refurbished. It was a full three stories high with stones walls more than a foot thick. You could tell the thickness of the walls from the inside by the twelve inches of depth for the window sills. The older house would suit their need. At $2000 a month it was the least expensive. The first floor in the farm house had a living room, dining room, kitchen, and smaller sitting room with adjacent bathroom with a shower. So Bern could have his own bathroom. The second floor had four bedrooms and a bathroom with combination tub shower which would be perfect for Kristen and the boys. Kristen and Bern would have separate bedrooms on the second floor. The best thing was the newly refurbished, fully carpeted, third floor. It had a small bedroom, but the rest of that floor we called the "super room." It was a great place for Kristen's and Bern's children when they had to be indoors. No longer would Kristen have to worry about the neighbors below. Bryce had first choice of the remaining bedrooms. He chose the bedroom on the third floor. Trey would have the bedroom adjacent to Kristen's on the second floor. That left the remaining bedroom on the second floor for Bern's children.

As good as the house was in providing for Kristen's needs, the rest of the property would provide more entertainment than any child could hope for. There was a private lane that led to the house from Bertolet Mill Road. The first part of the lane ran for three hundred yards until it came to a stream that meandered through the property. To the left of the path was a large open pasture with no cows. To the right of the lane was a wooded area through which cows from the local farm often roamed. It seemed the cows were in the wrong place. The lane was a great place for a walk. The next spring Bryce would turn six years old and learn to ride the bicycle on that lane. A few months later Trey, not yet five, would also learn to ride his bicycle on that lane. What boys wouldn't love a stream on their property? The fish were bigger than the one in Kristen's fish bowl. You had to cross over a rickety wooden bridge to get to the other side. You could hear the cars from the house as they crossed over the bridge. On the other side of the stream, the side with the two houses, there was a spring house with adjacent pond formed from stone walls. There were frogs in that pond and other things that would provide fun for the boys and me. There were several big trees on the property and porch in front of the house for shade in the summer. There were other buildings including a large barn. At the time it was only used for storage. For the boys and me, it would be a place to explore. Ten cats called it home. The cornfield behind the barn looked like it went on forever. At the time Kristen moved there the corn was already five feet high. The height would double the next month. A lot of lawn, several acres, surrounded the houses and other buildings on that side of the stream. Bryce was in paradise. He loved to mow even at age five. I bought Bryce a push mower, not power, before Kristen moved to the farm. It did not matter what pattern he used. There was a caretaker who would unceremoniously wipe out Bryce's unique patterns with a lawn tractor. Which would a child prefer, 10 hours in daycare, or 10 hours on the farm?

Ms. Dautrich: After those nine months, where did you live?

Kristen: Then what ended up happening was I felt that the apartment was very confining for Bryce, so I was looking into single homes to rent. Well, that wasn't—because my, you know, income being as low as it is, I was having trouble finding a home to rent by myself that I could afford. So, you know, I was looking around. And I did find this beautiful house out in the country which I felt would be great for the kids. Unfortunately, I would have to find a roommate if I wanted this home. And originally my thought was I gotta get Bryce out of this apartment because it just wasn't working for him.

Ms. Dautrich: Now, the house that you lived in that you just discussed in the country, was that the one where Bernard Harrison was the roommate?

Kristen: That was the roommate I found. That was the only person I knew, you know, looking for a place to live. Because at that point, he was living with his brother in row home in the city. And he wanted his kids to have, nice big yard, nice big home, a lot of room to play.

Ms. Dautrich: And did you ever live with anyone else other than your parents and Mr. Harrison from the day you and Harry split up?

Kristen: No.

In court, Harry would only say a little about the farm house. He would not say anything nor would Kristen have the chance to say anything about the great time the children would have living on the farm. I wish Kristen would stop using the word roommate to describe Bern. They shared a house not a room.

Zimmer: Now, mother's prior residence was three stories, correct?

Harry: Yeah, it was.

Zimmer: Where did the children stay at mom's house most of the time?

Harry: Well, Bryce had a bedroom—well, basically they called it the super room or the great room or it was the third—floor attic. The whole thing was Bryce's. Trey was on the second floor across the street from—across the hallway from his mom. So Bryce was up there. Now, Trey didn't use that room. He slept with his mom. (So, her roommate was Trey, not Bern.) He still does.

Zimmer: Do you believe that's appropriate?

Harry: No.

Zimmer: Why?

Harry: He should be independent. He's five years old. He needs to sleep in his own bed. He did that up until the time of the 50/50 custody arrangement happened. And now that's not the case.

Stop right there, Harry. So how do you know where Trey sleeps? How do you that the whole third floor is Bryce's? It is not. Only the separate bedroom on the third floor is Bryce's. He decided he wanted that for his own. Why is it that you do not mention the fact that Trey was afraid to be in any room by himself at that young age? Trey was less than four when Kristen moved to the farm house. When Mary Lynne babysat, Trey would always ask her to go with him when he needed to go to another room, even the bathroom. Trey told us that he slept between Harry and his boss for a number of weekends when staying overnight. Harry had pictures for the court in his exhibits that showed that the boys had separate bedrooms. The truth is that Trey would not sleep in his own room by himself. The boys share the same bedroom at Harry's house. How many times has Trey slept with Harry? When you said that Trey slept in his own bedroom before the time of 50/50, are you saying that when it became 50/50 you could no longer get Trey to sleep in his own bed? That must be the case. As usual, Harry's testimony is as clear as mud.

Zimmer: How is it that you're familiar with the layout of Miss Hall's home?

Harry: Bryce—Bryce is a very intelligent kid, and is very detail oriented. I know he had a third floor bedroom. I know that Trey had a second floor bedroom across the hall from mommy's bedroom. I know that he played video games at night when mommy was asleep.

The Court: So all your testimony comes from Bryce what you heard from Bryce?

Harry: Yeah.

The Court: All right.

Harry: He told me on three separate occasions he was playing video games and mommy was asleep.

Zimmer: Have you ever been in that house?

Harry: I've been to the front—no, never been in the house.

So that is the extent of what Harry knows about the boy's lives on the farm. Life on the farm is when you play videos at night while your mommy is sleeping. Perhaps, I should write a chapter about Bryce and his video games. Why did Judge Lash listen to and allow testimony of what Harry said the five year old, Bryce, said? Judge Lash would not allow me to testify to what I heard Bryce say. Why do Harry and Zimmer admit to using a five year old as a spy?

What was life on the farm like for my wife, my daughter, the boys, and I? They would be some of the best days of our lives. For the whole time, almost a year, Kristen had 50/50 custody? That meant for two or three days a week we, my wife and I, were the babysitters. On those days I would be at the farm by 4:30 am so that Kristen could leave for work by 5:00 am. When I got to the house I would first look at the stars and then proceed to the third floor bedroom to check on Bryce. That was only for the first half of the year. Bryce heard a thump in the night. People should not talk about ghosts. Thereafter, Bryce, for sleeping purposes, would takeover Trey's bedroom on the second floor. On occasion, Bryce would also take over the other third of Kristen's queen size bed. After checking on Bryce, I would proceed to the sofa on the first floor. About 6:00 am Bern came down the stairs to go to the first floor bathroom and shower. He would leave shortly for work. For the first four months he served his duty as overnight supervisor. Mary Lynne would arrive each morning after Bern had left. By the time the boys had started waking up their mother had already been "raptured." That is what it would be like to the boys. She left with the only trace being what she had worn to bed that night. One of the reasons she had allowed Trey being in bed with her overnight was the fact that he could not be with her as he woke in the morning. At least he was with her when he went to sleep. Trey had problems getting to sleep. Bryce, on the other hand, had already expended enough energy during the day that he went to sleep early. He would not play videos overnight.

Bryce loved to mow. I asked him why. He said he liked the sound and watching the grass fly. He let a lot of grass fly. Bryce and I were buddies. My forte is thinking up different things for kids to do. My wife calls me Peter Pan. Or, was it Robin Williams when he played Peter Pan? Bryce and I found a cool thing to do at the frog pond next to the spring house. Find a stick, a broken branch from a tree, six feet or longer. It had to be that long to reach down into the pond. The surface of the pond was three feet below ground level. In the summer the surface was covered with algae or green organic "yuk" I called, "scum." Reach into the scum with the stick and twirl it gathering up scum as you would when gathering cotton candy on one of those paper cones. Carry the scum over to the creek and flick the scum off the stick into the creek. Bryce and I would repeat the recipe. I would quit, but Bryce would continue for hours until the pond was free of the scum. It would take two weeks for the scum to completely cover the pond again. It would be time for Bryce to find another stick. The frogs did not seem to mind. They croaked, but not in the "dead" sense.

I would not want to be a rodent on that property. There were at least ten cats. Someone must have been feeding them. We saw some of them run into the barn. The boys and I followed. In the barn were several dishes for food and water. On several occasions, early in the morning—some would say the middle of the night – a man would come to feed them. When he turned on the water spigot about 200 feet from the house, the pipes in the farm house groaned. That was eerie at 5:00 am. I would eventually get to talk to him. He said he came at that time to feed the cats so that he would not scare anyone. I wish he would have scared me in daylight. It would not have been as scary.

Anyway, my daughter could not resist feeding the cats. She put food under the porch roof. The cats came to eat. When anyone came close to them they ran. They were "scaredy" cats. One day that winter another cat appeared that was different. The cat was young and did not run, but came to us. That spring the cat had two kittens in the back of the farm house. Kristen could not help but give the three a home for the first few weeks in the laundry room. She could not afford a washer and dryer. She could afford a monthly installment for the three cats. That was the only place they would be allowed in the house except for the path through the kitchen to the back door. Except for the fish in a bowl, the boys did not have a pet at Kristen's house. They would get to watch the mother with her kittens. The boys and I would follow the other ten cats into the barn. The barn became a fun place to explore when it was filled with the large rectangular bales of hay.

The lane and other parts of the property made it available for all types of riding toys. Bern had brought a battery operated riding toy to the farm that he had for his children. His children would only be there on the weekends. He allowed Bryce and Trey to use it at anytime. Bryce had gotten a similar toy for his fourth birthday when the whole family was still living together. Of course that had remained at Harry's house. At the time for his sixth birthday, Kristen was still living at the farm. She asked Bryce what he wanted for his birthday. She always tried to get the boys what they asked for. Bryce says, "The battery powered monster truck." Yes, it was not a little toy, but one which you would actually ride and drive. It had two seats. When Bern's children came to the farm all four children could be driving or riding at the same time. When Kristen had the boys by themselves each could be driving. Besides, it would it was a bargain at $350. Kristen knew when purchasing the monster truck that she would soon be giving it to Harry. She would have to move from the farm to an apartment in few months. By giving it to Harry when she moved, each would have a riding toy at Harry's house. She purchased the toy with $200 dollars she got from pawning the engagement ring she got from Harry eight years earlier. The rest would come from the monthly child support from Harry. To the custody evaluator one month after that purchase, Harry would say, "Trey would get whatever he asked for, but Bryce would only be punished harshly."

As said, the lane was great for riding bicycles. The boys had already been riding bicycles with training wheels in the basement of Harry's house when Kristen still lived there. Trey had still not turned three when he was riding in the basement. Occasionally, I watched as they crashed. Harry raced bicycles as a young adult and he had many trophies in the basement from those races. I thought he would be anxious to teach his boys to ride without training wheels. Kristen bought bicycles for the boys for Christmas of 2006, but the boys were too small and the bikes too big. It was early March of 2008, when Bryce came to me asking to be helped in riding the bicycle without training wheels. I did. Bryce was successful that same day. Two months later, Trey would also be successful. It was a great place to ride. My wife and I brought our bicycles to the farm and the four of us would ride together. A month after writing my letter to Judge Lash, I wrote a letter to Harry saying that I was sorry I taught them to ride before he did. I wanted to give him the first chance first to teach them, but that was not happening. Bryce asked. I responded.

There were many other things the five of us loved about living on the farm. Mary Lynne loved exploring the cemetery, walking the lane, saying hello to the cows, and just sitting outside looking over God's creation. In the summer, Bryce loved jumping off the rock into the stream. Trey loved the fact that he could enjoy it all with his mother. Kristen loved the fact that she could enjoy the farm with the boys, both of them. The only thing I ever learned that the boys loved about being at Harry's house was the dog.

Chapter 20 - Computer Whiz

Bryce's Expertise on the Computer

One day I noticed something different on my user account page on my computer. The little picture on the page seemed different. I wondered why I never noticed that before. A few weeks later it was different again. I would learn it was not the picture computer changing the picture. It was Bryce. He was only four at the time he started changing the picture. Bryce would show me years later how to do it. Bryce was a computer whiz at age four.

One day we took Kristen and the boys to Trexler's Game Preserve. At least, that was the name I knew for the place before being renamed the Lehigh Valley Zoo. To me the best part is when you exit the zoo. You have to ford a creek driving through it in your car. You then pass a large enclosed area in which elk are residing. A large herd of buffalo is scattered throughout the last enclosed area. The exit road climbs as you continue to exit. At the top there is a lookout off the road with a 360 degree view including that of the zoo some distance below. Be careful as you exit through the open area for the last mile. You might run into some free roaming deer. That day, I took pictures all along the way. I downloaded the pictures onto my computer. The boys and I looked at the pictures from that trip. When we got to the picture of the buffalo herd, Bryce wanted control of the computer. I had shown Bryce previously how you can zoom in and out on a picture. That was what

Bryce wanted to do on the picture of the buffalo herd. He zoomed as far as he could on the picture and still be discernable. The thing discernable was a nice size pile of buffalo dung. I am not trying to buffalo anyone. Bryce laughed. Many times he has come to our house and gone straight to the computer. He would go through all the necessary steps, seven of them, to get that same laugh. He was not yet five and he was a computer whiz.

We would get the game, "I Spy," for the boys to play on the computer. Bryce had not started kindergarten when he started learning words through playing that game. On one occasion, he was at the computer playing the game when his three cousins, all girls with the youngest his age, came to visit. He felt like "big stuff" having the three of them and his brother play the game with everyone as he was in control. He was the computer whiz.

Bryce was five and a half when it was time for him to be starting full day kindergarten. That was the way Harry wanted it. It might cost him less for daycare when he was to have the boys. Most of the time that first summer would be spent outside for there were plenty of options to entertain two boys on the farm. As the days shortened more time had to be spent indoors. The super room was great for lots of activities, but none would be sufficient to entertain Bryce. Bern, Kristen's house mate and night time supervisor, would come forth with what was needed to entertain a computer whiz. Harry would testify about that entertainment at the custody trial.

Harry: Bryce was talking about the video games he was playing. I can't think of the name of them. He played good games, but there were some other ones there. Grand Theft Auto was one, Mortal Combat. Grand Theft—and for Bryce with his issues, he shouldn't be playing violent video games. But these games are—the whole point of the game is to steal a car. You have got to shoot cops and pick up hookers, and I mean that's what the game was. And the Mortal Combat was just a fighting game. Bryce described an incident where you just kick a guy in the head until—

Ms. Dautrich: Objection as to what the children said.

The Court: Overruled.

Zimmer: Are you generally—

Harry: Bryce described the video game Mortal Combat where he said if you just keep kicking him in the head time after time, the blood starts running down until he slips and he falls. That was the kind of thing Bryce was doing.

Zimmer: Are you generally familiar with these games?

Harry: I've known of them. I don't play them. I don't have them.

Zimmer: Have you ever?

Harry: I've seen them.

Zimmer: Have you ever seen them play them at mom's house?

Harry: No this all happened after the kids were at her house.

Zimmer: With regard to these video games, were they playing the video games up on the third floor unsupervised?

Harry: Yes.

Ms. Dautrich: And I'm just objecting because I don't believe Mr. Hall has ever been at that house, and I'm not sure what his knowledge—basis of knowledge is for any of the things he just describe.

I say "a-men", Jamie Dautrich. From whom does Harry get this knowledge? How does a child five and a half learn to play the video games he described without being supervised? I was there watching Bryce as he played. So Harry is lying. I had watched Bryce play many times on the third floor. By the way, there never was a "they" that played the video games. Trey never played the video games when the boys lived on the farm. Therefore, Harry's last "yes" was a lie. The two games Harry mentioned were those owned and played by Bern. It was Bern that used those games to demonstrate to Bryce how to use the controls for video games. Bern had his play station hooked up to his TV in the living room on the first floor. It was there that Bern taught Bryce how to play. Bern would eventually hook up his old play station to the TV on the third floor for Bryce. I have not tried to learn how to the play the video games. When Bryce played Grand Theft he was only interested in driving the cars. He never tried to shoot cops. He just drove into them, which is what I would do all the time while losing control of the car. I never noticed as he played that he was stealing the cars. I thought he got in the next car because he wrecked the previous. I guess I hadn't paid attention to the title of the game. I didn't know some of the people he ran over on the sidewalks were hookers until I read the above from the transcript of the trial. Neither Bryce nor I understood the point of the game. Why does Harry know so much? I never learned how to pick up a hooker. Where do you hang one once you pick one up? I do know Bryce learned to operate the controls to drive the cars from that game. That helped so Bryce was able to play the games that he would get from Kristen. Most of those games are making something go somewhere and picking up things, not hookers, along the way. Bryce's two favorite things to do with Grand Theft were crashing into the glass windows of a lobby and driving the car down the beach until he went into the ocean.

I also watched Bryce play Mortal Combat. I don't understand why it is Mortal combat when the participants get to fight another day. I thought in mortal combat people die. To me, they did not look like real people. Bryce understood they were not real people. He treated it as a game, not real life. The thing that was amazing to me was that playing the game made Bryce calmer. It kept him from fighting with Trey. On the other hand, two years later Harry enrolled Bryce in wrestling. That did encourage fighting with Trey. The thing that intrigued Bryce about the game was trying to earn points to unlock other characters. He would not come from playing the video game to chasing Trey with a weapon. Weapons were for the game. And Harry, I never saw one of those characters kick the opponent in the head until the blood ran down so that they would slip on it. Each character I saw had a unique weapon. Maybe we've discovered a means of coping with "Asperger's" Syndrome. Being able to play and succeed in those games has given Bryce self-esteem. He enjoyed being watched by me, his brother, and others who took the time to watch. Trey appreciated the time that Bryce was playing videos because it was then that Bryce would not be destroying the things he was trying to play with or build. But, Harry, what do you do with Bryce and video games?

Zimmer: Do you agree with the children playing those types of games?
Harry: Absolutely not.
Zimmer: Do you let them play these types of video games.
Harry: No. Don't own any like that.
Zimmer: What type of video games do you have?

Harry: It's the Wii System, Interactive. And all the games are "E" for everyone. They're kid games.

Bryce told me about the game he and Harry played together on the Wii. He says the object of the game is to shoot and kill your opponent. Sounds like a nonviolent game to me. He says in some of the games you try to destroy the other player's tanks. Hum, sounds like a war game. I don't think it sounds like a game for a pacifist. I would say "no tanks" to that game. Maybe it is not a game for everyone. We should ask the computer whiz.

In one of my letters to Harry, written a few weeks after the letter to Judge Lash, I wrote about two items. One of those items was apologizing for having taught the boys to ride their bikes. The other item was to say that I believed that Bryce learning to play video games was a plus. It was sometime after I wrote that letter that Harry bought the Wii System. It had kept Bryce out of trouble for hours for us when it was not possible to be outdoors. Harry realized he had found a "nanny" that he could use to help himself with Bryce. I didn't, however, spend hours watching him play the video games at the farm. I preferred to take Bryce outside where there was much we could do. However, he has learned to read from playing some of the games. He has gained self esteem. He has become a computer whiz.

Chapter 21 - Stall Tactics

Harry Lands a Third Lawyer

In November of 2007, Kristen would receive word that her 24 hour supervised visitation provision would be lifted. To Harry, an opportunity was lost. Kristen had not faltered during that time. Harry was unable to entrap her by finding her with the boys without a registered or approved supervisor. We thought that there were times when the three of us were being observed, possibly by a private eye, as was the case at the time Harry filed the first PFA. During that time, Mary Lynne and I were the only ones that had the boys without Kristen while under her custody. She never left the boys alone with the other supervisors. In addition, there had been no incidents during that time that would enable Harry to make another false charge of child abuse. Spending a lot of time outdoors on the farm could leave many opportunities for an accident that could cause an injury. Harry would certainly use such an incident to his advantage. We had, however, successfully negotiated that period of time without breaking parole.

Kristen was satisfied with 50/50 custody. That was all she sought. She asked Harry for fair monetary child support when the 50/50 arrangement began in April. Harry would not pay that support without having it brought to a hearing with a Child Support Officer. With that "stall tactic," he was able to push back making payments for several months. Harry would have to start making $600 payments in August of

2007, a year after he filed the first PFA. It should not have felt like that much money to Harry. He had been and would continue to receive the $300 a month stipend for Bryce. As mentioned previously, that support was acquired thru Kristen's efforts. Of course, Harry was still not very happy. He believed that because of the "founded" verdict of child abuse from the bump on the head of Bryce that he would receive primary custody. The result of primary custody would have Kristen paying child support to him. That was his ultimate goal. He would continue to fight for primary custody.

As of November 2007, Harry would still not have a good case to win primary custody. One of his problems would be with his second lawyer, Jeffrey Karver. He was the lawyer who, after the "blue bowl incident" made the directive to both parties that a parent should speak to the other parent before going to an authority. Harry did not follow that directive in the "squirty bottle incident." I am sure that did not sit well with his lawyer. In the custody trial, Harry said he went first to the doctor. Next, he went to CYS. He never told Kristen. Harry, in the custody trial, never mentioned that he went to Jeffrey Karver to report the incident. It would be difficult for Harry to keep him on as his lawyer while he was going against the directive. Harry would say that he fired his lawyer. The truth may be that his second lawyer resigned because he would not do the unscrupulous actions Harry wanted him to take.

There was a tactic for which Harry could use this lawyer. It would be the "stall tactic." Harry and his lawyer had used the tactic before, they would use it some more. The original order for the scheduling of pre-trial conference was written 5/17/07 to have it on 6/14/07. On 5/25/07, an order was submitted to change the date from 6/14/07 to 7/24/07. Why push back the date? Simple, Harry needed more time to get another bump on the head accusation against Kristen. The blue bowl bump occurred before the 5/17/07 date but was called "unfounded." That would not be enough to win the case for primary. The time between the June and July dates was Harry's window of opportunity. That was the time when the "squirty bottle incident" had to occur in order for Harry to be able to get a "founded" verdict of child abuse. It did. There seemed to be a pattern of abuse. It seemed Harry had a plan. Was Jeffrey Karver in on that plan? I think not. On 7/23/07, the pre-trial conference was changed again to 9/6/07. It was another stall. On

9/6/07, the pre-trial conference was changed to 12/11/07. Also, on that date, 9/6/07, it was asked by Harry's lawyer that in lieu of the dismissal the case should remain open an additional 180 days. Harry's lawyer, Jeffrey Karver, would do one more act. On 12/7/07, he wrote an order that the pre-trial conference date be changed to 1/10/08. The notice for that change was sent out on 12/10/07. Kristen had not received the notice. She showed up for the pre-trial conference that day and no one was there. It was not the first time that she made arrangements to take off from work and then not have the scheduled conference. It would not be the last. All those changes in scheduling, all those stalls, were done in Harry's behalf. Harry did not feel that he could win at those times. He had to wait for something else to happen that would guarantee victory.

Jeffrey Karver would not appear with Harry for that 1/10/08 pre-trial conference date. There was an order given on that date to allow the case to be open an additional 60 days from that date. The order was not written by Jeffrey Karver. The case docket for the date 12/20/07 states: "the withdrawal appearance of Jeffrey Karver Esq for Deft Harry Hall with appearance of Mark Zimmer esq." Mark Zimmer would continue, where necessary, that pattern of using "stall tactics." Not only would Mark Zimmer use "stall tactics" in rescheduling dates, his use of that tactic was obvious in his manner of the questioning Harry on the witness stand. It is interesting that Mark Zimmer, his third lawyer, would miss that scheduled 1/10/08 pre-trial conference date. It would not even be rescheduled. Instead, more than two months later, Mr. Zimmer would file, in behalf of Harry, another Petition for Special Relief.

The order of 3/20/08 issued Kristen to show cause and to schedule a hearing for 4/2/08. So what does Mark Zimmer do? On 4/2/08, he is able to have the date rescheduled for 6/4/08. On 6/4/08, he is able to have that continued to 6/25/08. The court date would finally be scheduled for 8/26/08. My wife and I would be given a plan for something to do for our 41st wedding anniversary.

Kristen related to us a story told to her by her lawyer, Jamie Dautrich. Jamie had been in her first meeting with Judge Lash and Mark Zimmer to discuss Kristen's case. She told Kristen that Judge Lash said something like "so here is the new person to do the dirty work for Harry." These are probably not the exact words. To get them exact from the judge, to

Jamie, to Kristen, and then to me would be a stretch. However, if the words were passed at anytime, by way of Harry, then they would be exact. I am being facetious! Jamie goes on to say that Mark Zimmer retorted, "For three thousand dollars and three hundred dollars an hour, I will do whatever my client asks." We do know, from other sources, Mark's reputation. He usually wins. He gets for his clients exactly what they want. Why? I have not been impressed by his performances in court. But, he is very good at "stall tactics."

Harry, however, is not so good at "stall tactics." The first custody evaluation was held in November of 2006. The custody evaluator said 50/50. It had been over a year since that took place. Judge Lash ordered another evaluation. At a conference in March of 2008, Judge Lash asked why the second custody evaluation had not yet taken place. Harry pipes, "it's because Kristen had not made her payment yet for the evaluation." Kristen pulls out a receipt showing she had already paid her part, $500 worth, in January. Harry had no such receipt. Harry lied. Did Judge Lash take notice? Harry was not so good at stalling.

Chapter 22 - The Biting Incident

The Doctor Says Three

There was nothing on the docket summary from 1/11/08 to 3/16/08. Harry, however, was up to no good in February. About twenty minutes before Kristen was to receive the boys from Harry, she called us. Harry had just called her. He told her that Trey had bitten Bryce on the chest that day. Why did he call her about the bite before the transition? I don't know. Kristen did not know. That was why she called us. Was he in some way following the directive of his former lawyer, Jeffrey Karver? Perhaps! As Harry had said, there was a bite mark on Bryce's chest. That weekend, Trey would get in two more bites, one on the arm and the other on the leg. Those two bites would be the last of the bites. We would think no more of the biting. Harry would. What Harry thought about the biting can be read in a report by Dr. Johanna Kelly written on 2/25/08.

> Bryce is a 5-year-old little boy, where there is a history indicating report of child abuse in the past and a custody battle going on. Comes in today because of several marks on his body that Dad wanted me to check. He showed me one on his leg that is a bruise. Looks consistent with a bite mark. Asked him what happened. Said his brother bit him. His brother admitted that he bit

him. There is also one on his upper right arm. That does look consistent with a bite as well. Asked who did it. He said his brother Trey did it, and Trey admitted he did it. There is also one on his chest. Again, Trey said he did that one too. There are several bruises on his left forearm as well. When I asked Trey what happens to him when he bites, he said nothing. (Does that mean he answered not, or did he answer with the word "nothing"?) I asked Bryce what happens when Trey bites him, and first he said, "He gets in trouble." Then he said, "Only I get in trouble when I bite him. He doesn't get in trouble." (Bryce just self-incriminated himself by admitting he bites Trey. I believe he learned that from Harry. Pardon the interruptions.) So it seems a little inconsistent, what they're saying happens. However, the fact that he has so many bite marks on him is a concern, because there are multiple, as stated in dictation. Probably discipline techniques should be looked at, and the younger child should be evaluated for why he is biting at his age and not using words. There is definitely a problem with that at his age. (Does anyone remember any stories of adults biting?)

At what age? Dr. Kelly forgot to mention that Trey was only four. Why ask for an evaluation? Why did she not ask Trey why he bit Bryce each of those times? It is a simple question of motive. Bryce gives plenty of reasons that might cause Trey to bite him. Trey liked to build and set up things. Bryce, almost always, comes around to destroy the things Trey sets up. Why does the doctor fail to mention the fact of Bryce's special behavior problems? Does she have any knowledge of Bryce being diagnosed with Asperger's? Harry would tell her of the history of indicated child abuse that he filed. But, he makes no mention of Bryce's special behavior problems that could have resulted in Trey's reasons for biting Bryce. What does the doctor mean when she says Trey should have used words? I have no idea. Was he supposed to swear at Bryce? Why is it not mentioned anywhere in her report under whose supervision the bites occurred? They could have occurred under Harry's supervision. Dr. Kelly does not include in her report that Harry said they occurred under Kristen's supervision. Trey says he did not get disciplined for biting Bryce. Why did Harry not discipline Trey? Harry said he knew Trey bit Bryce. Or, why did the doctor not call Kristen and ask her personally about the bite marks and other bruises? Why did Harry not tell Kristen that he took the boys to the doctor about the bite marks and other bruises? Kristen and Harry, despite their separation, were supposed to be working cooperatively in raising the children. Mary Lynne said in court seven months later, "both parents should be on the same page." Kristen had no idea about this page.

Harry would not discuss the biting incident with Kristen, but he would discuss it with Dr. Peter Thomas in the custody evaluation held on April 22, 2008. Harry would give Dr. Johanna Kelly's report to Dr. Thomas. Kristen had not known or seen Dr. Kelly's report. However, the biting incident would be discussed in the custody evaluation with Dr. Thomas.

> Mr. Hall talked about an episode in which "Bryce had 7 or 8 marks on his body." He states that Bryce said Trey bit him. Mr. Hall was asked about Ms. Hall's statement the Bryce was bitten once at his house and came to her with one bite mark. Mr. Hall stated, "I never made that call," referring to telling mother that Bryce had been bitten at his house. He states there were "7 bite marks. It was not accidental."
>
> In several instances in these discussions, Mr. Hall overstated the case against Kristen Hall. He stated there were seven bite marks when indeed the doctor indicated three.

I would ask Dr. Peter Thomas why he did not question Harry's motive for taking the boys to the doctor about the bite marks in the first place. Dr. Thomas also talked to the boys in that custody evaluation. Why did he not ask them about the biting incident? He had the report from Dr. Kelly. He could have asked the same questions I had about that report.

Again, Harry had gone to a doctor without going to Kristen first, as was directed by his lawyer after the blue bowl incident. I do not understand. Was Harry now free from following that directive because he had a new lawyer? Or, did he feel he followed that directive when he made that phone call to Kristen, the one he then denied making when talking to Dr. Thomas? The biting incident would accomplish three things for Harry. It would be the physical abuse part of his next PSR, Petition for Special Relief. That PSR was filed only weeks before the custody evaluation. It was used in the custody evaluation as part his of arsenal for the war against Kristen. Dr. Thomas describes their relationship as a war. Third, Harry would use it against Kristen in the custody trial held in August of 2008.

Zimmer: Have the children acted out against each other?
Harry: Yeah. Actually, Trey more so lately than—actually, Trey, he was biting Bryce. He came from mom's home one weekend with eight bite marks on him. And when I asked the kids about them, you know, Bryce said Trey did it. Trey said, "I did it." And I specifically asked him about all the marks on him because he left with none, came home with eight. So that was the thing.

Give me a break Harry. When do boys like Bryce and Trey never have bruises of some type, especially having a father that encourages them to jump off furniture and "rough house?" The testimony continues. The wasting of time and stalling continues.

Zimmer: When was this?
Harry: I don't recall the exact date. It was several—maybe five months ago. We have a report from the doctor on that.
Zimmer: What did you do as a result of seeing these bite marks on your son?
Harry: I took Bryce to Reading Pedes to get—
Zimmer: Which doctor?
Harry: Which office?
Zimmer: Which doctor?
Harry: Again they have a couple of doctors. I don't recall the doctor's name, which specific doctor it was who saw him.

Get on with it you two. Is this an Abott and Costello routine? Who's on first?

Zimmer: Were there any recommendations made that you're aware of?

Harry: Actually she recommended that because Trey was doing this biting, that somebody should maybe evaluate him for why he was doing that and, not using his words, why he was acting out.

Zimmer: And did you obtain a doctor's report with regard to the fact that this incident occurred?

Harry: I did.

Zimmer: Are you familiar with Exhibit No. 3?

Harry: Yes. This is the report from Johanna Kelly at Reading Pedes about the incident we discussed with the multiple bites on Bryce from Trey.

Zimmer: And is this report issued after you had taken the child to the doctor with regard to the bite incident?

Harry: Yes, it was.

Zimmer: Did you commence any follow-up care as a result of this incident?

Harry: Again, the bites were just things that healed. There was no long-term follow-up care other than just making sure the kids know not to bite each other and that if they do, that they're going to get time-outs and disciplined.

Are there any questions about "stall tactics?" So, Harry did not follow through with any of the recommendations by the doctor. This whole incident sounds like self-incrimination against Harry. It was a job well done by his superior lawyer. Harry did not report to Kristen about his visit to the doctor at Reading Pedes for the "biting" incident, just as he had not for the "blue bowl" incident or the "squirty bottle" incident. Again, why is nobody asking why Trey was biting Bryce? Perhaps, the Court could have thought about asking that question. Did the Court fall asleep? Maybe Kristen's lawyer can make sense of this in the cross examination.

Ms. Dautrich: Okay. How about the time you took Bryce to the doctor in February of this year and that was regarding the bite marks? You indicated during your testimony, I believe, that there were eight bite marks?

Harry: (no audible response)

The Court: You have to say yes or no. (The Court woke up. Thank you.)

Harry: Oh. Sorry. Yes.

Ms. Dautrich: And to Dr. Thomas, you indicated there were seven. And the report indicates there were three.

Harry: The report indicates—what the doctor wrote was there was three bites, and she talks about the other marks. She doesn't specifically say those were bites. But they left with—I'm not done. They left with no marks, came back with eight. (Excuse me. Why does Harry say "they" when he only means on Bryce?)

Ms. Dautrich: I'm sorry.

Harry: I had not finished my answer.

Ms. Dautrich: I don't want to interrupt you. I just want to move things along. Did the doctor indicate in the report there were three bite marks?

Harry: Yes, she did.

Ms. Dautrich: Thank you. Now isn't it true that one—at least one of those bite marks occurred at your home?

Harry: No. Not true at all.

Harry, you lie. Kristen did call us about your phone call to her. So, Harry, "bite me!"

Chapter 23 – Good Dude or Bad Dude

Mike versus Harry

The end of November, 2007, was near. The original deal was that Kristen would pay $800 for the rent of the farm house and Bern the remaining $1200. The agreement was that there would be no romantic involvement. Bern would pay the oil bill and Kristen the electric bill. Bern changed his mind on two of the three conditions. He was still okay with the oil and electric bills. Kristen would only agree to one change. She would agree to change her share of the rent to $1000 per month. In August, Kristen started receiving $600 a month for child support from Harry. Her income from work was about $1200 a month. Do the math. It doesn't work. By the end of November she would have no her money for her share of the rent for December. She no longer had credit. She would need a "before Christmas" angel to enable her to stay at the farm with the boys. The alternative would be to sign over the boys to Harry. I was going to call this chapter, "Only an Angel to me." I changed it because of Harry's testimony in court on August 26, 2008.

Zimmer: Are you concerned that some of mother's negative judgment may have exposed the children to any potential harm?

Harry: Oh, yeah.

Zimmer: In what way?

Harry: The Mike Spadafora gentleman, he's a pretty bad dude.

Ms. Dautrich: And I object to that, ask that—

Zimmer: It's his opinion.

The Court: Overruled.

Ms. Dautrich: What's the basis?

The Court: Well, you have to give him an opportunity. Overruled!

Harry: It's based on a criminal report of him.

Ms. Dautrich: I'd object.

The Court: Sustained.

Later in the trial, with my daughter on the stand, Mr. Zimmer would bring out the criminal report numbered as Plaintiff's exhibit no. 6. The report was supposed to demonstrate a long criminal record. The truth was that our "Christmas angel" had no criminal record. The following is the dialogue concerning that report as given in the trial.

Zimmer: Are you familiar with how to spell his name?

Kristen: Yes.

Zimmer: I'd like you to look at a document.

Ms. Dautrich: For the record, Mrs. Hall is willing to stipulate that Spadafora is S-p-a-d-a-f-o-r-a and Michael is normally spelled M-i-c-h-a-e-l. However, we are objecting to the admissibility of this document.

The Court: It hasn't been moved yet. Any further questions, Mr. Zimmer?

Zimmer: You just heard your counsel spell Mr. Spadafora's name. Is that accurate?

Kristen: Yes.

Zimmer: Now, the document I just gave is a criminal background check. Is Michael Spadafora spelled the same on this document as your attorney spelled it?

Kristen: Yes.

Zimmer: do you have any knowledge as to whether this is the same individual or a different individual than we are discussing?

Kristen: This looks to be a different individual because he's 41 years old. And this birth date here is 10/1974. That would make him 34.

Zimmer: Do you know the date of his birth.

Kristen: No, I didn't know his date of birth. I knew he was 41 years old.

Zimmer: Okay.

The Court: He was 41 when? When you last saw him?

Kristen: Yeah, yes.

Zimmer: Well, there are three different individuals in this document. (Sounds like a fishing expedition to me.)

Kristen: Okay.

Ms. Dautrich: And, again, I have no clue where this document came from or how my client can interpret it. Because I can't even—

The Court: This is cross-examination.

Ms. Dautrich: Okay.

Zimmer: The second document has a Mike Spadafora born in '66 who lived in New Holland, Pennsylvania. Do you happen to know where he resided?

Kristen: He lived in Alsace Township.

Ms. Dautrich: And I'm not sure what relevance of a $137 fine is, so I'm still objecting on the relevance ground.

Zimmer: It's just a question.

The Court: Proceed.

Zimmer: I'm asking if she knows who this person is or not.

Zimmer again: Do you know whether Mr. Spadafora—strike that. Do you know why the information you provided your counsel was never turned over to me?

Kristen: I don't know. I don't know why.

Ms. Dautrich: Who gave you the spelling of his name?

At least I know that "What's His Name" is on second. Who was Mark Zimmer talking about in this dialogue? Why did he not at least narrow it down to one Mike Spadafora? So where is this criminal report Harry claims to have? Let's hear what Mr. Zimmer asked Harry three hours earlier in the trial.

Zimmer: Are you concerned with regard to mother's judgment?

Harry: Yes. Her—she's had several men in her life in the last year or two that I don't want my kids around, long criminal records, serious, serious issues there.

Zimmer: Are you familiar with the facts surrounding mother receiving money from an individual?

Harry: Yeah. There's a gentleman name Mike Spadafora. I don't know much about him other than he gives mom or has given mom, you know, a thousand dollars a month.

Ms. Dautrich: I'm just going to object, requesting what the basis is of this knowledge.

Zimmer: It's is Dr. Thomas's report, for one thing. So mother must have discussed it with him.

Ms. Dautrich: I—

The Court: Well lay a foundation. How do you know this?

Harry: It's in Dr. Thomas's report. I heard—I also heard Miss Dautrich tell my attorney that in this courtroom months ago. So I know it's a fact.

Well at least Harry and his lawyer were on the same page that time. What was in Dr. Thomas's report that Kristen told to him about Mike Spadafora? The following is from that report.

> Mr. Hall had complained that some individual gives Ms. Hall $1000 in order to use her car. He is concerned that this car is used for illicit and criminal behavior. Ms. Hall states, "I have a friend. I met him at the hospital. He's a married man with four children. He has a lot of money." She states that they had lunch together several times in the hospital. She states that this man gave her $2000 for rent and to buy Christmas presents for the kids. She states that this man helps her. She states there is no romantic or sexual relationship. She states that her previous boyfriend was very upset about this man. Ms. Hall states that this man asked if he could use her car to go into Reading. She states that he has vending machines or game machines and goes into Reading

to take care of them. She states that he has a friend who went in the same car and eventually got robbed and mugged. She states this man asked to borrow her car once but he never went through with it and never actually used the car. Ms. Hall was asked how much in total this man has given her and stated that he has given her $4500.

Harry would say that the proof of Kristen allowing Mike to use her car was written in Dr. Thomas' evaluation report. There, it is stated, "Mr. Chalmers said that this man uses mother's car so he can engage in 'shady' deals." Who made this statement to Dr. Thomas? It was Harry Hall that made that statement. Harry Hall gave Harry Hall's proof. Is there anything wrong with this picture? Harry complains this man is helping Kristen survive this period of high rent and good times on the farm for the boys. Without the money she would have given up. It is no wonder that Harry was angry. How dare Mike spoil Harry's plan.

Kristen would get to describe her relationship with Mike in more detail on the stand.

Ms. Dautrich: Now, about this Mike Spadafora? Is he ever around the kids?

Kristen: Maybe one time he dropped off popguns that he had gotten from Cabella's. He dropped them off one morning. My parents were babysitting. He knocked on the door, and he gave mehe gave my parents, actually, the popguns. But the kids were in the home at that point.

Ms. Dautrich: But other than that—

Kristen: Nope. He was not around my children.

Ms. Dautrich: And how did you meet him?

Kristen: Mike, I met while I was working at St. Joe's Hospital. He was in with a family member who was having a heart catheterization that day. I work as receptionist in the waiting area in the heart institute. I sit there all day long with family members. And he sat there and talked to me for I think six hours while his family member had a procedure that day. That's how I got to know Mike. That's how I first got to know him.

He then—after that day, he started coming to the hospital. I'd see him. He didn't—he didn't have a nine-to-five job, so he didn't work much during the day. So he was in a lot, bringing friends in that were sick or whatever, had appointments at doctors' offices. He'd come in to see me a lot, take me to lunch every once in a while down in the cafeteria.

At one point in time, he questioned me. He said, you can't be making more than $10 an hour sitting at this job. How do you afford a thousand dollars a month rent making $10 an hour? And I said, I don't really do well. I said, like this Christmas, I have no money to buy Christmas presents. So out of the goodness of his heart, he gave me $2000 to buy Christmas presents for my boys and my family. I asked him how he had so much money just laying around. And he said, well, I work in the amusement business. He goes, I have poker machines in bars and stuff like that. I have those little grabber machines that grab toys, you know, in malls and stuff like that. That's what he told me. And he said, I make a lot of money doing that. I didn't question him much further. I did say, seems a little shady maybe, I said, I believe you when you make a lot of money doing this amusement business.

He also—Mike also gave me $300 in gift cards to Weis/King's. He bought little plasma cars. This lady made blankets. He brought me three blankets one day. He said don't worry about your rent. He said, at the end of the month, I'll be there with you. He said, "You got me. I'm your friend for life." I said, okay.

And I—you know, at first I didn't want to take the money from him. But he said to me, he said, you know Kristen, you're a good person. He said, I give money out to my family. They don't appreciate it. I give money out to other people that don't appreciate it. He said, you're using this money for a good cause, your kids. And he said, I'm gonna continue to help you out. And I was like, wow, this is like Santa Claus to me. (I wish she would have said a Christmas angel.)

So he also continued every month up until April to give me that thousand dollars a month. I used—sometime for rent I used the thousand dollars. I also used the thousand dollars to pay for the custody evaluation. I used the thousand dollars a month once to pay for four new tires on my car.

So that man, Mike, who was, you know, supposedly a bad man in my life, he actually helped me out a lot and my kids.

Ms. Dautrich: Now, did you ever try to hide this or lie about where you got the money?

Kristen: Never, just went out to dinner a couple of times and lunch. But that wasn't dating to me.

Ms. Dautrich: Do you know if he had a family?

Kristen: Yes.

Ms. Dautrich: Meaning a wife and kids?

Krsiten: He lived with his wife and four children.

Ms. Dautrich: Were you romantically interested in him?

Kristen: Never.

Ms. Dautrich: Did you ever have reason based on what he told you to believe that he obtained money illegally and then gave it to you?

Kristen: I didn't have any reason to believe that, no.

Mark Zimmer would cross examine Kristen.

Zimmer: Okay. Now, you stated that this Mr. Spadafora was giving you a thousand dollars a week out of the goodness of his heart. Does that sound about right?

Kristen: No, it was a thousand dollars a month?

Zimmer: I'm sorry, a thousand dollars a month. But still out of his generosity?

Kristen: That's how I felt, yes.

Zimmer: Okay. Didn't it raise any concern to you that this is an odd situation?

Kristen: Yes. And I talked to Michael about that, yes.

Zimmer: Okay. And in light of the things that you know now, the fact that an individual who identified themselves as a DEA agent has spoken to you, you still don't have any concerns about Mr. Spadafora?

Kristen: I don't have concerns about Mr. Spadafora. I have questions, yes. But I have no way of knowing if these accusations against him are true or not.

Zimmer: The last time you spoke with him was sometime after Mr. Hall filed a Petition for Special Relief raising concerns such as is Mr. Spadafora related to drug activity?

Kristen: I talked to him after the Petition for Special Relief came out. When that came out, I talked to him about that. And he said, well, this is a lie. He said, I will go with you to your attorney's office and, you know, don't worry. We'll take care of this. This is all lies. You're a good mom. You know, he—you know, he told me that he doesn't drug deal. That's what he told me.

Zimmer: Is he here today to testify?

Kristen: No, he's not.

So, Mr. Zimmer, why did you not subpoena Mike Spadafora? Zimmer continues with questions about the car.

Zimmer: Does he own a car?

Kristen: Yes, he has a car.

Zimmer: Did he ever request to use your vehicle?

Kristen: One time he talked to me regarding using my vehicle to go—see, his job entails for him to go into Reading and take money out of gambling machines basically from bars throughout Reading. And a friend of his is also in the same business. And the friend of his would go to the same bar the same day every week with the same car ended up getting jumped, and his money got stolen. So Mike told me one time that, you know, if I go downtown in Reading, I don't want people getting to me in my car, whatever. So that's why he asked to borrow it once. But he never actually borrowed it. I never gave him the keys to my car. He never once set foot in my car.

There was one story about Mike Spadafora that Kristen would not relate to either Dr. Thomas in the custody evaluation or Judge Lash in the custody trial. What Mike said to Kristen would greatly encourage her trust in her decision to accept his generous offer. Kristen did relate this story to my wife and me about the midway point of the four or five months of her relationship with Mike. She had told us about receiving the money from Mike from the beginning. She showed us the wad. We wondered when she first rented the farm house how she would be able to survive financially. We thought it would be impossible. As much as we wished, we knew we would be unable to provide enough help for her financially to stay at the farm. From our work in Christian ministry, even though mostly as volunteers, we had become well acquainted with stories of generosity that may seem "unbelievable" to a person such as Mr. Zimmer. God Himself has been generous to mankind beyond "reasonable" logic. About now, you are saying, "don't give me a sermon tell me the story." Okay. Kristen relates the story.

> "Mike and I were talking one day about my custody case. Mike was inquiring on who was the judge in my custody case. When I told him that it was Judge Scott Lash, Mike replied, 'I know Judge Lash. He and I are buddies.' Mike told me that he was recently before Judge Lash for an issue regarding his daughter's boyfriend. Mike stated that the boyfriend was going to be sent to boot camp. Judge Lash approved Mike Spadafora to be a guardian over this youth in his home. The youth would serve out his time under house arrest at Mike's home instead of going to boot camp. More and more I trusted Mike to be a good person. After all, Judge Lash approved him to watch over a delinquent youth. Mike visited me at work with that youth. I saw the youth. I was familiar with the house arrest band as I has been a Correctional Officer and Counselor at the Juvenile Detention of Berks County."

I challenge each of you, based on your present knowledge, to answer the following questions with either the name Mike or Harry. Who has exploited the children for financial gain? Who helped Kristen to be able, financially, keep the boys on the farm? Who helped Kristen provide a good Christmas for the boys, or who was the real Santa Claus to the boys? Who destroyed Kristen financially? Who caused emotional harm to the children by keeping them away from their nurturing mother? Who encouraged the mother of the children emotionally by saying and writing, "You are a good mom."? Who defamed unjustly the character of the boy's mother? So, who is the "good" dude? Who is the "bad" dude?

I say that Mike was Kristen's "helicopter." There was a man who drowned in a flood and had gone on to heaven. He says to Saint Peter,

"I prayed to God to help me escape from the flood, but God never came to save me, why?" Saint Peter says, "Do you remember when the sheriff came to your door as the flood waters approached? Do you remember when the man came to your window in the row boat? Do you remember the time when sitting on the roof top the rope was lowered to you from a helicopter? So, Kristen took the rope from the helicopter, Mike Spadafora.

Mike would not put Kristen in harms way. Kristen would only see him one day after that meeting in her attorney's office in April. He came to take a game machine out of the third floor super room. Bryce and I played the golf game on that machine. He liked hitting the ball into the water. Maybe Mike is guilty of what some have accused him. Maybe he is not. Either way, he was an angel that provided a way for Kristen to survive and be with the boys for those months from December of 2007 thru April of 2008. He gave Kristen the strength to carry on. That came not from the money but from the affirmation, "You are a good mom." Those who name "Christ", take notice.

Chapter 24 – Unholy Alliance

The Jilted Lover

Dr. Peter Thomas writes the following as part of his summary for the second custody evaluation held on April 22, 2008.

> My primary concern about father is his continued degree of attack toward mother. In my opinion, when he accepts involvement from Mr. Chalmers he has created an "unholy alliance" in which Mr. Chalmers' motives can certainly be questioned, the validity of all the material is very much in doubt, etc. I am concerned that Mr. Hall continues to be focused on his attacks on mother.

Kristen knows the importance of custody evaluation reports. She knew that from her experience working in Domestic Relations. She also had first hand experience with her first evaluation with Dr. Thomas. Dr. Thomas had recommended 50/50 and that was what she obtained. She still had 50/50 in spite of the "founded" verdict from the "squirty bottle" incident. The result and recommendation of this evaluation would largely determine if the 50/50 custody would remain in tact or Harry would receive primary.

She would be interviewed for the first 15 minutes, Bern would be interviewed, and finally Harry for the remaining time. Therefore, Kristen would have to anticipate what Harry would be telling Dr. Thomas. Kristen did have some idea of what Harry would discuss. Harry had filed another Petition for Special Relief against Kristen only weeks before this evaluation would be held. Perhaps, the timing of those events was not coincidental. Perhaps it was part of a plan. There were two different hand writings on that PSR. Some of the writing was Harry's. The other writing was that of Rob Chalmers. Dr. Thomas would write the following of what Kristen would say in regards to Rob Chalmers.

> Ms. Hall talked about additional events. She states, "Harry got together with an ex-boyfriend of mine." She states that she had been seeing a man named Rob Chalmers for two months. She described him as "very controlling." I didn't want him in my life. She talked about a tumultuous break-up with this man. She states this man broke her car windshield. She states that this man went through her desk at her workplace at St. Joseph's. She describes him as being very angry with her. She states that this boyfriend has joined with Harry to say negative things about her. She describes him as a "jilted lover." She states that this man said that she abused her children.

If this is all you would know about her relationship with Rob Chalmers, then you would certainly get the wrong impression. Kristen had known Rob Chalmers before those two months that began in December of 2007. Kristen and Rob were high school classmates twenty years before that December meeting. They dated a few times when she was only 21. They met by chance in the Mall while Kristen was shopping with the money she had gotten from an angel with the first name of Michael. After shopping and talking, Rob said he wanted to show her something he had in his car. It was not a puppy. Rob showed her a picture that he had of her as Homecoming Queen in 1988. Rob told her he still had the same crush on her that he had from that date.

After two weeks of dating, they were talking marriage. Rob was more than just a "jilted lover." She would get a bit closer to telling the truth of her relationship in the custody trial held four months after the evaluation.

Ms. Dautrich: What about this guy, Rob Chalmers? Does he have some kind of extensive criminal record?

Krsiten: No.

Ms. Dautrich: Were you involved with him romantically at one point?

Kristen: Yes.

Ms. Dautrich: And what happened that ended that?

Kristen: Rob and I went to High School together, graduated from high school together, dated briefly when we were 21. Rob always told me he had this crush on me. Well, anyway, we ran into each other Christmas shopping this past year. And I wasn't dating anyone. He's like, why don't we get together and start hangin' out. I said, okay. I said we can get together. So the end of December, it was actually December 31st, we went out on Rob's birthday. And we started seeing each other. We started dating for about six weeks

Rob, I thought, was a good guy. He graduated with me from high school. I, kind of knew, you know, some of his history. He worked for Twin Valley School District in the special needs, you know, with special needs kids. So, I thought, hey, that's a good thing. He understands Bryce. He also worked with mentally challenged people. And I thought that was—you know, that was something good about him. So I thought Rob was a good guy. So I'm like, okay, we'll try this out.

So I dated him for about six months (it was really six weeks as said above) until I started noticing some very controlling aspects about him. I was concerned that if I ever have the kids over at his house and they would do something at his house, like ruin his paint job. He would flip out a little bit. So I was like, you know, I'm not sure this guy's right for me. So I told Rob—you know, told Rob this. And, you know, he was pretty much begging and pleading to let's stay together, let's work this out.

And the next week after I told Rob that, we were still, you know, I guess talking, Rob and I. I had a male friend over at my house one night.

And this male friend I knew from the hospital. Rob came over to my house that night without being invited, found the other male friend in the home. I wasn't home because I was out getting pizza, and the male friend was just waiting at the house for me. Rob, of course, had words with the guy. Both of them were on their way leaving, you know, pretty much yelling at each other back and forth. And Rob proceeded to smash my window that night. He was angry because I talked to another guy, smashed my window that night, and also went into my place of work that night. It's all on camera because I sit at my desk. He also contacted my supervisor that me and this male friend were having sexual relations in the consultation rooms. Basically he was harassing me, this Rob Chalmers. So pretty much it was over at that point with that guy. He flipped out in a way that I never want to see again.

So what ended up happening was the night after he, you know, threw the rock through my windshield,—he knew where I met Harry to pick—drop and pick up the kids at Weis/King's. He was in the parking lot when we did the drop-off that night, handed Harry a piece of paper, including his phone number on it. I found out later on, Harry proceeded to call him that night. Rob and him proceeded to get together. I don't know when it was, but they proceeded to get together after this incident occurred. And that's when they drew up the Petition for Special Relief. That was a bunch of lies about me, about me being, you know, with Mike Spadafora drug dealing back at the house and that's how I was getting money. And it was all a bunch of lies.

Ms. Dautrich: And how did that make you feel about, you know, Harry's motivations with joining up with Mr. Chalmers?

Kristen: First of all, what Harry needed to do,—I warned Harry that night in the parking lot, don't talk to him; I'm filing charges against him. Harry, of course, doesn't listen to anything I have to say. So I was like, why would, you know, the father of my—children get in cahoots with a man to try to bring the mother of his children some more, you know. It's been all a plan. All of his allegations of child abuse, it's all a plan just to get primary custody of these children from me. I feel like I've been harassed because there's been a lot of lies about me, and I'm constantly—I have to—it's like I've been defending myself for two years. It's a complete defamation of character, that's what it is.

Just what did Harry tell the custody evaluator that was supposedly told to him by Rob Chalmers which in turn caused the evaluator to question its validity? Harry communicated that Mr. Chalmers quoted Kristen as stating that she only wanted custody of Trey, not of Bryce. Kristen denied saying that to Mr. Chalmers. Harry said Mr. Chalmers communicated to him that Kristen hit Bryce and called him names. Kristen denied that. She stated that Mr. Chalmers only spent about 7 hours total with her and the boys. She said, "No way did I do that." He stated he learned from Mr. Chalmers that Kristen was receiving $1000 a month from Mike Spadafora. Now that was the truth! Rob did ask Kristen early on in their relationship how she was able to afford living at the farm. She told him unashamedly right then, "it is because of Mike's generosity." Harry states that Mr. Chalmers said that this man, Mike, uses mother's car so he can engage in "shady" deals. Of course, that did not happen. We don't know if Mr. Chalmers told that to Harry or Harry just embellished on the truth that Kristen told Rob that Mike had asked to use her car. Mr. Hall stated that Mr. Chalmers related material about Kristen that she hates Bryce, that Kristen blames Mr. Hall for adopting Bryce, and that Kristen tells the boys that Mr. Hall is gay. Why did Harry have to use Mr. Chalmers' name for things he would like to blame on Kristen for his own purposes? Harry wants to think he is keeping himself pure by placing blame on someone else for saying those things. I believe strongly that Harry intentionally blames Kristen for things that in reality are only his own thoughts.

Harry goes on to state that Mr. Chalmers described Ms. Hall as disciplining Bryce by sitting on him. Did Rob see her do that? No. Harry states that Mr. Chalmers describes Ms. Hall as slapping Bryce in the head and calling Bryce a liar? No and yes. Bryce does lie a lot. I doubt that Mr. Chalmers related that to Harry. Harry lies a lot. Dr. Thomas asked Harry if the family counselors are aware of those things Kristen does to Bryce and Harry stated, "No, no, of course not. She puts on a good front." Stop! I have a question. If Kristen can put a good front on for the family counselors, why can she not put on a good front for someone she had planned to marry? Up until the brick throwing incident, Mr. Chalmers wanted to marry Kristen. Rob Chalmers never saw any of those things Harry claimed he saw.

A number of accusations against Kristen that Harry related in court attributed as coming from Bryce were really things that Rob Chalmers told him. These were things that Kristen confided to Rob. Harry embellished on those items in court attributing the knowledge of them as coming from Bryce. Included among those items were the stories of Bryce playing video games through the night. Kristen had related to Rob that she came downstairs one morning and found Bryce playing one of Bern's video games on the TV in the living room. At the time there was no video game player on the third floor. That day had to be on the weekend; otherwise, Kristen would have been at work. It was remarkable that Bryce was able to turn the game on by himself. Harry embellished that story to say that Bryce said he played video games thru the night on the third floor while mommy slept.

Harry would go on, as reported by Dr. Thomas, with another explanation of the event described by Kristen in court four months later. Harry explains, "Mother was found in bed with another man by Rob Chalmers. Mother was fully clothed but I speculate about the reason for being in bed. Bryce was in the house at the time." I can not imagine what Dr. Thomas thought of this story. Apparently, this event took place at the farm house. Why does Harry say Bryce is there? Men don't usually come to visit Kristen when she has the boys. Where is Trey? Why did Harry not say the boys? The boys were not at the house that day. It was Daddy's custody day. Rob knew that the boys were not with Kristen that day. Kristen's bedroom is on the second floor. How is it that Rob Chalmers just walked into that house right up to the bedroom on the second floor? Does he have nerve or what? Actually, Rob did do that. And what did he see in Kristen's bed? Was it the big bad wolf? No, it was a man. Kristen had gone off to buy pizza. The man was a friend and fellow worker at St. Joe's. He worked for many hospitals because he was an expert on heart pacemakers. He was always on call for emergencies because he had to be there when pacemakers were installed. He had asked Kristen if he could come to the farm because it was better than driving the additional 40 miles home and then have to be called back if something was not right. She said it would be okay. She did not have the boys that day. So he came to the farm to rest up. Rob and that man had a discussion. It was almost finished when Kristen got home with the pizza. I wonder what Bern, Kristen's housemate, thought about the whole scene. Bern was there, Bryce was not. It is no wonder that Dr. Thomas doubted the validity of Harry's testimony of what Rob said.

Mr. Hall was asked why Mr. Chalmers is involved in this case at all. Mr. Hall affirmed that Mr. Chalmers went out of his way to insert himself into this process. Mr. Hall responded, "Yes, he was hurt. He was jealous and hurt." Mr. Hall adds that Mr. Chalmers works with children and "it weighed on him that my kids would be in that environment." Did Kristen file a complaint of harassment against Rob Chalmers? Yes. He was convicted of harassment against Kristen and was given a year on probation.

In court, Harry would admit that since the first PFA, two years before the trial, he did not have a chance to witness any of the negative accusations of child abuse he claimed about Kristen. His testimony for the custody trial consisted of things that supposedly happened as told to him by Bryce and this man, Rob Chalmers. In the trial, Harry would be asked for proof of some of his statements. He said, "It's all in Dr. Thomas' second evaluation report." The supposed proofs from that report were what Harry said that Rob said.

Dr. Peter Thomas states that there was no evidence that father questioned the motives or reliability of reports for Mr. Chalmers. I say that Dr. Thomas should have questioned himself on the reliability of any of Harry's testimony as to what he said that Mr. Chalmers said. I say that Dr. Thomas should question his own discernment in recommending Harry as primary custodian of the boys. With that recommendation, Dr. Thomas did award the "jilted lover" a measure of revenge.

Chapter 25 - It's all about the Money

Revenge through Finances

The custody trial was held one day more that two years from the date that Kristen, my wife, and I were in the courtroom for the hearing discussing the filing of the first PFA. In the custody trial, Harry was seeking the primary custody he long desired. For the last 14 months he only had 50/50 custody. Kristen is in the courtroom, while my wife and I are being sequestered in the hallway outside the courtroom. Harry is on the witness stand.

Zimmer: Have you asked Miss Hall for contribution to the cost of daycare?

Harry: No. I think our—there's some—Bryce gets a stip—stipend through Berks County for his special needs, and we included that in my income. And through Domestic Relations, we've determined the support amount so it all kind of washes out. So, I don't ask her for any cash towards that.

Let's see. Harry puts the children in daycare when he has custody of them. So, we are supposed to consider Harry as being magnanimous in that he does not seek cash from Kristen to help pay for daycare. We,

Kristen's parents, babysit the boys when she has custody and is working. So why should we pay part of his daycare bill? Her mother had already given up her job to provide daycare for Kristen. Who made up this question this line of testimony? How was it determined that the stipend should be included in Harry's income? What does Harry's answer to the cost of daycare have to do with the stipend? What does he mean it all washes out? What really happened with the stipend?

The stipend of $300 per month was originally in Kristen's name because she was the one who made all the necessary arrangements to earn that stipend. She was the one to notice Bryce's special problem at the early age of 18 months. She had him tested by BCIU when he was only four and they agreed with Kristen that there was a problem. Harry always claimed Bryce had no problem and his behavior was because of Kristen's parenting. Of course, Harry was unable to do anything himself to improve that behavior. The "we" who determined that the stipend should be given to Harry was Harry. The week after having removed Kristen from house through the use of the Oley Police, he took the check written payable to "Kristen Hall" and destroyed it. He proceeded to have the check rewritten payable to "Harry Hall." He told the necessary authorities that he was primary custodian and the checks should be in his name. It has been that way since. It was not until after receiving a year's worth of those checks that the meeting with Domestic Relations to determine child support payments occurred. That meeting only occurred because Kristen filed with Domestic Relations to receive child support that was due because of the 50/50 ruling. Was Harry's action in tearing up the check in Kristen's name criminal? At the time he destroyed Kristen's check no determination of custody, whether temporary or permanent, had been made.

But how does this all wash out? It would be much later in the trial that the answer to this question might be understood. Zimmer questions Kristen.

Zimmer: You know, you mentioned before when you were talking about Mr. Spadafora the you needed that thousand dollars a month because you needed additional income. Isn't it true that Mr. Hall pays you $600 in support?

Kristen: He does.

By the time of the custody trial, Harry had received 24 checks of $300 each for a total of $7200. Meanwhile, Kristen had received 12 checks of $600 each for a total of $7200. Harry was correct. It all washed out. Harry paid her with the money Harry received through the stipend for Bryce. So, in reality, by that time Harry had paid nothing at all. Is that what is meant by money laundering? It all washed out.

I would like to ask Mr. Zimmer if he actually thought that the $600 a month support was a fair and just amount. Harry would pay that amount to Mr. Zimmer for two hours of work. I would like Mr. Zimmer to show me a monthly budget for a single mother with two children and an income of $1800 a month. There is another stipulation. A separate bedroom must be provided for the children.

Six months before the trial Kristen had signed an agreement with Harry that she would not seek alimony. She wanted the marriage to be officially over. She understood that she did not have the financial resources to fight any kind of battle. She might have thought differently if she had known Harry would file another PSR a few weeks later. I don't know why she was feeling confident that she could survive with only the $600 from Harry. Oh, Mike was still giving her a thousand dollars a month. A month later, Harry would cut off that supply. Harry in the divorce settlement did give her $5000 from one fund. There was another worth $11,000 from another she was to receive. She has never been given any of that money. She has given Jamie, her lawyer, the right to fight for that money in lieu of payment of services which Kristen could not pay. Jamie has not been successful in retrieving any of that money from Harry. Harry is a financial genius.

There was another reason why Kristen wanted to get that divorce settled in March of 2008. By that time the 50/50 custody agreement had already been in effect for a year. So Harry and Kristen agreed that both could declare one child as a dependent for income tax purposes. Kristen knew that would benefit her greatly for filing income taxes on April 15. She would be able to file as "head of household" with one dependent. She would claim Trey, and Harry Bryce. With that refund from the IRS, she would able to survive the few remaining months left on the year lease for the farm house. In October of 2008, two months after the custody trial in August, Kristen received a letter from the IRS. They said she was required to redo her tax forms. Harry had claimed both boys as dependents on his Federal income tax return. Harry did have primary custody of the boys the first few months of 2007. Therefore, legally he had the right to claim both boys. It did not matter to the IRS that Kristen had the agreement with Harry. That was a clever "dirty tactic" by Harry. Kristen owes the IRS a lot of money she got as a refund for the 2007 tax year. Harry should write a book on the use "dirty tactics" in finances for fighting a war.

The IRS "entrapment" was not the only "dirty tactic" used by Harry. There was another reason why Kristen agreed to signing the divorce agreement without asking for alimony. Harry told Kristen he could not afford to pay alimony. He said if he had to pay alimony he would lose the house. Kristen did not want the boys to lose their home. Kristen had received from the bank holding the mortgage on the marital residence a notice of foreclosure. Harry had stopped making payments on the mortgage when he started making the $600 payments to Kristen for child support. Harry knew Kristen well enough to realize that she would not let him lose the house for the boys. Therefore, she agreed to no alimony. Is it not interesting that at sometime during those five months of none payment of the mortgage Harry was able to hire Mark Zimmer as his lawyer for $3000. Five times $600 is $3000. See how it all washes out? In my letter to Judge Lash I wrote that Harry abused a bank. I was talking of this time when Harry let his house go into foreclosure. Harry knew at the time banks were having problems with foreclosures and were willing to make adjustments to not have to do them. Harry used this to his advantage in pulling this "dirty tactic" against Kristen.

Harry would say in court, "I've always done fair. I've got several agreements I put together with Kristen that were 50/50 straight up, even better than 50/50. She just never agreed to any of them." He said earlier in court, "I always agreed to give Kristen her fair share. I made many, many 50/50 offers with Kristen." Earlier, Mr. Zimmer had objected to that line of questioning saying, "We're heading into equitable distribution again." Kristen never heard of any such agreement. I never heard of any such agreement. Would it be considered "perjury", if Harry when asked to show one of those agreements could not provide one? What does Mr. Zimmer mean by saying, "equitable distribution again"? There never has been anything "equitably distributed" on the part of Harry Hall. Harry gave Kristen $10,000 dollars in exchange for a house valued at more than twenty-five times that amount. He traded even up giving Kristen $4300 for the family Durango worth twice that amount. He gave her none of the family furnishings or appliances that they had purchased together for the house. He did keep some of the items for himself that Kristen had brought into the household. He kept some of the items her parents gave her for the marital residence. Harry even kept her dog.

Early in the custody trial, Harry through Mr. Zimmer's questioning would give a thought about child support.

Zimmer: If you got primary custody of the children, would you file for child support?

Harry: No. No. Kristen's income is not very substantial. It wouldn't impact me in any great way, and it would hurt her. I want her to have a place for the boys.

Zimmer: If you filed for child support, do you believe that that would hurt her ability to provide for the children?

Harry: It would hamper her, yes.

Mr. Zimmer does it again. Harry answers the first question with it would "hurt." Mr. Zimmer asks in the second if it "hurt." Harry did provide the apartment the first year with the $10,000 in lieu of the house. That would be the last of his supplying a place for Kristen and the boys.

Anyway, Judge Lash would commend Harry in his final report for saying he would not file for support if he was awarded primary. Judge Lash should not be commending a person on a deed not yet done. Would Judge Lash award Harry primary? If he did, would Harry seek support? It is all about the money.

Chapter 26 - Easter Holiday PSR

The Event that Provokes a Letter

The date for the second custody evaluation with Dr. Peter Thomas was April 22, 2008. Easter that year was on the last Sunday in March. In Dr. Thomas' evaluation report was a paragraph of Harry's version of what occurred that Easter.

> Mr. Hall expressed concern about an event that happened at Easter. He states it was his holiday. He states he went to the Oley Police but urged them not to talk to Kristen in front of the boys. He states the police talked to Kristen on the phone. He states in spite of his request, Kristen told the boys what was happening.

Does this make any sense? How are the police to know where the boys are in relationship to Kristen while she is answering the phone? How could Kristen not tell the boys what is happening when she would have to be bringing them to the police? So what was Harry's concern? Why did Harry have to bring up the Easter event to Dr. Peter Thomas? Harry believed he had to refute my story of the Easter event. The custody evaluation took place only three weeks after my letter to Judge Lash. A lot had happened in those weeks. In my letter to Judge Lash I included an article I had written concerning that Easter holiday. The article, "Easter – Whose holiday is it?" is as follows.

Kristen and Harry have an agreement for custody of the boys over the holidays. They agreed to alternate holidays. For thanksgiving 2007 my wife and I planned to take Kristen and the boys for dinner at the Golden Oaks and then to Longwood Gardens. Christmas was to be Harry's holiday with the boys and his family. That left New Year's Day for Kristen. So Harry had the boys New Year's Eve. New Year's Day came and Harry and his family were having a special dinner. Harry wanted the boys for that day also. Kristen gave up the argument with the agreement that she could have the boys for the next holiday which would be Easter. No problem, Harry agreed.

Easter weekend 2008 came. It was Kristen's normal weekend in the schedule. So, she really did not gain another day with the boys according to the holiday schedule. So Harry made out pretty well in not giving her another day with the boys.

For Saturday we planned to take Kristen and the boys and our son's family with their three daughters to Longwood Gardens. When Kristen got to our house to leave for the trip she was very upset. She said that Harry had just called her and said that he was picking up the boys at 9:00 am on Easter Sunday morning. He insisted it was his holiday. She insisted it was hers. The last time she talked to Harry was 8:30 pm on Saturday. She thought she had finally convinced him of the truth. Even with the upsetting phone call earlier in the day, we all had a great time at Longwood Gardens.

Easter morning came. We hoped we were clear and would not hear from Harry. That morning I started out on Mt. Penn with my brass group playing for the Easter Dawn Service. I then went to FPC to teach a special Easter lesson to the children in Children's Church. We had an 11:30 reservation for dinner with Kristen and the boys at the former Fleetwood fire hall. It would not be very glamorous, but at least it would be inexpensive. Nine o'clock came and went and we had not heard from Harry. While on the short drive from Blandon to Fleetwood, with all of us in the car, Kristen got a call on her cell phone. It was the Oley Police. They told her she had to bring the children immediately in order to give the boys to Harry. Of course, Kristen became very upset and the boys likewise. They understand now and believe that a talk with the police may mean that they are going to be taken from their mother again. This is the abuse that the boys fear, that of losing their mother. We took the boys out of the car to walk to the fire hall. Meanwhile, Kristen negotiated with the police to explain it really was her holiday. It was quite a "horrific" experience for all of us. Kristen did not give in. She eventually got back to Harry and he finally agreed he would take the boys at the normal 7:00 pm time that evening.

The boys were anxious to get back to Kristen's house that afternoon. Two of their friends would be coming and we would have an egg hunt, which we did. The rest of the day was ruined to some extent because we feared what Harry would pull the next day.

We were correct to fear, for the next Kristen received her latest, I don't know what to call it, back door "PFA" and pack of lies. Harry was inspired again. This time Harry thought he found a good ally for his evil plans. Unfortunately for Harry this ally may be to his detriment. His present ally is waiting for a hearing on "harassment" charges. He has problems. This time Kristen said "no" after 4 weeks and he "flipped out." So he has joined Harry to seek revenge. Harry told him he needed an "ally" because the court favors women in custody trials. Rob only spent a few hours with the boys. All his accusations are simply mimics of Harry's lies, things Kristen had told him she was accused of by Harry, and other half truths (lies). Rob's lies are written in his own handwriting on PFA #5.

Now I know what I called a "back door" PFA is really a PSR, Petition for Special Relief. The article above was the first of sixteen I would eventually write in the five months before the custody trial of 2008. Those articles where written about the events that started two years before the custody trial, starting with the filing of the first PFA by Harry. Three months after the custody trial the number of articles would be thirty. By June of 2010, seventy articles were written. It was time for me to start writing a book.

One of the items included in that PSR was the biting incident. That was the only item for which physical abuse was demonstrated. Before the filing of the PSR, we did not know that Harry had gone to the doctor with Bryce and Trey in order to accuse Kristen of poor supervision because of those bite marks. Three weeks later Harry would include the doctor's report concerning the bite marks in the evaluation with Dr. Peter Thomas. Dr. Thomas did have an interesting short sentence in his evaluation report. It read, "She bit the children." Even Harry did not come up with that idea. I laughed to myself when I read it. Maybe his typist hit the "b" instead of the "h."

Many of the accusations in the PSR were in Rob Chalmer's handwriting. They were not things he observed. They were lies. Harry would have to admit months later in the custody trial that he was not able to observe Kristen in her parenting since being removed from the marital residence with the first PFA. He would use Rob Chalmers as his source of knowledge of Kristen's parenting. Also, the accusations by Rob Chalmers in the PSR were those used by Harry in his interview with Dr. Thomas. They were the reason that Dr. Thomas would call Harry's teaming up with Rob Chalmers an "unholy alliance."

Not long after filing the Easter Holiday PSR there would be a hearing. My wife and I would go to court that day to give Kristen moral support as we did for the first PFA twenty months before. By that time we understood that we would not get to participate in the hearing. As for the other events, we could have added the truth to refute Harry's lies in the PSR. The actual discussions for the case would be closed door as it was only a hearing. Harry would have one person with him for support that day. Harry must have believed that that person could speak in his behalf that day. The person seated next to him was Rob Chalmers. Harry must have thought he could have Rob speak because Rob helped him write the PSR. Before the discussion of the case began, Judge Lash would, unceremoniously, have Mr. Chalmers removed from the premises. Rob was eventually convicted of harassment.

It was the filing of the Easter Holiday PSR that led me to write my letter to Judge Lash. I enclosed the "Easter Holiday" article along with that letter. From the trial transcript I learned that Harry liked my use of the word "horrific" in my "Easter Holiday" article. He would use it to describe other accusations he would make against Kristen from the witness stand in the custody trial. I wonder what other words from me he will learn to use when he reads my book.

Chapter 27 - Wanting Justice

My Letter to the Judge

Your Honor Judge Lash,

I am presently Children's Ministry Director at First Presbyterian Church. For thirty-five years I was a math teacher at Berks Career & Technology Center. Before taking the position at FPC in June of 2007, I taught for four years for the YMCA in its Youth Outreach Program. I know what it is like working with children with "extra" problems. All children have some. I also know the requirements of law to report suspected cases of child abuse. So I must report this case of child abuse.

I am enclosing an article concerning myself that was written for our church paper, IVY TOWER. Also enclosed is my resume for Christian service I used for applying for the job. My summers had always been used to do volunteer work for youth. Upon receiving the position, I was given a book describing the Presbyterian code. The statement on the page that struck me immediately was that we as Christians must fight against "injustice." The greatest case of "injustice" I know is the one perpetrated by Harry Hall against my daughter, my wife, my grandsons, and myself. I must now begin the fight.

Harry Hall calls us the "evil triangle." For twenty months the "evil triangle" has been silent. It has not been because of indifference, but because we have not been given the chance to speak in defense of our daughter or ourselves. Harry, on the other hand, had been able to tell his lies over and over again to the court, Children's Services, lawyers, police, doctors, and others. Worse, he was able to get action on those lies. Our daughter, my wife and I, and our grandsons have been punished without trial or chance to speak the truth.

This case is supposedly child abuse by my daughter against her children. There has been no such abuse. There has been, however, much abuse by Harry Hall. He has abused the court system. He has abused his wife. He has abuse my wife and I. He has abused all those he involved as accomplices in his crimes. He has abused those with whom he has done business, including the bank. He has abused the Christian religion. Most of all, he is the real abuser of the children. This case is not about child abuse, although his abuse of them is part of it, but it is really about Harry's attempts at revenge and financial gain. It is not about his love for the children. If he had love for them, he would want them to be with their "loving" mother, a mother who was willing to give him 50/50 custody so that the children would have a relationship with their father. I do not agree with her in this respect because I do not think a person of Harry's character should be fathering anyone. The words I would use to describe his character are condescending to women, unforgiving, untrusting, hateful, unscrupulous, deceiving, arrogant, and controlling.

As the other parts of the "evil triangle," Harry's hate is directed towards my wife and I. He has been jealous of our relationship with the boys. We are the ones who have helped her with the boys from the beginning and even more so now. Harry wants us removed from this position. From the beginning he has denied that Bryce needed help. It was Kristen who fought for that help. However, he has been willing to accept that check given for Bryce. The checks were in Kristen's name originally, but Harry ripped up the check when he filed the first PFA and had them continue in his name.

Harry says he wants primary custody of the boys. He has never given one positive reason why he should have them. He has none. He has given only negative lies against Kristen.

This past week, the boys came up with a solution to the situation. Trey, the four year old, said, "Mommy should have us 100 days and daddy one." Bryce, the now six year old, is a little more understanding of the calendar. He said, "Mommy should have us six days and daddy one." Later he said, "No, mommy should have us ten days." I asked Bryce what he likes best about daddy. He said, "The dog." If only Harry was as good as a dog.

Thank you for taking time to read this. I will be giving information to substantiate my claims. I am enclosing an article with this letter telling of Harry's exploits the past two weeks. The most "damming" of these can be verified by the Oley Police Department. I also will be filing a PFA against Harry.

My ending was "Wanting Justice." I signed, "David Rathman, father of Kristen Hall." In my last line of the body of my letter I said I would file a PFA. I had to keep my word. I tried. That same week I went to the Children's Services building. It has sixteen floors. I never had the occasion to be in the building before Harry got us involved with the first PFA. I would get to visit many other floors of the build in the ensuing months, even years. There are hallways connecting the Children's Services building to the Berks County Courthouse. One day I had used one of those hallways to go into the courthouse and run up the stairwell to a courtroom. That was the day I caught Harry in the lie to Kristen in the hallway of the stairwell. This time I only had to go to the first floor of the Children's Services building. The office where the PFA's were filed was on the first floor.

I entered the waiting room and signed in. The receptionist was in the office talking to a client. The door was open, but it did not matter. My four semesters of Spanish in college forty years before would not be enough for me to know what they were saying. At YOP I was fortunate that our secretary was bilingual. I was the only person in the waiting room. Forty-five minutes later the client left and the receptionist gave me the necessary forms to file a PFA. She said I had twenty minutes to have it ready for the judge. I quickly wrote about the biting incident. It worked for Harry. The biting had started at his house. I also had my Easter Holiday article which I attached to the application. I knew not what I was doing.

I was sent off with my writing to a courtroom in the courthouse. Once again I was on my way through the hallway. I met a man outside the courtroom who said he would take my PFA application to the judge.

I remained outside the courtroom. I found out Judge Lash was not on duty that day. A few minutes later the man came out the courtroom. He said my PFA would not be considered by the judge on duty that day, but they would keep record of it on file. I thought that was odd. Kristen told me that judges always sign the PFA's in order to protect them selves. I guess I am not very dangerous. Or, could it be that Judge Lash had warned the judge on duty that I might be filing a PFA? Had Judge Lash read the last sentence of my letter that said I would be filing a PFA? Nah, he said he only read enough of my letter to surmise what case it referred to so that he knew to what counsel it should be given.

Why, five months later in court, did Judge Lash say that my writing a letter to him was improper? On occasion, I watch FOX News. Judge Napolitano said you should write to your judge. Kristen's first boyfriend, after Harry filed the first PFA, wrote a letter to the judge on Kristen's behalf. He put it under the door of Judge Lash's office at the courthouse. Bern, Kristen's house mate and supervisor, said I should write letters to the judge. I thought he should know. He had spent nine years in prison. I would learn, after receiving the transcript of the custody trial months later, that Judge Lash allowed as an exhibit a letter written by a friend of Harry. That friend would not even be at the trial to testify. It was written more than a year before the trial and addressed "to whom it may concern." Judge Lash said he would consider the exhibits. Did he consider that letter?

Why didn't Judge Lash ask me, when I was on the witness stand, why I wrote my letter to him? If he had read my letter, then he would have understood I was reporting child abuse. I did not know to whom I could report the abuse. I could not report it to Children's Services. We tried that and three months later Kristen was slapped by CYS with an unjust charge of child abuse. In addition, they passed the unjustified condition of 24 hour supervised visitation onto Kristen which would also affect my wife and me. They were entirely in Harry's camp.

You would think that Judge Lash would know that it is a requirement of the law for a professional that works with children to report suspected child abuse. I thought it was true. I looked it up on the internet. There is an act called CAPTA which stands for the Child Abuse Prevention and Treatment Act. All 50 states have passed some form of a "mandatory child abuse and neglect reporting law" in order to qualify for funding.

Does Judge Lash think that I, as a Christian, should not become involved when I see "injustice"? I feel it is my Christian duty to become involved. I stated in my letter that I was inspired to seek justice to some extent by a section in a book I referred to in my letter. It stated that "justice is the order God sets in human life for fair and honest dealing and for giving rights to those who have no power to claim rights for themselves." It states "there is no peace without justice." I will have no peace until there is justice. The section finishes with the statement that we, as believers, should commit ourselves to be reconcilers seeking justice and pursuing peace. I am committed. Did Judge Lash think my letter was about him? It was supposed to be about Harry Hall. It was not about Judge Lash. I was not saying that he had dealt unjustly with us the first twenty months of this case. I was saying decisions were made based on Harry's lies. I was saying that I was willing and able to testify to the facts of the case. I was saying the facts were not given a chance to be heard.

Did Kristen get to say anything in defense of herself when the 24 hour emergency PFA was filed by Harry? No. But that night she was punished by being removed from her home. The children were punished by losing their mother. Was it justice when Harry followed through with the PFA that increased to fourteen more days the time that she would be kept from her children and her home? Again, Kristen and the children were punished without her having a chance to tell her side of the story. It was accomplished with a simple signature from Judge Lash. Judges have to sign those PFA's. For the next eight months Kristen was punished by the family justice system with the brand of "child abuser." The last five months of that time period she would only have her children four days a month. Her side of the story was heard by the custody evaluator, but the children were still being punished by being alienated from the Kristen.

Then, there were the two bumps on the head accusations. She never got to tell either of the doctors from Reading Pedes how the bumps occurred. The second bump resulted in the accusation being called "founded." CYS would not listen to her explanation of how Bryce got that the bump. Their decision was based only on the words of Harry and the boys. It was defamation of character. It meant that her career in social work was forever finished. The college degree she had earned was made useless in gaining employment. She was served a lifetime sentence. Another result was that Kristen would be unable to accompany her children in activities with other children. Thus, she would not be able to participate with me and her boys in the activities I planned as Children's Ministry Director at FPC. When the boys would be in a school activity she could not accompany her own children. In addition, CYS punished her by making her sign the paper to agree to the 24 hour supervised visitation. Does it seem like a lot of punishment for a single bump on the head, based on the testimony of a five year old diagnosed with "Asperger's", his three year and a half year old brother rehearsed by his father, and a father wanting primary custody at any cost other than his own? We three, Kristen, my wife, and I, knew the truth about the bumps, but the decision was made without our voice.

I stated in my letter that Harry used many accomplices against Kristen with his lies. Let me elaborate on those I knew at the time I wrote the letter. There would be more accomplices I could add in the five months time between my letter writing and the custody trial. I will elaborate on those later. When I say "he used," I mean that in the sense that he "lied to." Harry used three different doctors from Reading Pedes – one for the "blue bowl" incident, one the "squirty bottle" incident, and the last the "biting" incident. Besides Judge Lash, he used a district judge for the 24 hour emergency PFA. He used three Oley Police, two to remove her from her home and one to make the Easter phone call. He used two state police to come to the house for a 911 call for the "recording" incident. At least, he has not, according to their instructions, tried to use them again. He hired and used three lawyers. He used a number of workers from CYS including the supervisor and solicitor. Also used from CYS were caseworkers who had to visit Kristen because of his child abuse charges against Kristen. There was the woman from CYS who made the threatening phone call on Harry's behalf. There was Bill Clemons who wrote the charge that Kristen would have the record as a "child abuser" until Bryce would turn 23 years old. Bill Clemons was the one who had to admit that Harry was lying to Kristen about the results of the first charge using CYS – the "blue bowl" incident. He was the one from CYS that was present when Harry's lawyer made the directive to both parties. There were other counselors, psychologists, caseworkers, including the custody master and custody evaluator who Harry tried to influence with his lies. We knew he had at least one private investigator that followed us at various times. What did he tell him or them? Harry used his supposed knowledge of Kristen's past history with boyfriends against her. He formed an "unholy alliance" with Kristen's "jilted lover." They got to lie together. For me, however, the most grievous use of accomplices was that of using his sons, Bryce and Trey. Yes, he lied to them.

I stated in my letter that Harry is the real abuser of the children. The article on mandatory reporting of child abuse listed items considered as child abuse. It stated that abuse would be any act which results in imminent risk of serious harm, death, serious physical or emotional harm, sexual abuse or exploitation. The serious emotional harm done to the boys has been, from the first PFA, the alienation of the boys from their mother. Of course, the perpetrator of that crime has been Harry Hall. We could add as an accomplice the family justice system of Berks County. They assisted Harry at every step. The boys have been used by Harry Hall for exploitation in gaining revenge. That revenge is based on his jealousy of our relationship with the boys. We were there for the boys when Harry was there for the money. Harry's obvious goal was that of winning primary custody. He wanted Kristen to pay him support. That does not work out well when you kill the goose that laid the golden eggs. Does anyone understand the analogy?

Why was it that the only words in my letter that Mark Zimmer deemed worthy of repeating to the court were, "if only Harry was as good as a dog?"

Chapter 28 – Super Granddaddy CMD

More from the IVY TOWER

Besides the Easter Holiday article, I enclosed two other items with my letter to Judge Lash. One of those items was the Christian service resume that I used in applying for the Children's Ministry Director position at FPC. The last item enclosed was the following article written for the IVY TOWER, which is FPC's monthly newsletter. Written by Evelyn Marker, it appeared in the November 2007 edition. By that time I had already been the CMD for five months. I included it with my letter to Judge Lash to demonstrate that indeed I was working with young children. Also, I wanted to demonstrate that I had much experience in working with children of all ages. Perhaps, I would be able to handle with some degree of expertise the position of grandfather. Consider this article to be a biography of the author. The title was, "Getting to Know You"

This month we would like to introduce, First Presbyterian's Children's Ministry Director.

When Dave was seven years old he went forward in a revival meeting to accept Christ. He told the assembly, "I was going to wait until I was an adult, but I felt it would waste a lot of years." Based on this experience,

Dave says, "I believe children can learn a lot from the Bible at an early age."

Dave grew up in the Fleetwood Bible Fellowship Church. His father was the young men's class Sunday school teacher for 20 years and Dave's teacher from 7th thru 12th grades. "My dad had only a ninth grade education, but as a young Christian was able to attend some Bible College classes in Providence, Rhode Island, and Philadelphia. I gained a sense of "awe and reverence" from him concerning the scriptures. He studied early every morning to prepare for those lessons." Dave says, "I want our children here to have that same sense of awe."

Dave's years in the Fleetwood school system were full of many interests and accomplishments. He studied trumpet, later switching to baritone horn; and earned placement in a number of county, district, and regional state bands. He lettered in soccer, basketball, and baseball; and upon graduation was named the top senior athlete, as well as best musician, and the student with the highest average in mathematics. Dave then enrolled in Kutztown State College, where he majored in math, earning a BS degree in Secondary Education. He was the second Kutztown State College athlete to win an individual PSAC gold medal; winning the high jump in 1966. Dave also served as KSC band president. Three years later he completed his MS in education at KSC.

While in college, Dave started attending West Wyomissing Chapel where he met his future wife, Mary Lynne. "We sang a duet in an Easter cantata, and a year and a half later we were married." The name of the cantata was "No Greater Love." Dave and Mary Lynne have two children, Todd and Kristen, and five grandchildren. Much of Dave's Christian education experience came about as it related to his children as they grew up. It started with Children's Church, then Vacation Bible School, followed by Bible and Sports Schools, and finally Music Camp at Greenview Bible Camp.

Dave taught Sunday School in every church he attended. At West Wyomissing Chapel he also served as Sunday School Superintendent. (Note: This is my justification for using "super" in the chapter title.) His involvement in music, sports, and Christian education led him to develop the Bible and Sports School form of VBS. He directed and taught in 45 such schools in ten churches from 1977-2001. He held his 46th Bible and Sports School at FPC this summer. For these schools, Dave wrote the curriculum, designed the teaching materials, chose the music, and even wrote some of the theme songs. He formed an orchestra comprised of adults and youth for each school. "Music was an important part of these programs. Everything I do music will teach something. We have so little time to teach children, we don't sing just for fun." Dave is presently writing the Christmas pageant for FPC's children.

Music has been important throughout Dave' life, but mostly as it related to serving or praising God. "In my teen years I dreamed of getting together a marching band that played religious music," Dave says. He organized brass groups in every church he attended, and his brass ensemble from West Lawn United Methodist Church started playing for the Easter Dawn Service on Mount Penn in 1992. In 1997, he organized the BRASS IN PRAISE ensemble, a large group of brass players from Berks County and beyond. BRASS IN PRAISE has played for the Easter Dawn Services, the Gring's Mill Hymns Sings, in churches, in nursing homes, and at various community functions; and recently gave its 170th performance. Dave writes the orchestrations for the group. More than 200 musicians representing 50 churches have played with Dave.

Dave is in his 41st year of teaching mathematics on some level and is currently teaching College Algebra at Penn State, Berks Campus. Dave taught for 35 years at the Berks Career and Technology Center. He also taught four years in Reading for the YMCA in its Youth Outreach Program. Dave summarizes his teaching career in one sentence. "The math I teach is important for this life, but when I teach from the Bible, its values are for eternity."

For me, the position as CMD at FPC was a dream job. I do not mean a job where I could sleep on the job and still get paid. It would be unique in that I would be getting paid for things I had done as a volunteer. For nearly forty years, I invested my summers in teaching children from the scriptures. My CMD position was a dream job because of the subject matter. I enjoyed the challenge of making the scriptures as real to children as it was to me at an early age. Over those many years I gained at lot of experience in writing curriculum. I would put all I had learned into this effort, starting June of 2007.

The average attendance for Sunday school for the children's department from age 3 to grade five the previous year was thirty. It was an "older" congregation, if you know what I mean. They, however, were interested in teaching the children. They had more adult volunteer helpers than children. The person that handled that scheduling was still on board. Otherwise, my dream job would have been a nightmare. I would handle the curriculum and the music. I would be a proactive CMD, meaning I would be involved with the teaching and activities of the children. I announced the curriculum for the summer of 2007 in the IVY TOWER.

Two post graduate courses will be offered for the students who will be completing a grade from kindergarten to 5th grade this June. First, in the Sunday School hour, Dave will be teaching a course on what it means to be a Christian. A song entitled, "To Be a Christian", will be introduced. It is based on five key words from the book of Romans. Second, in Children's Church, Dave will teach a course entitled, "It is finished." The lessons describe what Jesus accomplished for the world and us in his death on the cross. This will be open to children who have completed any grade from 1st through 5th this past year. It will be held, as in the past, when the children are dismissed from the worship service. The third post graduate course offered in July will be for anyone who has completed a year of life this past year. It will be offered as part of Vacation Bible School for the Family from July 23 thru July 27. The theme for the school will be based on the words to the song, "I See God." It is a first course in apologetics giving five good reasons why we can believe in God. It will be for all ages. A unique feature of the school will be the "Bible and Sports Challenge" for children from kindergarten age to 5th grade.

I had other items on my "bucket" list. I had orchestrated music and written a few songs for my Bible Schools. As an Assistant Sunday School Superintendent I was given the task of directing the Christmas Pageant. Yes, I wrote the Christmas Pageant. The title was, "The Christmas Story as Told by Matthew and Luke to Isaiah and Micah." My "bucket" list item was to write a cantata. My plan was to write the fall curriculum for Sunday School in a way that could demonstrate what the children had learned that fall. Each oral presentation would be followed by singing. It would be like a cantata. I wrote a theme song and used a number of songs I wrote for past themes. As the November article had stated, "Dave is presently writing the Christmas pageant for FPC's children." Below our some words from the January 2008, IVY TOWER:

The cover page for the program announced the following: "Shadows of Christmas". It is a celebration of the Christ of the New as found in the Old, based on the Holy Scripture, written by the prophets of old, produced by FPC's Children's Ministry Team, and presented by the children of First Presbyterian.

In order to see the "light", the audience was put in the dark. Under the white light only the event from the Old Testament could be seen as a shadow. When placed under the black light the Christ of the New Testament was revealed. Each of the twenty shadows was introduced by a scripture quoted by a child. As the fourth shadow was place under the black light a bright rainbow appeared and there were a few "oohs" and "aahs" from the audience. The promise of that shadow seemed to provide a sense of anticipation for the remainder of the program. The program concluded with everyone singing "Shadows of Christmas." The final line concluded, "It now has been told."

Perhaps, the above line should conclude this book, or at least this chapter. I am getting there. Three weeks before the pageant I had still not determined how I would include the children of preschool age. Someone reminded me of that fact. There were seven children in the 3 to 4 age group. The probability of having all girls is 1 to 128. It happened. I asked if we had any angel costumes. The answer was yes. I was lucky I did not have to convince a boy to wear one of those angel costumes. Each angel would get to announce a special birth recorded in the Old Testament. I wrote a song for the angels entitled "Special Birth." Below are the words to that song. My inspiration for the second verse was my daughter's adopted son, Bryce.

We are God's special angels, telling of Special Birth,
And that birth most special was when Jesus came to earth.
Now we sing glory to the Highest Special Birth,
Now we sing glory to God in the highest, peace on earth.
Now every birth is special, whether a girl or boy.
God created each special to bring to all great joy!

Mark Zimmer, inspired by the writings of Judge Lash about myself and my wife, would write his own unique words nearly a year after my words above in a report after the custody trial held in August of 2008. I do not believe his words were put to music. His words: "The children's relationship with Maternal Grandparents was addressed at the trial and Father believes that until Maternal Grandparents can learn to accept Bryce for the special and unique child that he is and treat Bryce the same way that they treat Trey, that a relationship with Maternal Grandparents is not suitable at this time." Apparently, Mr. Zimmer and Judge Lash think that this "granddaddy CMD" is not so "super."

Chapter 29 - Twice Resigned

A Resignation Clothed in a Suit

So, how did the Christmas Pageant go? Thank you for asking. Compared to the nightmare rehearsal the week before, it was a dream. I included the dream in the following month's IVY TOWER article for Children's Ministry. The following words, excluding the names to protect the innocent, are from that article.

> Thanks to all participants in the program. Despite the weather, the program was well attended. Only one child expected to participate was absent and that family has more than an hour to church. There was more than one volunteer willing to take the part. Each child had a part to say. A number also attempted some solo singing and all sang as much as they could. A 5th grader controlled the black light with his remote control system.
>
> Besides the children, others helped in pulling off the program. Four teens helped with the moving of the shadow charts. Another teen played the trumpet, and one filled in at the last minute operating the house lights. The most difficult task was the interchanging of the song charts. The children sang 25 times as the 30

song charts were "juggled" by a parent. Our pianist has done an excellent job during Sunday school all fall and for the program. Other teachers "pitched in" helping children get to where they should be.

There were many favorable comments about the program. One parishioner exclaimed, upon leaving after the program, "Now that was the Gospel!" He caught it, that is, the message. He saw the Christ of the New from the Old. At our staff meeting, Pam, our church administrator, told us that a parent said it was the best Christmas pageant she ever saw. Pastor Keevil was not so exuberant. He would comment, "Maybe you could have—." I forgot what he said. He did miss the first ten minutes or so. The program lasted an hour. It was all program; no announcements, no commercials, and no pats on the back. How do you pat God on the back for a job well done? Christmas is all about what God did. Dr. Keevil had missed my special song called "Special Birth", sung by myself and special angels, written being inspired by a special child whose name was Bryce.

Apparently, Dr. Keevil was less impressed then even I suspected. I was told I should cease writing curriculum and choose a commercial product. I said I would and I did. I just did not understand why. I would write a series of lessons for January and February as the new quarter, for which I would order material, started in March. My series of lessons was based on the characters from Hebrews chapter 11 and the word "faith". I call it the "Hall of Faith" chapter. I had written a theme song many years before entitled "By Faith." Dr. Keevil also informed me that he wanted the new Music Director to take over the singing for the children's Sunday school opening. She would choose the music so that they could learn songs to sing for the worship service. She was well qualified to teach children music as that was her full time job in an elementary school. The first song she would choose would be an oldie with a lot of Hallelu's. Like I said, "We don't sing just for fun. It has to teach something."

I was not a happy CMD. I would no longer be doing the two items which I believed were my greatest contributions as CMD. I still would have control of the curriculum for Children's Church which had an average attendance of 10. I rotated with the three other teachers I had procured. I would be there early every Sunday morning to help out with the younger children before the older children came for their lesson. There was a period of at least 20 minutes between Children's Church and Sunday school. For this time I invented projects for the children and taught games I invented, including "blind man's wallyball." (Space does not permit explanation of the game.) I was not satisfied with the materials that we had to use for S. S. even though I chose them. I felt I was no longer worthy of the $21,000 per year salary.

An important meeting was scheduled for the first Saturday in April of 2008. I believe it was with the board called Session. The heads of most of the organizations in the church were there to give reports. The report was to include accomplishments from the previous year and goals for the upcoming year. Pastor Keevil had advised me to include as one of my goals, "an increase in attendance of the children in Sunday school of 50%." Remember the story of David in the Old Testament? Remember his great sin? No, I am not talking about that one. David's sin was that of numbering the people, his army. Read the story. I would not be presumptuous enough to say I could bring about an increase in attendance even though I can do increase problems in mathematics. God alone can bring the increase. My first goal would have been that I continue to be faithful in the presentation of the gospel and the scriptures to the children. My second goal would have been to continue to be a faithful witness demonstrating the love of Christ thru the influence of the Holy Spirit in my life.

It was my turn to give a report. I told the assembly of twenty, "I have no report. My goal is to resign." I told the assembly I was grateful for the opportunity given me to present the gospel to the children. I left the room and went back to the office. A few moments later, Dr. Keevil showed up in my room asking for an explanation. Basically, I told him I felt unworthy of the position. There was not enough that I did to earn my pay. He asked me to come back to the meeting. I did. They convinced me to stay on as CMD. I said as long as they wanted me I would stay. They would have to ask me to leave. I would be there only one more Sunday.

There was something else going on in my mind the week before that Saturday in April of 2008. A few days before, I had sent my letter "wanting justice" to Judge Lash. At that time my daughter was still under the sentence as a "child abuser." She could not come with her children into a group of other children in a Sunday school class. Secretly, I thought, "here I am teaching other people's children and not my own grandchildren. Is there something wrong here?" No, we consider all children God's, not our own.

I was in my office the next Tuesday morning. Dr. Keevil came in holding a piece of paper. The piece of paper was my letter to Judge Lash. He hells me there will be a meeting Wednesday afternoon. There were two other persons at the Wednesday meeting with myself and Dr. Keevil. One was the church secretary and the other a representative from the Law Office of John Roland. Dr. Keevil proceeded to tell me that the church was being threatened with a lawsuit because I had written my letter on church letterhead paper. I do not remember the lady's name from the law office representing the church. She said they were not sure how to handle the situation. She said she recommended to Dr. Keevil that I be suspended without pay. I would like to have known at that time how it was that Dr. Keevil had my letter. Was it sent to the church in his name? Did someone simply hand it to him? I never would find out how he got the letter.

A few days later my wife and I would receive a letter from a law office. It was from an attorney of the Law Office of John Roland. His name was Jonathan Phillips. His said that he was unable to complete our "will" due to a "conflict of interest." We had been to see him about three weeks before. We were trying to find a lawyer who would help us in a suit of Harry Hall. We had our notes on one sheet of paper. He said we did not have enough for a suit. We asked him then if he could do a "will" for us. He said, "Yes, for $300." At the time he said it would only take a few days. He did ask if he could keep a copy of our notes on Harry Hall. I said, "Yes." I thought maybe he would come up with an idea. He did happen to mention that he was going through a divorce. I know a good divorce lawyer. His reputation is that he usually wins. His name is Mark Zimmer. What is this "conflict of interest" that would disqualify Mr. Phillips from doing our "will?"

We had received the letter above about the same time I sent my letter of resignation to the church. I would receive a confirmation letter of my resignation from Dr. Keevil on April 22, 2008. Ironically, that day is the same date on my daughter's second evaluation report from Dr.

Peter Thomas. His report would decide the fate of six lives. My letter to Dr. Keevil meant that a church would again be searching for Children's Ministry Director. Below are Dr. Keevil's words in acceptance of my resignation.

> Pursuant of your letter regarding resignation, I accept it with regrets. I have already informed Session by email and a sufficient number have responded for me to be able to confirm that Session has also accepted it. I regret the events which led to this. I understand that we all make mistakes with unintended consequences. This must be a difficult time for you and your family. Please know that we bear no ill will only regret that this happened at all. We pray God's blessing on you and your family with hope that the issues that lead to the writing of the letter will be resolved soon.

He regrets the events. What events does he regret? Is it the fact that I wrote a letter? Or, was it only the fact that I wrote it on church letterhead? Is he actually saying he regrets that we have been going through this injustice in the family court system? He states we must be having a difficult time. Was he willing to hear about that difficult time? Did he ask me why I wrote on church letterhead? He did say it was a good letter. He probably understood why I used the letterhead. Would he have let me use the letterhead if I had asked? I am sure he would have said no. It does seem that he is telling me that it was a mistake to write the letter. I have a thought. Did Dr. Keevil put one and one together to make one? Did he consider my letter writing and resignation as part of the same event? That was not my intention. I wrote my letter to Judge Lash before I had thoughts of resigning. My serious thoughts of resigning came after the talk about goals with Dr. Keevil a day after my letter was sent.

I do not regret writing the letter. I was as compelled to write that letter as I have been in all my ministries of teaching, praising God, and witnessing for Christ in all that I do. As a young person, I remember a simple testimony given by some in Wednesday night prayer meetings. I usually tried to be more original, even at the age of ten. But, the testimony still rings true. It was, "I'm glad the Lord saved me, and is keeping me, and I want to keep on living for Him." I do not consider my letter a mistake. It was meant to be. Does that sound a bit too much like predestination? I accept the consequences. I am not saying I have not made mistakes. Did I just write a triple negative?

Will good come from my having written the letter? I say and sing, "Amen! Amen and amen!" It already gave me a title for a book. It has already given a demonstration of the character of one named Harry Hall, and an attorney by the name of Mark Zimmer. Who would try to sue a church? You could say that my letter was "clothed in suit."

CHAPTER 30 - EGREGIOUS ACTS

More from the Second Custody Evaluation

Before I would take the stand in the custody trial in August of 2008, there would be a discussion concerning my letter. I would not learn of this discussion until Christmas of 2008. I learned about it from reading the trial transcript my wife and I had purchased as our only Christmas present to each other.

Ms. Dautrich: I think most of what would be new would be regarding the lawsuit that Mr. Hall had against the church that led to—

Zimmer: There's no lawsuit, Your Honor. Show me something that's filed.

The Court: Well, the testimony was that Mr. Hall has not or will not be filing any lawsuit. And you are saying that's not an accurate statement?

Ms. Dautrich: Well, if it wasn't filed, it was the threat of the lawsuit that ended up leading to the—my client's father being let go from his job basically because of that. The agreement was he would not file the suit basically if my client's father was removed from

Zimmer: That's not true. There's no such stipulation. No document was ever drafted. That's not true at all.

Ms. Dautrich: I think that may be protected under—

The Court: Well, how is that germane to the custody, the best interests of the children?

Pardon, would the court please look at the content of the letter? The content of the letter is germane to the best interests of the children. It was written by someone who is and has been fully vested in the interests of the children. They continue with the discussion. Sorry for the interruption.

Ms. Dautrich: It's just germane to Mr. Halls assertions that—

The Court: How would that impeach Mr. Hall? The letter came to me. I started reading it, saw that it was not appropriate, sent it to counsel. And, that's the last I knew about it. And apparently it went to the church and the church attorney, and that may have been the basis for him being suspended.

Zimmer: I believe it was. I sent it to the church. They sent it to their counsel. Their counsel called us.

The Court: All right.

Zimmer: That was the end of it.

The Court: Has Mr. Hall authorized you to take action because of that correspondence, Mr. Zimmer?

Zimmer: We did not open a separate file. We didn't take any separate action. I merely sent a letter to—I didn't. My associate sent a letter to the church. Their counsel called us up, and Mr. Ulrich dealt with it. I did not. But I know that there has been no action taken. No settlement was reached. We're told it was terminated..

The Court: Why would the church lawyer call you if you weren't representing Miss Hall's father, if you were involved in the correspondence? Why would they call you?

Zimmer: I believe they were in contact with Mr. Ulrich. I believe Mr. Ulrich was pursuing whether or not—

The Court: I mean you.

Zimmer: Right. We were pursuing whether or not there was a viable claim and discussed it with the church's counsel. And that was the end of it. Nothing was pursued.

The Court: All right. So you were considering whether there might be a claim against the church?

Zimmer: Correct. He did not know whether or not he was under the church's authority, what he was doing. Once we realized that he pretty much did it on his own, he just put it on church letterhead. That was the end of it. The church didn't know he did it.

Exactly, that was what I said in my letter to Mark Zimmer. The church knew nothing about my letter. I still have some questions for Mr. Zimmer. Why did you send my letter to the church? Did you think you could possibly make some money on the deal? What does that say about your character, Mr. Zimmer? Are you saying that Harry had nothing to do with the attempted suit of the church?

But what did Harry say to the custody evaluator four months before the trial and only two weeks after my letter was sent to Judge Lash? Dr. Thomas interviewed Kristen first in the custody evaluation. Kristen would tell him of my letter. Dr. Thomas included the following paragraph in his report.

> Ms. Hall expressed concerns about an issue. She states that her father had written a letter to the judge. Apparently her father is employed as a youth minister at the church. Mr. Hall states he is suing the church because the letter was written on the church's letterhead. Ms. Hall states that her father is now suspended without pay from his job.

Again at another place in his report Dr. Thomas writes that Mr. Hall was asked about Ms. Hall's message that Harry is suing First Presbyterian Church. He states he is doing that because Ms. Hall's father wrote on church letterhead – "He completely trashed my family." Dr. Thomas should have read my letter. I said nothing about Harry's family in my letter. It would have been simple for him to discover Harry is a liar. As noted previously, Dr. Thomas questioned the reliability of what Rob Chalmers supposedly said to Harry. Dr. Thomas should have questioned the validity of all of Harry's testimony in the interview.

Dr. Thomas would comment on what he thought of Harry's attempt at suing the church. He would say, "Father's act of suing the Presbyterian Church is, in my judgment, particularly egregious." Egregious is defined as "conspicuously bad." It is interesting that Dr. Thomas thought that about Harry's suing the church, while Judge Lash thought it not worthy to being even mentioned in his final report from the custody trial. Also, it seems to me that Mr. Zimmer and Harry Hall should have decided between themselves who should get credit for attempting to sue the church before they went into court.

I used the word "acts" in the chapter title not "act". I could tell of many acts of Harry that I consider particularly egregious. One of the egregious acts was to use lies about what he claimed his spouse was supposedly doing or had done to Bryce. I say supposedly because Harry was not an eye witness to many of his claims. Through this whole experience I have learned the egregiousness of a lie. How can you talk about something that never happened? How do you answer a lie?

The following are some statements by Harry to Dr. Peter Thomas from that second evaluation. Many of these are the same as given by Harry in testimony on the witness stand in the custody trial held four months later. Harry was the only one to testify against Kristen in the trial. His testimony is laced with deception and lies.

> Harry's first main issue was, "The child abuse. I don't believe Kristen has the ability to cope. When Kristen gets angry she hits Bryce." He states that Ms. Hall hits Bryce in the head and calls him names.
>
> Mr. Hall states that Bryce and Trey both told the doctor and Children and Youth that mother hit Bryce in the head. He states that mother hit Bryce on the head with a bottle. He states that Trey and Bryce affirm this.
>
> Mr. Hall's next main issue was, "Kristen's feelings for Bryce are not the same as for Trey."
>
> He states that Trey gets whatever he wants while Bryce gets disciplined harshly.
>
> Mr. Hall states that he did institute a PFA against mother on Bryce's behalf. He states it was thrown out.
>
> Mr. Hall talked about an incident where Bryce came home with many bruises that over a few days became

more evident and severe. He states he was told it was too late to report that. He states he took photographs.

Mr. Hall repeats that there is disparity in love and affection given to the boys.

Mr. Hall also complained that Bryce gets to play video games all night.

Mr. Hall complained that Ms. Hall allowed Bryce to go to a public bathroom alone. He states she would never allow Trey to do that.

Mr. Hall talked about the episode in which "Bryce had 7 or 8 bite marks on his body."

Mr. Hall stated Kristen Hall would go to daycare at noon and take Trey out but leave Bryce in daycare.

Mr. Hall states, "She calls me names with the boys in the background." He states that Bryce used to say things to him like, "I'm going to use the words that mommy uses," referring to swear words.

Mr. Hall expressed concern that, "In the last few weeks Kristen is working the boys," programming the boys to say that they want to be with her.

There must be humor somewhere in Harry's statements. I felt ridiculous and a little silly typing them. I should add some commentary for each of his statements. This is a matching test. I will try to make it easy. I will put my answers in the same order as Harry's statements above. Or, you may take this a true or false test. Or, should I say, "Truth or lies"?

Since filing the first PFA, Harry has never witnessed Kristen being angry with Bryce. If there was a body hit in the head by Kristen, then it should have been Harry. Would it not be more appropriate to say "on" the head? Maybe it is true that Kristen can get "in" someone's head.

Sorry Harry, both Trey and Bryce told the doctor that it was a "cup," not a bottle. Also, the person from Children and Youth said it was a "squirt gun". You said a bottle. Might it be that you were the one to hit Bryce with the bottle. At least in this statement you said "on" the head.

Were Sarah's feelings the same for Ishmael as Isaac? No Harry, not your mother, Sarah, I meant the Sarah whose husband was Abraham.

Harry has a short memory. He knew a month before the evaluation that Kristen bought for Bryce's birthday exactly what he wanted. It was a battery driven, ride a toy, monster truck which cost more than $350. Only a few months later the monster truck ended up at Harry's house because Kristen had to move to an apartment. What Harry didn't know was that Kristen sold her engagement ring from Harry to pay for the monster truck.

It was not thrown out. Harry agreed to drop it because Kristen agreed to sign temporary custody to Harry. It was Kristen that was thrown out of the house with the first PFA.

People trafficking in child pornography take photographs.

Harry, are you the boy not getting love and affection? Have you shown disparity? Biblically speaking, why are one circumcised and the other not? The boys have noticed the difference. You promised Bryce years ago. Why did you name the second son, Harry III? Sounds to me like disparity. Bryce said one time, "I guess that makes me Harry II?" Does that sound a bit confusing? I believe it is time, Harry, to tell Bryce he is adopted.

Harry, don't be jealous. You may play video games all night. The truth is Bryce, with his hyperactivity, is so tired by night time that he is the first one asleep. Every time I checked on Bryce at 4:30 am he was sleeping.

Bryce does not appreciate his mother going into men's restrooms with him. Trey, on the other hand, can not wait until he is 18 so that he does not have to go into the ladies restroom with his mother.

Hmmm! I wonder if a book about biting would sell. I heard of a boxer who bit. I did not mean a dog. Anyway, I already covered the "biting" incident.

Did Bryce have a bag packed with pajamas and clean underwear for the next day?

I get it. Mommy is singing and the boys are background singers. Actually, Bryce is such a good singer that he should take over as lead singer. Kristen should be a background singer along with Trey. I could write the music and words for the group. The words not used would be those of Harry Hall the first who Harry Hall the second accused of being a "verbally abusive alcoholic."

We don't have to program the boys to say that they want to be with their mother. I wrote in my letter to Judge Lash that very thing. Those statements were made almost year before I wrote my letter. Harry read that in my letter only a week before the evaluation. Perhaps it would be interesting to find out what the boys said to the evaluator. Especially, since we know Bryce as a "storyteller." We also believed Harry was "programming" Bryce for the interview with the evaluator as we believed he may have done for the doctors and CYS.

When Kristen received the custody evaluator's report, the only thing she wanted to know was the final recommendation of Dr. Thomas. She knew what she said to him. She knew some of the lies Harry had stated. She only read a bit of Harry's interview and had to quit. It made her sick. Mary Lynne will not read Harry's words to Dr. Thomas. I only read the full report after we had gotten the trial transcript months after the trial. We should have digested the full report before the custody trial. We should have read the report of the boy's interview with Dr. Thomas. If we had, we would not have been so surprised with Bryce's testimony at the expungement hearing nine days later, May 1, 2008. Below are excerpts from those interviews held by Dr. Thomas on April 22, 2008. At that time, Bryce was 6 years month old and Trey 4 years 7 months.

> Bryce discussed a number of his favorite things including video games, pets, and food. Bryce was asked for three wishes but could not think of any.
>
> Bryce was asked to describe what he likes and disliked about each parent. With father he states that he likes – "he is nice to me". With mother he stated "she liked me too". Bryce was asked what he did not like about each parent. With the father he stated that he did not like that "when I say I want to ride my bike, he doesn't want to." When asked what he did not like about mother he stated "when I want to ride by bike she says no."

One can see that these responses were quite minimal and quite even handed. Also, Bryce frequently responded "I don't know" to questions. Behaviorally, Bryce was quite restless and mildly agitated through these discussions.

Bryce was asked if he feels mother treats Trey differently than him. He indicated that he does feel that way. He was asked what the difference is and stated "she's nicer to Trey and badder to me." Bryce denied that father treats the two boys differently.

Bryce was asked if father ever hit him and stated no. He was asked if his mother ever hit him and stated "yes". He was asked again what happens when mother hits him for an example of that. At this point he stated "she spanked me." He talked about this and stated he was referring to a time the family was still together.

Bryce was asked about the toy which mother allegedly hit Bryce on the head. He was asked about that story and stated "I don't really know." Bryce denies that his mother ever told him that she did not love him.

Bryce was asked if he was afraid of dad and stated that he is not. He was asked if he was afraid of his mother and stated he is not.

Bryce was asked if dad ever hurt him and stated that he did not. He was asked if mom ever hurt him and stated that she did not.

It is obvious Bryce was not in a talkative mood. He was not interested in being interviewed that day. Bryce can talk. He can tell stories. He tells many. He usually completes them with a snicker. Dr. Thomas did not get to see the Mr. Bryce that day. Perhaps he would have more luck with Trey.

Trey entered the interview setting with more comfort and discussed a number of his favorite activities. Trey went on to talk about other things he enjoys. He talked about liking to play at mom's house and "I like to eat good food at my mom's and I like to go to t-ball with my mom." (Trey did not play t-ball. He liked the fact that he had mom to himself as Bryce was in the game.)

Trey was asked what he likes with his dad and stated that he likes "when he makes deer horns." He was asked if there was anything else he likes and stated "no, just that".

Trey was asked what he does not like about mother and stated he could not think of anything. He was asked what he does not like with father and stated "when my dad is on the phone, if it is something hard for me, he can't help." (It could be noted that Harry was busy, the few weeks before these interviews, preparing for this evaluation. He probably was on the phone discussing how he could sue the church. Ha! Ha!)

Trey was asked if father ever hits him and stated that father does not but his brother does. (In court, Harry would say that the brothers are very close. You can't get any closer to a brother than having him hit you. So why, as Bryce says, is mother nicer to Trey?) He was asked if his mother ever hit him and stated she does not.

Trey was asked if dad ever hit Bryce and stated that he does sometimes. Trey was asked to elaborate about that and stated "sometimes dad does in a dream." He was asked if dad does that in real life and stated that he does not.

He was asked if mother ever hits Bryce and stated that she does sometimes. He was asked what happens and stated "when he would be bad, she tries to get him away from me. She tells him to go play video games." Trey was asked where mother hits Bryce and stated that she hits him "on the butt sometimes."

Trey was asked if there was an episode in which mother hit Bryce with a bowl or a bottle. He stated that she did not do that. He stated that Bryce pulled mother's hair and he pulled mother's hair.

And Harry says over and over that the boys said that mother hit Bryce on the head. Harry said it was all written in the evaluator's report. Obviously, the boys did not say to Dr. Thomas that Kristen hit Bryce on the head. The only one saying it in the report was Harry. I will, however, vouch for the hair pulling statement. On a trip home from the Great Adventure Safari, Kristen was sitting in the back seat which is our normal way of traveling together. The boys started pulling Kristen's long blond hair and giggling. Luckily, we soon came to a service area on the turnpike. Kristen took the driver's seat and I sat in the back between the boys. They did not pull my hair. I think Kristen should have her hair cut.

What did Trey mean by "in a dream?" Did Harry, in the middle of night or early morning before taking Bryce to the doctor, hit Bryce on top of the head with a bottle? Maybe that is why Harry said Bryce was hit with a bottle. Or, was Trey in some sort of hypnotic trance when Harry hit Bryce? The boys sleep in the same room contrary to the pictures Harry had as exhibits. Trey may have been slightly awake as Harry went into their bedroom to administer a little bump. It might have seemed like a dream to Trey. Or, am I simply slipping into the "Twilight Zone"? Get it. Is twilight early evening or morning? I found a definition of twilight. It is defined as a state of imperfect clarity. I am definitely there.

Anyway, I consider what Harry has done to his wife and children to be "egregious acts."

CHAPTER 31 – Go! Go! Go! Go!

The First Expungement Hearing

From the IVY TOWER, April 2008 edition:

JOSEPH AND THE AMAZING TECHNICOLOR DREAMCOAT

This musical will be presented by the Reading Civic Theater, May 2nd through May 4th at the Sovereign Performing Arts Center. The tickets range in price from $15 to $40. Dave has a block of tickets for the May 4th, 3 pm performance at a cost of $13.50 each. See Dave for tickets to join your family with our church family to enjoy this performance together.

The story line follows the Bible story of Joseph very closely. One line in a song says, "As found in Genesis thirty-nine." To help our children enjoy and learn even more from the musical, we will be teaching the story of Joseph in Children's Church and Sunday School on May 4th.

The billing is posted on the Children's Ministry Board. On it you will note that our own Kevin Cooper is the Music Director and Conductor for the musical. My wife, Mary Lynne, and I would like to attend with our church family, but we will not be able to join you in the balcony. We will, however, be viewing the proceedings from the stage.

Performing in a musical was one of my wife's "bucket list" items. My wife and I had sung together in choirs before and since are marriage, more than forty years. We first performed with the Reading Civic Theater in 2003 for the musical "My Fair Lady." We were part of the ensemble. The program playbill for me read, "He and his wife are delighted to be a team for this new adventure." For Mary Lynne it read, "This puts a new meaning on family togetherness." Our next musical, in 2005, was "The Sound of Music." We did not play any of the children. Mary Lynne, however, got her wish. She became a nun. She also played a baroness, while I was the baron. I also got to play the priest who performed the marriage. Shortly, I would become the "Nazi" soldier chasing the couple and the children through the Abbey. Besides the finale, the only thing I got to sing in that musical was "Good-bye."

We jumped at the chance to perform in the musical for the spring of 2008. There are not many musicals in which we would feel comfortable performing. A musical based on the Biblical character Joseph would certainly be suitable for a CMD. Even before auditioning, I had in mind that I would try to get children from FPC and my five grandchildren to attend a performance. Fortunately, Mary Lynne and I were accepted into the ensemble. For the playbill I wrote, "Dave's next musical will be the Biblical epic 'Methusalah'. I will be old enough for the lead." I believe, at age 61, I may have the record for being hired as a CMD at the oldest age. My wife's words for the playbill would be more meaningful. She wrote, "Reading Civic Theater has been a great way to experience the magic of a musical with my husband, Dave, and the musical talent of Berks County."

Doing this musical would be a bit of a stretch for both of us. We would get to sing a lot. That would be great. The catch was that we would have to do some kind of motions a bit more complicated than those with "the rain came down and the floods came up." Some people might even say we were "dancing" and "singing" at the same time.

I say the word "dance" with trepidation, meaning "a nervous agitation." Trepidation is also defined as "a tremulous motion." My dancing can be described by both of those definitions. Both my wife and I grew up in very conservative churches. By that I mean "dancing" was considered one of the seven deadly sins. Mary Lynne reminds me, on occasion, that a "prayer meeting" was held on her behalf when she went to her Junior Prom. But, I do believe it says in scriptures to praise the Lord with dance. I found a reference. Psalms 150:4 reads, "Praise him in the dance." In Exodus it speaks about a calf, a dance, and three thousand people dying. Where is my delete button? Imagine our horror when our son said he was having dancing at his wedding reception. My wife and I signed up for ballroom dancing lessons. Stop laughing! It did help years later when I had to waltz in "My Fair Lady." One, two, three! One, two, three!

We had to rehearse many hours outside of rehearsal time to learn the words and motions for the musical about Joseph. We had a CD with which to rehearse. Everywhere we went it was "Go! Go! Go! Go!" The best part about the whole experience was that often Bryce and Trey were learning with us as we drove along. Many times it was the five of us going somewhere together. By the time of the performance on May 4th, the boys knew the words to most of the songs. I hope they were not too annoying while singing along during the performance. We still put in that CD as we travel and sing-a-long.

There was another aspect of doing this musical that would make it intriguing. That would be the storyline. It is a story of miracles. It is a story of "injustice" turning to "justice." I had been planning to tell the story of Joseph to the children at church on the morning of May 4th. Of course, by that time I had already resigned as CMD. I would have told the children the many ways in which Joseph's life mirrors the life of Jesus. Joseph is a "type" of Jesus, as Adam is the "anti-type." In the fall the children had been taught how the Christ of the New could be seen in the Old. We sang that principle with the words I wrote for the Christmas pageant.

There are shadows of Christmas as seen in the Old.
They tell of His story. It needs to be told.
They tell along how he planned to come to the earth;
To give the gift of salvation by giving New Birth.
There are shadows of Christmas as the prophets foretold,

With meanings more precious that silver or gold.
With a message of hope, and a message of glory,
A message eternal, it's all in this story.
There are shadows of Christmas as seen in the Old.
They tell of his story, it now has been told.

As we rehearsed for the musical, we related the story of Joseph to our own. On May 1st, the day before our first performance, we would have our miracle. Scheduled for that day was Kristen's expungement hearing. It was her appeal against the child abuse ruling of "founded" from July of the previous summer. She filed against that ruling in October of 2007. The hearing would be held before our first presentation of "Joseph and the Amazing Technicolor Dreamcoat."

Kristen had her response ready. Basically the whole case was based on Bryce's testimony to the doctor that mommy hit him on the head with the "squirty bottle." At that time, we did not realize that other terms had been used to describe the weapon to the doctor and CYS. Kristen's defense was simple. She knew how the bump occurred. She did not cause the bump. She also knew she had to offer more than just her testimony.

There were three parts to her defense. First and foremost was that Bryce was a "storyteller, liar". She had many examples of Bryce's lies for his teacher and daycare workers. For a month after the incident, Bryce, when admonished for bad behavior would say, "I am going to tell that mommy hit me with a squirty bottle." Apparently, he thought that would get the reaction he wanted. Also, a caseworker for Bryce had come to the house and witnessed Bryce say that same statement. Mary Lynne and I also witnessed Bryce use that statement. Perhaps, using that statement was encouraged by Harry Hall. Several months after the incident, I asked Trey how he knew that mommy hit Bryce with the squirty bottle. He said, "Daddy tells me everyday." I admire Harry's persistence. Why had both boys, in their first interview on the incident, said to the doctor the weapon was a "cup?" When did Harry and Bryce decide the weapon was a "squirty bottle?"

Kristen's second point was that there was no evidence or proof of "severe pain." The doctor had admitted that there was no need for treatment. If there was a bump causing severe pain, Kristen would have told Harry. She would have followed the directive of Harry's lawyer after the "blue bowl" incident. If the bump had caused severe pain, then Bryce would have told me, my wife, the caseworker, or daycare worker that next day. All these people had seen Bryce the day after the bump occurred. Third, Harry was supposed to first report to Kristen, according to the directive, if he discovered a bump or bruise. He was required to go to Kristen before going to a doctor or any other authority such as CYS. He did not tell Kristen he discovered a bump. What should be kept in mind was Bryce's age. He was five when the incident occurred. The hearing was nearly a year later.

Bryce would be taken into a room to be interviewed by an Administrative Law Judge of the State of Pennsylvania and personnel from CYS. Kristen, my wife, and I were allowed to be in a room where we could hear the interview over an in house phone.

After a few basic questions, the questioning turned to ask Bryce if he understood what it meant to tell the truth. Is it not interesting that in all the doctor's reports and CYS reports telling the "truth" was never discussed? It would be asked of Bryce in many different ways. Ultimately, and quite boldly, Bryce answered, "Yes!" Only Kristen in our room could hear Bryce's answer as she had held the phone up to her ear. Kristen began to whimper. We asked her what was wrong. She said, "Bryce said he understands what it means to tell the truth." I did not know if her whimper was for the good or the bad. I learned later she meant it for the good. A few seconds later, Judge Maloney came into our room. He said he heard the whimper over the phone and not to do it again. We did not know she could be heard over the phone in the other room. She would not whimper again, although it would be hard for her to not express emotion after Bryce's next response.

The next question was, "Did mommy hit you on the head with the squirty bottle?" Bryce answered, "Mommy did not hit me on the head. Trey did." We had our "miracle." We had to weep for joy silently. This was the first time we had heard Bryce admit that the bump was caused by his brother, not his mother. For the next ten minutes, Judge Maloney and personnel from CYS tried desperately to get Bryce to recant that testimony. He would not. Neither would he snicker as he would usually do after telling a lie. We thought at the time that Kristen had won the appeal.

Kristen in her interview would bring up the fact that no one that was with Bryce the day after the bump, which happened the previous evening, gained any knowledge from Bryce about a bump on the head. Mary Lynne had washed his head that morning. Later before taking Bryce to daycare, I had taken Bryce to our house to trim grass. He said nothing about a bump. I only learned about the bump when Kristen told us that Harry had gone to CYS again. Bryce told no one at daycare about the bump.

CYS would call for another hearing. They needed help to keep their verdict secure. They did not want to admit that they may have made a mistake. They would subpoena Harry and the doctor to come to that hearing. Mary Lynne and I would also be allowed to testify at that second hearing. It would be scheduled for July 30, 2008. The custody trial would be a month after that hearing.

Go! Go! Go! Kristen, you'll make it some day! We had been inspired for our weekend performances of "Joseph and the Amazing Technicolor Dreamcoat" with our own "miracle."

Chapter 32 – The Gang of Four

The Second Expungement Hearing

Attorney Mark Zimmer questions Harry about items concerning his ex-father-in-law.

Zimmer: Do you know if mother's father has spoken negatively of you to the children in your presence?

Harry: He's written—I don't know if he's spoken negatively to the children about me. I know that when I'm near father-in-law, my little guy, Trey doesn't—hegets—tied. I ran into him in the building over a couple weeks ago. And when I came out the elevator, I bumped into them. And my little guy clammed up. He didn't know who to go to. He was standing his—his grandfather and me. Bryce came over and jumped on me, but Trey just didn't know where to go.

Zimmer: Now, you say you ran into them at a building over here, was this surrounding—

Harry: Yeah. It was actually the appeal hearing for Kristen's indicated charge. I was coming out of the elevator, and my father-in-law was in the lobby with the two boys at the time. We bumped into each other. Bryce ran over and hugged me, and Trey just stood there. I had to coax him over to me. And that's not—that is not our relationship. We're very close.

Zimmer: So does he behave differently with you and when Miss Hall's father is around?

Harry: Yeah, just like that. He doesn't know what to do. He doesn't know who to love.

I hope Trey can love both Harry and me. I do not get the point of Mr. Zimmer's last question. How am I supposed to be incriminated by that question and Harry's response? That day was a very unusual circumstance. It was only the second time in two years that I was with Harry and the boys in the same room. The other time was when I went to collect my balls left at Harry's house. Maybe Harry had this elevator event discussed in the trial because I wrote about it in one of my articles. The article was called "The Gang of Four." I wrote the article only a few days after the event. The following is the first paragraph from that article. In that paragraph I describe our, that is, Harry and I, "bumping" into each other. Bryce did not "jump" on Harry. Harry can not describe even the simplest event truthfully. The building where the event took place was the State Office Building. The judge was an administrative law judge for the State of Pennsylvania.

> After concluding my testimony at the second expungement hearing, I took Bryce and Trey down the elevator from the fourth floor. We needed to do something to take up time while we waited for Kristen and Mary Lynne. The boys and I took a walk outside around the perimeter of the building. We spent some more time outside and then came inside to wait in the lobby. I was sitting and facing the two elevator doors. One elevator door opened and I saw four people in the elevator seemingly having a good time together. When they saw me their fun stopped. Three of them quickly scurried out the building. The fourth person walked directly toward us, dropped on his knees, and said, "Come here." It was Harry Hall. He opened up his arms to the boys and tried to get the boys to come to kiss him. Trey would not. Bryce gave "raspberries" on his Harry's cheek. Harry left. I did not why Harry was

there to testify. Who were the other three? It was the lawyer or solicitor for Children's Services, and two other employees of Children and Youth Services. They were the gang of four. Two minutes later, out of the other elevator came Kristen and Mary Lynne.

The boys and I were surprised to see Harry come out of that elevator. I did not know that Harry was subpoenaed by CYS as a witness for that second expungement hearing. For the boys, this was a mommy day, not a daddy day. Therefore, Trey in his young mind, going on age 5, thought he was supposed to be with mom and that meant he would be with his maternal grandparents. That was the case for that day. Like I asked above, "Mr. Zimmer, what was the point of that line of testimony?"

Who were the three persons representing CYS in that second expungement, the three with Harry in the elevator? In a real sense, they were also representing Harry in his quest against Kristen. Besides the solicitor for CYS, there was Bill Clemons and a supervisor. The supervisor was the one who certified Kristen's supervisors for the 24 hour supervised visitation period. Bill Clemons was the person who declared, officially, the verdict of "founded" for the indicated child abuse. He was also the person who had Kristen sign that paper to agree to the 24 hour supervisory conditions. Judge Maloney suggested that it was odd that Kristen agreed to sign that paper for a case on only one bump on the head that required no treatment. We would learn that Kristen would not have had to sign the paper. It is supposed to be used for people who have shown a pattern of consistent or very serious abuse. So, Bill Clemons, why?

Bill Clemons was also the one that had to verify Harry's lie to Kristen in the stairwell. We felt at that time Bill Clemons was being fair in his judgment of Kristen. We realized at this hearing he was not. He really was on Harry's team. He was also the one from CYS who was there when the directive was given by Harry's lawyer. He knew both parties were supposed to report to the other party before taking a child to someone else to report a bruise or a bump. When I was interviewed at the hearing, I asked why CYS allowed Harry to talk to them before first talking to Kristen when Bill Clemons knew of the directive. They said that what Harry did was okay because they were told of the bump on the head by a third party. Judge Maloney seemed unsatisfied with that explanation. Why did CYS not ask Kristen to that party? They did not ask her about the bump before their verdict was determined. In the custody trial a month later, Harry said that he went to the doctor first. I guess he was the third party.

Mary Lynne and I were interviewed at that second custody hearing. I told of my experience in the stairwell of the courthouse. I told of Harry's lie to Kristen and of knowing that Bill Clemons had verified that fact. Mary Lynne and I both got to tell the fact that we did not learn of the bump until after Harry had reported it to CYS. We had been with Bryce the day after the bump and learned nothing of it at the time. I also told the judge and the CYS gang, who were there for the entire interview, that I believed Harry may have hit Bryce on the head before taking him to the doctor. That idea would not be considered. I thought CYS was supposed to be neutral. They would be looking out for the best interests of the children. A number of times the solicitor objected to my testimony. I thought objections could only be raised in a trial. It seemed that the solicitor was running the trial, excuse me, hearing.

Dr. Mark Reuben had been subpoenaed as a witness for the defendant, CYS. Kristen was really the plaintiff in this case. I had not thought of the hearing in this way. In effect, Kristen was saying the guilty party was CYS. They were guilty of making a wrong decision with their verdict. They were also guilty of administering punishment wrongfully with the enforced 24 hour supervised visitation provision. They had a lawyer, the solicitor. They needed witnesses. They needed testimony from the good doctor. The good doctor did not show up for the hearing. Judge Maloney called Reading Pedes. They gave his phone number. Judge Maloney was able to get Dr Reuben on the phone. He was on the golf course. His golf game was more important than the lives of those who had been affected by his saying that the bump from the "metal cup" was enough abuse to destroy another person's life. Remember, at the time we still had not realized that the doctor had used the term "metal cup" for the weapon of choice in his report. He said on the phone from the golf course that he really did not remember the case.

The other witness for the defense was Harry Hall. Kristen told me one important item that Harry said in the hearing. Harry claimed that he was not seeking primary custody. He said he had signed a paper agreeing to 50/50. He was using that statement to demonstrate that he had not taken Bryce to the doctor in order to gain primary custody. CYS agreed with Harry's statement. Kristen strongly disagreed. She told Judge Maloney that she had a paper that proved Harry was trying for primary. Judge Maloney asked if she would fax that paper to him the next day. She said she would and she did. The solicitor for CYS asked if she could also have a copy of that paper. I dropped that paper off at her office the next day. It was too easy to prove that Harry was seeking primary. The court date was already set. It was less than a month away. Harry had been caught in another lie.

We were a bit giddy over the prospects. Kristen had to win the expungement. She was told that expungements are only won about five percent of the time. Surely, this would be one in that five percent category of successes. In addition, she was her own lawyer for these proceedings. The result of winning the expungement should lead to a win in the custody trial. It should also lead to a condemnation of CYS. But, why had the "gang of four" been giddy as the elevator doors opened? Did they know something that I did not know?

Chapter 33 - DEA or DA

Real or Phony

A few days, maybe the next, after the second expungement hearing, Kristen called us early in the morning. She had just gotten a phone call from Harry at 5:15 am. On occasion, when she gets a phone call from Harry that seems strange, she calls us immediately. She did call us that time to tell of Harry's phone call concerning the biting. A 5:15 am phone call from Harry is strange. Kristen received the call as she was on her way to work. Mary Lynne and I were already at her apartment as we were on a day of babysitting. Harry told Kristen he was with Mike. Kristen did not know the meaning of the call. Perhaps, Harry was drunk with glee having found a new boy friend named Mike with whom he spent the night. I had an idea. Maybe, Mike was Mike Spadafora. A few weeks later and only week before the custody trial we thought we had learned the reason for the call. Kristen would describe that event in the custody trial.

Ms. Dautrich: To your knowledge, has anyone—has he ever had anyone surveilling you or following you or your moves during the day?

Kristen: Now, last week at work, I'm sitting at work at my desk. And two men come up to my desk stating that they were DEA agents from Harrisburg, federal DEA agents. We want to talk to you about Mike

Spadafora. I said, okay. I said, I have an elderly woman waiting for a man who's have a heart catheterization. We need to leave. I'll walk away from my desk for a while. So I went down to the cafeteria at St. Joe's with them, talked to them about Mike and how I knew Mike. I—Mike actually left—after the Petition for Special Relief was filed by Harry regarding the allegations in there about Mike and I drug dealing, he actually never spoke to me after that. So I don't know what that meant. But April of this past year, that was the last I even heard from Mike. And I told them—these men the same thing, that, you know, I haven't seen him since April; you know, I'll work with you. Because I have a custody trial coming up next week, this better not have any influence on what happens with me and my children.

Ms. Dautrich: Did they provide you with a card to contact them?

Kristen: They did not give me a card. They said, can I grab a sticky note? So they grabbed one of my sticky notes, and the guy wrote down his name and phone number.

Ms. Dautrich: By name, was it first and last?

Kristen: No, it was just Scott and his phone number.

Ms. Dautrich: So did they really seem like legitimate DEA agents?

Kristen: They had a badge, and it looked legitimate. And I said, okay, you know, this is serious. I don't want this going against me in court next week. So, you know, I followed them down. They questioned me. They pretty much knew everything about me, you know, since the last four months. So I think they've been watching me for about four months.

Ms. Dautrich: Have you, now that you had time to think about it, had any reason to believe they were not DEA agents?

Kristen: Yes. A friend of mine that works at the hospital is dating the supervisor of security at the hospital. And she told me any man, you know, anybody who is coming in as a DEA agent, they need to be cleared by security first. Nobody ever came and got cleared first. They just came right up to my desk at work.

Ms. Dautrich: Were you given the office address or office phone number for this person?

Kristen: No. Nothing. They just showed me their badge. It's the only way.

Thus, we were given an idea of why Harry called Kristen that morning. Could it be that Harry called her so that she might try to contact Mike? Did these, supposed DEA agents, follow Kristen from the morning of Harry's phone call until the meeting with her at St. Joe's? Were these men real or phony DEA agents? We leaned towards an answer of phony. They were just more men working for Harry. Harry had to do something before the trial. Harry had just lost big at the expungement hearings. He thought it would be good for his case if he could catch Kristen meeting with Mike Spadafora.

What did these men tell Kristen? For one thing, they told her they had seen her at the Gring's Mill Hymn Sing. That event was only the day before they met Kristen at St. Joe's. That weekend Kristen had custody of the boys. Mary Lynne was watching the boys at the Hymn Sing, while Kristen was at the bottom of the hill playing the French horn with 50 other musicians. I was at the bottom directing BRASS IN PRASE. I hope the DEA agents, real or otherwise, enjoyed the music. Maybe, they joined in the singing. They also told of following her to King's, the tanning salon, the Laundromat, and other places. They said they saw her, when she was moving from the farm house to the apartment, go into the office to pay for the rent. How did they know it was to pay the rent? She would have had to pay the rent before moving in. Other events they described could have been told to them by Harry before they met Kristen at the hospital. Harry knows she goes tanning. There was one item that almost convinced me that, indeed, they did follow her at least once. They told her she drives too fast. I've told her that. But, Harry also could have told them that fact. So, were they real or phony DEA agents?

At a hearing for reconsideration a month after the trial, Harry and Mr. Zimmer would try to convince Judge Lash that the above meeting never occurred. They said that it was a product of Kristen's "paranoia" just as Kristen's other claims of Harry using others for surveillance. If the two people that came to Kristen's desk wanted to remain unknown to others, they did not do a good job. A coworker was nearby when they asked and left to go with Kristen to the cafeteria of the hospital. They were also recorded and seen by security with the surveillance camera that focused on her desk. I told Kristen she should have tried to get the tape before the trial.

I wish Kristen would have asked them how they knew that she would be a person of interest in the case of Mike Spadafora. There is no mention of Harry by Kristen in her testimony of that event. Was Harry involved with these men? Let's look at Harry's testimony earlier in the trial.

Ms. Dautrich: So then do you deny hiring anyone to go approach Kristen at her work to ask her about the same people that this gentleman performed background checks on?

Harry: Could you repeat the question?

Ms. Dautrich: You didn't hire him to approach Kristen at her job?

Harry: I never hired anybody to approach Kristen at her job.

Ms. Dautrich: You didn't hire anyone to approach Kristen regarding Mike Spadafora?

Harry: I did not hire anyone.

The above testimony was in the cross examination. The following testimony is from the redirect examination.

Zimmer: You were asked about Mr. Spadafora, how you've come to know him.

Harry: Uh-huh.

Zimmer: Were you approached by the Berks County District Attorney's Office regarding Mr. Spadafora?

Harry: Yes, I was.

Zimmer: When did this occur?

Harry: Some months back, after I found what his name was and he contacted me,—

Zimmer: Who's he?

Harry: The DA contacted me and was curious about anything I might know about Mike Spadafora.

The Court: The District Attorney.

Harry: The District Attorney.

Zimmer: Well, when you—

Ms. Dautrich: I'm just—

Zimmer: The district attorney or an assistant district attorney?

Harry: Scott Erickson. (He didn't ask for a name, Harry. He asked, "DA or ADA?")

Ms. Dautrich: I was just objecting because I don't think those people are here to testify. I think the substance of what they discussed—

The Court: We're not there yet. Overruled!

Zimmer: Have you been questioned formally? Have you been brought into—

Harry: No.

Zimmer:—the detective's office?

Harry: It was an informal conversation about Mike Spadafora and—and him, what he is and what he does.

Zimmer: Was this during the period when Mr. Spadafora was visiting Miss Hall?

Harry: It was after I found out about Mike Spadafora. And I'm not sure if he was still visiting her at the time or not. It was recently.

Zimmer: Do you have knowledge as to what they were investigating Mr. Spadafora for?

Harry: Yes.

Zimmer: What is that?

Harry: Sellin' drugs.

Ms. Dautrich: Again, objection based on hearsay.

The Court: Sustained.

Zimmer: Are you currently in contact with the police or the District Attorney's Office with regard to that investigation?

Harry: No.

Krsiten's attorney would call for a re-cross examination of Harry.

Ms. Dautrich: And you indicated you were approached by the District Attorney's out of the blue about Mike Spadafora?

Harry: I didn't say out of the blue.

Ms. Dautrich: So, you approached them?

Harry: No. You had brought up Guillermo Jalil, who is a friend of mine. And I spoke to Guillermo about Mike Spadafora because of what I had heard, the kind of person that he was and the things he was doing. I was very concerned for my kids. So I contacted Guillermo Jalil to get some advice, and he recommended that I talk to the local police about him. And I didn't feel comfortable doing that. But he did call the Exeter police and asked them and found out the kind of person Spadafora was. And he called the DA, and then the DA called me.

Who is this Guillermo Jalil that the Exeter police would give him that the information? Would not that information be confidential if there was an investigation ongoing? I did not learn of this testimony until after my wife and I received the trial transcript on December 24, 2008. In the custody trial, held August 26, 2008, the date of our 41st wedding anniversary, Harry and his lawyer presented criminal record checks on Mike Spadafora. They were bogus. A few weeks after the trial we tried a criminal record check on Mike. There was still no criminal record. It had been March of 2008 that Harry and Rob wrote in their PSR against Kristen that Mike was supposedly selling drugs. They also claimed the Kristen was involved. When did this supposed contact with the DA take place? When did Harry go to Guillermo Jalil to ask about Mike Spadafora? When did Guillermo go to the Exeter Police? When did the Exeter Police know about Mike selling drugs? Why would they give that information to Guillermo who would give it to Harry? Sorry, I already asked that question. Who is Guillermo Jalil? That is the question. Who is running this show? Is it the DEA or the DA?

I have one more "who" question. Who is Scott Erickson? It appears from Harry's testimony that he might be an Assistant District Attorney. It was several months after receiving the trial transcript that I came across this name. It only appeared once in the two hundred plus pages of testimony. Kristen was in our home when I read it. I asked her if she knew of a person with the name Scott Erickson. She said, "No." I told her I just read it from the transcript. She said that one of the DEA agents called the other "Scottie". Was he a DEA or DA or will he be DEAD if he is a DA playing a DEA? Or, are the names just a coincidence?

Chapter 34 – Discovery at Midnight

Uncovering the Mystery Man

It was less than hour before midnight. The custody trial was to be tomorrow—the day we worried about yesterday. Kristen got a phone call. It was her attorney, Jamie Dautrich. Jamie asked Kristen, "Have you ever heard of a person by the name of Guillermo Jalil?" She went on to say that she had discovered an email address written on a small slip of paper that was in a pile of official papers she had gotten from Harry's, attorney, Mark Zimmer. She looked up the email address on the internet and up came the title of a book whose author was Guillermo Jalil.

Kristen had an answer to Jamie's question. Indeed, Kristen had heard the name. Perhaps she remembered it because it was unusual. The truth is she remembered it because it was an unusual circumstance to which she related that name. Kristen met Guillermo Jalil in the fall of 2005 at Harry's class reunion for 1985 graduates of Exeter High School. Guillermo was one of the persons that shared a table that evening with Harry and Kristen. Kristen learned that Harry and Guillermo had also competed in bicycle racing. Guillermo also left an impression on Kristen because he had been a juvenile probation officer in Berks County, which is something Kristen had inspired doing. And Kristen also remembered when she came back to the table that Guillermo gave Harry what looked like a business card. It would be the summer of 2006, less than a year after the class reunion that Harry filed the first PFA.

Jamie would go on to tell Kristen that she was able to pull up the book on her computer. She only had to read a few pages to discover that tactics suggested in the book were those that Harry seemed to have followed. In court the next day, she would question Harry about Gillermo Jalil.

Ms. Dautrich: Isn't it true that there were times when you tape recorded Kristen's conversations, had surveillance performed on her whereabouts?

Harry: Yes.

Ms. Dautrich: Including when she first came to my home—my office, there was a private eye following her at that time, right?

Harry: I don't know. I had a private eye follow her one day.

Ms. Dautrich: So you say you haven't had anyone following her recently?

Harry: I haven't, no.

Ms. Dautrich: So then who is Guillermo—do you know a man named Guillermo or Bill?

Harry: Yeah, I went to high school with him.

Ms. Dautrich: And what was his function in your surveillance or investigation of Kristen?

Harry: He is actually a private investigator himself. And way back in the beginning when all this started, he was familiar with things I wasn't. So I would ask him questions about, you know, how do you—I've never did have a private eye, how do you do that kind of stuff?

Pardon my interruption, but, did Harry a few lines above say he had a "private eye?" Now, in the last line, he says that he never did have a "private eye." Does that mean he really had a "public eye?" Maybe he meant he had "public eye," which could be a county detective. Maybe, we just caught Harry in a lie. I would like to know what he means by "that kind of stuff." Maybe we will find out. We will continue with the testimony.

Ms. Dautrich: You're aware that he—of his federal indictment for selling on the Internet fake diplomas or degrees?

Zimmer: I'm going to object to that as to relevance and laying a foundation.

The Court: Well, let me ask you this? Did you hire him to do some investigation?

Harry: No.

The Court: So you just went to him for advice?

Harry: Yeah he's a friend from high school.

The Court: And you're not aware that he did anything, whether it's on your behalf or anyone else's behalf?

Harry: He did get a criminal record check on some people for me that were involved, some of Kristen's boyfriends.

The Court: Background checks.

Harry: Background checks.

The Court: So you hired him for that purpose?

Harry: Yeah.

The Court: All right.

Judge Lash just did an excellent job in catching Harry in a lie in court. Is that considered "perjury?" The score is one to one. Let us proceed to see who can break the tie in the game of "Catching Harry in a lie." Jamie Dautrich is up next.

Ms. Dautrich: Did you utilize this gentleman, Guillermo—what is his last name?

Harry: Jalil.

Ms. Dautrich: J-a-l-i-l?

Harry: uh-huh.

Ms. Dautrich" Did you utilize him to protect your assets in divorce?

Harry: I talked to him way back in the beginning about divorce. And his actual job is to do just those kinds of things. And he told me to get Kristen to sign something and shelter your money and do this, that, and the other thing. And I wasn't comfortable with any of that. I always agreed to give Kristen her fair share. I made many, many 50/50 offers with Kristen. So that is what he does, and suggested that. And I never did any of that.

Ms. Dautrich: So you never followed any of his suggestions regarding—

Zimmer: Objection. We're going far afield here. We're heading into equitable distribution again.

Is Mr. Zimmer crying, "Foul!"? It seems like Miss Dautrich has just racked up a lot of points. I believe Harry did do "this, that, and the other thing." We know Harry did not give Kristen her fair share. We know of zero 50/50 offers. Harry's purpose in this trial is to take away the 50/50 custody agreement. What should be the minimum number of points awarded? Sign, shelter, this, that, and the other thing should be worth 5 points. In the fair share category at least 4 points could be awarded for housing, transportation, material possessions, and the dog. The dog was Kristen's. Harry did not give her half of the dog. He kept the whole dog. For offers of 50/50, at least two points should be awarded, one point for each "many." And, one point should be given for the "never" leaving a total of 12 points. Let us continue the game of "Catching Harry in a lie."

Ms. Dautrich: Well, if you let me proceed—

The Court: Go ahead. Ask the question.

Ms. Dautrich: Regarding making allegations of abuse or filing PFA's?

Harry: No. I never got any advice from him in that regard whatsoever.

Ms. Dautrich: Or regarding support?

Harry: No. No.

Ms. Dautrich: Regarding custody?

Harry: No.

Four more points awarded to Miss Dautrich – one for each "no". Let us continue.

Ms. Dautrich: And you never utilized his book on how you should fashion your testimony at trial?

Harry: No. Didn't know he had one.

The Court: What do you mean his book? He wrote a book?

Ms. Dautrich: What I'm referring to is the book, PROTECTING YOUR ASSETS DURING DIVORCE.

Harry: Never heard of it. Never read it. I've always done fair—I've always—I've got several agreements I put together with Kristen that were 50/50 straight up, even better than 50/50. She just never agreed to any of them.

Ms. Dautrich: Right. And I'm just not referring to property here but other things that may be addressed in that book. But you indicate that you never had a copy of that or used it?

Harry: No.

How can it be that Harry does not know his friend wrote the book? When you look up the email address that Jamie found it brings up the advertisement for the book. Why would Harry's friend not verify that he wrote the book to demonstrate to Harry his expertise in the arena of helping people win in divorce cases? I award Jamie one point, believing that Harry knew of the existence of the book. Sometimes the referee has to make a judgment call.

Is another point awarded for the repeating of the same lie? Let us say yes. Therefore, Jamie is awarded five more points earning two for the word "never," two for the word "always," and one for the phrase "even better." That brings us to a total of 19 points for Jamie.

It is difficult to ascertain the validity, or point value for our discussion of Harry's last answer of "no" to Jamie's last question. Harry did indicate previously that he did not know of the book. So a consistent answer should have been "yes". The question was did he "indicate" that he had the book. It was not, "did he have the book?" Therefore, the point is awarded to Jamie. That brings Jamie's total to 20 points. If this was ping pong, one more point by Jamie and she wins 21 to 1. I believe Judge Lash needs a time out.

The Court: Let's take a break. We'll reconvene at 11:20.

Chapter 35 – Battle Plan

Questions for Harry on the Witness Stand

Jamie had a long range plan. Let Harry keep throwing his accusations. They are his ammunition in his war against Kristen. In the second evaluation Dr. Thomas had written, "It is paramount that it is in the best interests of the children that the war between Harry and Kristen cease." Jamie thought that Harry was making himself look bad by firing all those bullets at Kristen. She would defend Kristen with the shield of "truth" in that she did not do those things of which she was accused by Harry. Kristen was also nice, in that she did not try to retaliate with accusations of her own. She would not use the illegal weapon of warfare, that is, lies, against Harry that he used against her. Jamie thought they would surely retain the 50/50 custody agreement. I never agreed with the 50/50 idea. To me, agreeing to 50/50 sounds like you are saying the guy is really an okay guy, an okay father type. Besides, should "good" ever compromise 50/50 with "evil?" At its best, the compromise would be "not so good." What Harry did to his children and the mother of his children is "not so good." He has used "lies" as his ammunition. I would have a different "battle plan" than Jamie. Perhaps Jamie did not read the part of the evaluation where Dr. Thomas called it a "war." I would attack Harry with the "truth" of what Harry had done not only in his attacks that are well documented, but also in his actions that had not yet been revealed. I wrote this plan of attack to give to Jamie a number of weeks before the trial. She would never get to read my "battle plan."

In addition to the article, "Battle Plan", I included fourteen other articles I had written before the custody trial. Some of these articles I had already sent to Harry's lawyer as I had promised in my "Letter to Mark." I know Mark read at least one of them. That article described what was going on at Harry's sister's house a few days after Harry filed the first PFA that concerned the attempted "stoning". Judge Lash signed Harry's PFA on Friday. Harry spent that weekend with the boys at his sister's house. Harry's parents had been living there for several months. His father died in that house the Monday after Harry filed the PFA. Harry and the boys, ages three and four and a half, were present at the time at the time of death. In describing the event in my article, "Let's Learn about Death", I had written that his father had died of liver disease due to alcoholism. It was from that article that Harry's lawyer would get the idea to say I was hurtful because I called his diseased father an alcoholic. As said before, I did not write that in either my letter to Judge Lash or my letter to Mark Zimmer. I did not know at the time of writing those articles that Harry, to the custody evaluator, had said that his father was a "verbally abusive alcoholic." It would be evident later in reading the trial transcript that other articles of mine had been read. It would also be obvious why they would not want me to take the witness stand. I thought Mark Zimmer was not interested in my writings. I was wrong. He used my writings to form his case. That was why events were brought up I did not expect. He knew as a witness I would be sequestered. I would not hear the items that were brought up with Harry as the witness. I would not get to refute his versions of each of the stories. I had salvos of "truth" which could have neutralized Harry's lies.

In formulating my "battle plan," I kept in mind that Dr. Peter Thomas called it a "war." A war has more than one battle. In the first battle, fought in the mind Dr. Thomas, the outcome was a stalemate. With the truce, 50/50 custody was awarded. Harry was not satisfied. A second battle was fought on the same battlefield, the mind of Dr. Thomas. Harry won that battle. Kristen would not agree to give Harry primary custody. The next battle would decide the outcome of the war. It would be fought in the courtroom and in the mind of the Honorable

Judge, Scott Lash. I believed victory could not be won if only pursuing 50/50 custody. Kristen must go for primary custody.

I formulated some general objectives for the campaign. First we would demonstrate that their never was any child abuse on the Kristen's part, but there was on Harry's part. Second, we would demonstrate that Kristen and her supporting army had already provided a better experience for the boys than Harry and his army. Third, we would cry "foul" in Harry's use of finances as an illegal weapon of mass destruction. Fourth, we would cry "foul" again in Harry's attempts of assassination of character of Kristen and me. Fifth, we would carry out our own assassination attempt using the "truth" as opposed to Harry's attempts using lies. These objectives would have to be accomplished through questioning Harry on the witness stand. We were told only three hours were scheduled for the trial. I would leave Harry on the stand the whole time. He would stumble over his land mines of lies. How would Harry answer each question? Mark Zimmer would try to remove those land mines saying, "Your Honor, I object."

Harry, did Bryce hit Trey with a stone? Did Kristen hit Bryce with a stone? Then, would you not agree it was Trey that was in "imminent" danger from Bryce?

Harry, were you brought up in a home where the language, in some circles, would be deemed inappropriate? Knowing Kristen's parents, do you believe she heard that same kind of language in her home as she was growing up? So, who do you believe would be more apt to use inappropriate language, you or Kristen?

Harry, would you please describe the bowl that Kristen used as a weapon to deliver the first bump on the head you reported to CYS? Did Kristen's parents go to your sister's house to show the "blue bowl" which Bryce claimed was the weapon? Were your boys and mother at that house at the time? Did the doctor conclude that the bump was of no consequence to be considered child abuse? Did he say the bump was too small? Do you still believe that Bryce could have received so small a bump with such a humongous ceramic bowl? Did you question the validity of Bryce's story? Did you ask Bryce why mommy hit him on the head with the bowl? Did you have someone from BCCYS call Kristen's parents the Saturday after the event to warn them that they should not interfere with the investigation?

On the day of the hearing for the "blue bowl" incident, did you try to get Kristen to sign some papers in lieu of your dropping the charge of child abuse? Did you tell Kristen that the incident was going to be called "founded"? Was this discussion in the stairwell outside the courtroom? Who came up the stairs as you were waving your papers in Kristen's face? Did Kristen's father tell her not to sign the papers and go straight to her lawyer? Did Bill Clemons, from BCCYS, verify that you were lying to Kristen about the doctor's verdict? Who was your lawyer at that time? Did Jeffrey Karver Esquire issue a directive to both parties the day of that hearing? Did he say that a parent should inquire of the other parent as to how a bump or bruise occurred before taking the child to a doctor or other authority?

A few weeks after the "blue bowl" incident, Bryce received a bump on the head at your house. Is that correct? Are you saying you don't remember the bump? It was the bump Bryce caused on himself when he stood up from the lawn tractor under the deck of your house. Did Kristen go to BCCYS with a charge of child abuse for that bump? Do you believe it was a bigger bump than the bump caused by the bowl? Are you saying you still don't remember that bump? Which bump?

Three months after the bowl bump, did you take Bryce to BCCYS to report another bump on the head? Before going to BCCYS, did you follow your lawyer's directing by asking Kristen how Bryce acquired the bump? Why not? Would you describe the item that caused the bump? Did you ask Bryce if he was telling the truth about how he got the bump? Why not? Does Bryce tell stories? Would you say Bryce is a storyteller? Does Bryce lie? Do you know why mommy hit Bryce on the head with the "squirty bottle"? Why not? Do you know if the doctor asked Bryce if he was telling the truth? Do you believe Bryce was in "severe pain" from that bump? Then, why didn't Kristen tell you that Bryce got the bump on the head? Kristen knew of your lawyer's directive, is that correct? Why did neither Kristen's parents, daycare workers, nor Bryce's caseworker hear any complaints from Bryce the next day after the bump? Why is it, two days after Bryce receives a bump on the head, he complains of "severe pain" only when at your house? Did you hit Bryce on the head with an object early that morning before taking him to BCCYS? That question should draw an objection.

Besides BCCYS, did you take the boys to a doctor? (Note: At the time of forming my battle plan I did not realize Harry went to the doctor before going to BCCYS.) Did Bryce need treatment for the bump? Did you discuss the case history with the doctor? Did you believe that this time the bump would be called indicated child abuse because this second bump would demonstrate a history of abuse? Do you want me to repeat the question? Did the doctor talk to Kristen about how Bryce received the bump? Did the doctor ask Bryce why mommy hit him on the head with the "squirty bottle"? (Note: I did not know at the time the doctor wrote the weapon was a "metal cup".) Did the doctor call the incident "founded" as an indication of child abuse? Did that make you happy? I know. Objection!

Did Kristen appeal the verdict to a state supreme court? Did you know, almost a year after the bump, May 1, 2008, Kristen had an appeal hearing with a state administrative law judge? Were you at that hearing? Why not? Are you aware that Bryce, at that hearing, said, "Mommy did not hit me, Trey did"? You were called as a witness for a second hearing to be held on July 30, 2008, is that correct? Have the results of that hearing been made known? Would you be happy if the verdict of "founded" was overturned? I know. Objection!

Did Kristen bite Bryce? Did you bite Bryce? Did Trey bite Bryce? Did you tell Trey to bite Bryce? Did you call Kristen before the transition to tell her that Trey had bitten Bryce? Are you aware that Kristen called her parents immediately after your call to tell them of your call to her about Trey biting Bryce? Objection! Did you tell Kristen that you were taking the children to the doctor about the biting? Why not? If you were concerned about the biting issue, why did you not discuss with Kristen your conversation with the doctor about the biting? Do you believe that every parent who has a child bite a sibling should be convicted of child abuse?

Are you aware that "emotional harm" can be considered "child abuse?" Then, do you think alienation of young children from a "nurturing mother" can cause emotional harm? Would you describe Kristen as a "nurturing mother" of Trey? Has she ever abused Trey? Your first PFA filed against Kristen resulted in Trey, not yet three, being alienated from his mother for fifteen days, is that correct? Is it correct that during those fifteen days there was no phone contact with the boys? So, for fifteen days the boys neither saw nor heard from their mother, is that correct? Do you think you may have caused emotional harm? Would that make you a child abuser? Objection! Is it true that Trey, even now, does not like to be in a room alone day or night? Are you saying that is not true? Is it true, that although you have separate bedrooms for the boys, you had to move the boys into the same bedroom because of Trey's fear? For the three months after the PFA, Kristen came to the home to babysit for you each day you went to work. Is that correct? During that time, which child would come running to Kristen to beg her not to leave? So, is it possible you may have been creating "emotional harm" to Bryce for those three months? Were you creating "emotional harm" through parental alienation for the next five months when Kristen only had the boys for two weekends a month? Yes, I know there will be an objection. Mr. Zimmer will say that Harry Hall is not qualified to determine what would be considered emotional harm. If that is true, I would say that Harry Hall is not qualified to be primary custodian.

For the summer of 2007 and this past school year 2007-2008, did you share 50/50 custody? When you had custody during the week that summer, would it be correct to say that the boys were in daycare from 6:30 am to 4:30 pm? Is it true that in the summer the square foot per child at daycare is decreased? When Kristen had custody during the week that summer, would it be correct to say that the boys spent their time on the farm? Would it be to correct to say that the area per boy available at the farm would be measured in acres? How many square feet in an acre? There are 43,560 square feet in an acre. Where do you think the boys enjoyed being that summer, daycare or the farm? Is it true that Kristen was under the 24 hour supervised visitation provision that summer? Is it true that Kristen's parents babysat the boys during the day until she got home at 2:30 pm? Is it true they remained as supervisors for Kristen and the boys until another approved supervisor could replace them? Get to the point. I will. At daycare, what would you say was the worker per child ratio? After daycare hours, who helped you in the supervising of the boys during the week? That's correct, no one. When you took a shower, who watched the boys? Did you say you showered with the boys? Sorry, strike that question. Kristen always had to have a supervisor with her when she had the boys that summer. Who had the better worker to child ratio that summer? So, whose army was the better for defending the boys, yours or Kristen's?

For the school year Bryce was enrolled in full day kindergarten. Is that correct? So Bryce went to day care, then to kindergarten and finally back to daycare; while Trey had to spend all ten hours in daycare each day under your custody. Is that correct? So do you understand why Trey said he wished mommy would have them for 100 days and daddy one? I can hear Mr. Zimmer say, "I highly object your Honor, the child is not hear to speak. From where does counsel get this information? And Jamie could say, "Your Honor. It was written in Kristen's father's letter to The Court only a few lines before he said, 'if only Harry was as good as a dog'."

In my letter to Judge Lash, I had written that Harry had many accomplices. Many of these I would call draftees. They may have not wished to participate for Harry, but it was necessarily part of their job. Among them were judges, doctors, police, caseworkers, and employees of BCCYS. In my analogy, you could consider his lawyers as the enlisted men. His first lawyer resigned, not willing to carry out Harry's orders. I would ask Harry, "Why did your first lawyer resign?" Harry claimed he fired his second lawyer because he was moving two slowly. First, I would ask Harry, "Did you fire your second lawyer because of the directive he issued to both parties on the day of the hearing for the 'blue bowl' incident?" That directive, rule of engagement, would seriously have hampered Harry in his battle plan. Harry would say no. He might add that he fired him because of moving too slowly. Then, I would ask, "Is it true before he was removed from your service that he wrote for you many requests for time extensions of hearing dates?" We move on to a question concerning lawyer number three. Did you hire, enlist, Attorney Mark Zimmer in your service because, for the money, he would do anything you asked? That question would certainly bring Mark Zimmer out of his seat with a hearty objection. Or, should I say, a hearty attack?

Every army needs an information network. We knew Harry used private eyes. They could be classified as spies. We had suspicions about Bill Clemons with BCCYS. He was the one who confirmed Harry's lie in the stairwell of the courthouse. We thought then that he was on the side of truth. Three months later, he was the one who made Kristen sign the paper to agree to 24 hour supervised visitation. He was part of Harry's special force's, doing covert activity within the domain of BCCYS. I had two questions for Harry about Bill Clemons. Was Bill Clemons in the hallway when the directive was given by your attorney at the time, Jeffrey Karver? Do you think Mr. Clemons was correct in assigning the 24 hour supervision as it was based solely on a single bump on the head told by a five year old well known for story telling? The objection would be that Harry does not have the training to answer that question.

In this war, Harry would form an "unholy alliance." Those were the words by Dr. Peter Thomas in his evaluation report concerning Harry's relationship with Rob Chalmers. How long have you known Rob Chalmers? Did you know he was planning to marry Kristen and was jilted? Did he help you write the PSR? Did he attend the hearing for the PSR? Did Judge Lash remove him from that hearing? Objection! Oops, I think that one came from The Court. Did you question, in your mind, the validity of the items told to you by Rob Chalmers? Why not? Did you repeat the items told to you by Mr. Chalmers in your evaluation interview with Dr. Thomas? Dr. Thomas had said in his report that he was somewhat troubled in that Harry did not question the validity of the testimony received from Rob Chalmers.

The most despicable use of accomplices would be that of using the boys as "human shields" he dangled before their mother. How many times did you use the boys as witnesses against their mother? To whom have you taken them? Before what doctors have you taken them? How many times have you taken them to BCCYS? How many times were they required to be interviewed by the evaluator? Of course, we already discussed that Bryce changed his testimony about the "squirty bottle" incident. Did it bother you that Bryce changed that testimony? Which testimony do you believe to be the "truth" concerning that incident? I do not know how Harry would answer that question. I believe Mr. Zimmer would get him off the hook with, "I highly object!" Again, I do not know which way to lean for the judge's response, overruled or sustained. Would you consider that Bryce's most recent response, no matter which was the truth, illustrates his love for Kristen and desire that she be in his life as much as possible? Harry would probably say, "He was programed by Kristen to change his story." Do you think the boys will have any animosity towards you when they become mature enough to understand how you used them to witness against their mother? "Objection as to relevance," pipes Mr. Zimmer. I should have said "fires." We are talking war.

As Gideon's army, Kristen's would become small in number. Her two foot soldiers were her parents. I did not mean they were each two feet tall. Her father was a trumpet player and in fact, a member of Gideon's International. Her mother could turn on the "light" to reveal the "truth." Both would be useful because they knew the terrain of the battlefield, that is, the children. Harry, what words did you use to describe Kristen's parents to the evaluator in the first evaluation? Did you say that they were good people, great people? Did you say, also, that you did not want to keep them, her parents, from your children? Then, why did you try to have Kristen's parents removed as supervisors during the 24 hour supervised visitation period? Of course, Harry will say he did not do that. Before filing the first PFA, whose side of the family was the primary care givers? Do you want primary custody so that the boys would spend less time with Kristen's parents and more time with your side of the family? Whose side of the family do you believe can provide the best care for your boys? Objection! That is for Judge Lash to decide. That is why we are here. If I was Mr. Zimmer, that would be my response.

We also had two good counter spies in our army, Joshua and Caleb; otherwise known as, Matt and Berne. Matt was primarily the day time supervisor. Berne was primarily the evening and overnight supervisor. Bern was interviewed by Dr. Thomas in the second custody evaluation. Matt would testify in the custody trial. Both would testify to a land flowing with "milk and honey." That is, they would testify that Kristen was a good mother. Harry, did Matt, as supervisor ever report any negatives concerning Kristen's parenting to BCCYS? Did Berne ever report any negatives? Do you know of anyway in which either Matt or Berne harmed the children? Did you try to form an alliance with them as you did with Rob Chalmers? Objection! That is speculation.

Another ploy Harry was using to win the war was finances. As of November 2007, Kristen was near surrender because she could not pay the rent. As Elijah gave help for the widow with the unending oil, Kristen would receive help from one whom we would call her angel named Michael. Can you imagine an angel having that name? Sorry, that was not a question for Harry. Michael would anger Harry by postponing the victory he would have achieved through the use of finances.

How, financially, did you expect Kristen to survive when you removed her from the marital residence with the first PFA? Why did you get rid of the computer on which Kristen did her work for CONCERN? Why did you assume you had the right to tear up the check in Kristen's name that was to be used for Bryce? Did you give her any of that money when she took care of Bryce at your house the three months after the PFA was dropped? Did you give her any money during that time? Why not? How was she supposed to survive at that time with no income? You were still married at the time, is that correct? Does it sound reasonable that you should have remained supporting someone who was a "stay at home" mom until a financial agreement would be reached? How do you justify giving Kristen no alimony? Did you stop making payments on your house when she was awarded child support? Did you let your house go into foreclosure? Did you tell Kristen that if she asked for alimony you would have to give up the house? Did Kristen agree to not seek alimony in order that the boys could remain in their home? Did you make Kristen go to court in order for her to receive child support once 50/50 custody was recommended? You think that you should not have to give Kristen alimony nor child support, is that correct? Objection, Harry does not have to think. Would it be correct to say your house is valued at $250,000? How much did you give Kristen in your divorce settlement for the house? Harry could say he gave her $10,000. So, you think, excuse me, you believe $10,000 is an equitable distribution? Objection! It is not the purpose of this court to determine equity. You gave Kristen $4300 for transportation, is that correct? Your Durango is worth approximate $9,000, is that correct? So you gave her everything 50/50? And a cry comes from Mr. Zimmer, "Objection! We are not getting into equitable distribution." I agree, there is nothing equitable in anything Harry does.

Harry, when you sought the child abuse charges to be upheld against Kristen, did you understand that if they were upheld as "founded", then she would be eliminated from many employment possibilities? So, do you deny understanding that possibility when filing the first PFA? Do you understand that if Kristen cannot afford a place for your children that she will have to sign the children over to you? Were you angered when you learned Kristen was receiving money from a man by the name of Mike Spadafora? Would you say it was Mike that made it possible for boys to be with their mother on the farm for those months he gave her money for the rent? Did it make you angry when you learned it was Mike that paid for Kristen's share of the cost of the second custody evaluation? Are you saying you did not know that? Well, knowing that fact, does that make you angry with Mike? Does it make you angry that the money Kristen received from Mike made it possible for her to purchase Christmas presents for your boys? Does it make you angry that money from Mike was used to feed Kristen and the boys? Would it have made you less angry if you had been giving the money?

Do you agree with the custody evaluator's recommendation that you receive primary custody? So you agree that Kristen should have three weekends a month during the school year? Would you agree that in general you spend more on children for food and activities during the weekend than while they are in school? Did you agree to give Kristen primary custody in the summer? How much per month would it cost you in daycare for the summer? Would Kristen be able to pay that amount per month? Would you agree that amount is more than her income for a month? In other words, do you agree that it would be financially impossible for Kristen to comply with the custody evaluator's proposal? Are you intentionally setting up Kristen for failure? Are you trying to get Kristen to surrender? And from Mr. Zimmer we would hear, "Your Honor, I object! This is not a war!" Sorry. Dr. Thomas did call it a war.

At what age did you recognize that Bryce had a special problem? Would it be correct to say that Kristen recognized the problem at an earlier age? Is it true you said Bryce was just your average active boy? Did you always blame Bryce's behavioral problems on Kristen's parenting? Was it in your mind to adopt Bryce when you first received him as a foster child? At what age did you plan to adopt Bryce? At what age did you plan to tell Bryce he was adopted? At what age did you tell him he was adopted? So, why has Bryce not been told he is adopted? Trey is younger than Bryce, is that correct? Yet, he is Harry Hall the third and you are the second. So, where does that leave Bryce? You do not have to answer that question for I just figured out the answer. That leaves Bryce as a Hall.

One day the five of us were discussing the fact that we call Harry Hall the third Trey. Of course, we explained we liked the sound of the word for three in Spanish. It was nice to have short different names for the two Harry's. It was more interesting that Bryce, immediately upon hearing Trey meant three, exclaimed, "If Trey is Harry Hall the third, then I am Harry Hall the second." Sorry Bryce, that just makes the real Harry Hall the second an idiot.

Do you feel you have adequately provided for the needs of the boys since you filed the first PFA? Near the end of the 8 month period of your temporary primary custody, did Trey have a dental appointment? Was it determined at that appointment that Trey had a mouthful of cavities? Did you provide for fluoride treatment and supervise daily brushing of the children's teeth? Why not? During the two weeks that Kristen was removed from the house with the first PFA, did you miss two special appointments for Bryce? You say that you do not remember? I can understand that knowing you had to make arrangements for your father's death? Is it not true that Kristen's parents offered to help you with the boys at that time? Would it have been prudent for you to have asked them to keep those appointments for you? Alright, the important appointment was needed for the diagnoses of Bryce's special needs. You know, the one Kristen tried for 6 months to arrange. Now do you remember? Thank you. Who did the custody evaluator say has a better grasp of Bryce's special needs, Kristen or yourself? No Harry, it was not you. What do you do special with the $300 you receive each month for Bryce to meet his special needs? I confess that I do not know what Harry would answer. Who bought the winter coats for the boys this past year? Did you boy any new clothes for the boys this past year? Kristen says when she sends the boys to you in the new clothes that you send them back in old clothes, is that correct? You are correct. By the time those new clothes get sent back to Kristen they are old.

How long did it take you to agree to Trey's adenoid operation? Did you ever get that second opinion? Why not? Does Trey breathe much better since the operation? That's good. So he suffered unnecessarily for a year longer. Would that be correct?

Would you describe the philanthropic activities you were involved with before your marriage to Kristen? How about since? Do you understand the question? Well, did you ever teach Sunday school? No, attending Sunday school at an early age is not a philanthropic activity. You are very family oriented, is that correct? Did you, as a young man, serve as an unofficial guardian for your nephew, Jeff? Was he on parole living in your sister's house when your father died? Before Kristen moved in with you at your apartment, was your nephew Billy living with you? Would you say you assisted and provided for Billy? Was Billy in prison at the time of your father's death? Is it true that you complained to the evaluator that Kristen was involved people with criminal records? Now, is it possible you are applying a double standard?

Did you complain to the evaluator that Kristen has allowed Trey to sleep in her bed? Have you ever said to anyone that you believe two men living together can make out well together? Excuse me, I meant financially. Is making out well "financially" your ultimate goal? Did you file for unemployment most of the last two months of 2006? Doing that, did you actually make money in that you did not have to pay daycare? In that same period of time to you work some hours for an employer whose name was Chris? Did you ever take the boys and visit with Chris overnight? Are you aware that Trey told Kristen that he slept between you and Chris on those weekends? I am waiting for Mr. Zimmer to fire his defense missile, "I object". Are you aware that Trey said at that time, "Mommy has her man and daddy has his man." Objection! Grammatically that is incorrect. The word "man" is not needed at the end of the sentence. Sorry, the word stays. That was what Trey said at the age of three and a half.

All salvos would have been fired if this were the actual battle. I was grateful it would not be used. I am grateful I was not the General in charge. Besides, Jamie had a better defense. It concerned the uncovering of Harry's secret "battle plan" from his strategist, Guillermo Jalil. If Harry was in a sub he would be blown out of the water.

Chapter 36 - A Sure Thing

The Custody Trial

Never bet on a sure thing. I teach logic and probability. It would be more appropriate to say "always bet on a sure thing." What should have been said logically is, "Never bet on what you think is a sure thing." I am sure that Harry thought, going into the custody trial, that he had a "sure thing." After all, the custody evaluator, four months before, had made the recommendation that he receive primary custody. Kristen, with knowledge from her experience working in domestic relations, had told us that judges rarely deviate from the custody evaluator's recommendation. I am not a betting man. However, I would bet that this would be one of those rare cases. To me the outcome was a "sure thing." Harry would not win the primary custody he sought.

We had waited two years for this moment. We were going to have another "Joseph" moment. All summer we three and the boys sang the songs from the musical. We three were to get our chance to interpret our dream before our pharaoh, Judge Lash. The thought that lessened our "anxiety" in the prospect of testifying was that we would only have to tell the truth. Harry should be very anxious since his testimony to the evaluator and others contained many lies. Judge Lash had already been an eyewitness to some of those lies. Harry had lied in the hearing with Judge Lash where he claimed that Kristen was the one who held up the custody evaluation with Dr. Peter Thomas by not paying her part of the fee. Kristen pulled out her receipt at that hearing which showed she had paid months before Harry. Harry had no receipt. Judge Lash knew of Harry's lie in the stairwell of the courthouse on the day of the hearing for the "blue bowl" incident. The trial would be different. Harry would have to swear to tell the truth. If he did not, he could be arrested for "perjury." At least, I thought that would be the case.

We were not completely surprised to learn Harry would be the only one to take the stand for his team. Harry had no witnesses because there was no crime on Kristen's part. There was no one that witnessed child abuse of Bryce by Kristen. The one witness Harry might have tried to use against Kristen would have been Bryce. Harry, evidently, realized it would take a lot more training to prepare Bryce for the witness stand compared to simply repeating a little phrase such as "mommy hit me with a blue bowl" or "mommy hit me on the head with the squirty bottle." I still am perplexed as to the weapon. Also, Bryce, at the expungement hearing, had said, "Mommy did not hit me on the head, Trey did." We had hoped to have the report from the expungement hearing before the trial. That did not happen. However, Kristen, Mary Lynne, and I could each testify of Bryce's testimony to the administrative law judge at the hearing.

Harry would have trouble being his own witness. In the past two years he only saw Kristen with the boys at transitions or appointments when they were with the boys together. In those two years he had few possibilities to observe Kristen interacting with the boys. He was not an eyewitness to any problem that Kristen had with the boys. In the trial he had to admit that since the first PFA he did not witness any wrongdoing by Kristen. Before the first PFA, Mary Lynne and I witnessed more interaction with Kristen and the boys than Harry. Harry was mostly absent. He was busy making money.

There was one possibility of a witness. That would be the one who joined Harry to write the Easter holiday PSR. That would be Rob Chalmers. He was the "jilted lover" convicted of "harassment" against Kristen. He was the one with whom Harry, according to Dr. Peter Thomas, had formed an "unholy alliance." He was the one Judge Lash had removed from the courtroom at the last hearing before the trial. Harry would not dare use Rob as a witness. Besides, what Rob wrote in that report he had not observed. He had only spent several hours with

Kristen when she had the boys. Most days he spent with the Kristen those six weeks were "daddy" days. Obviously Kristen did not have custody those days. The hours he spent with Kristen and the boys were at the time they were still intending to be married.

On the other hand, Kristen would have witnesses other than herself. Bern, who shared rent at the farm house, had already been interviewed by Dr. Peter Thomas and testified that Kristen was not only a good mother to her own children, but she was also liked by his children. They had shared rent for almost a year. Bern had helped Kristen survive the 24 hour supervised visitation time. We had his testimony in Dr. Thomas' evaluation report. We would not need his testimony as that report was an exhibit for the trial. Matt was the other male friend of Kristen who had been certified as a supervisor by CYS. He agreed to testify for Kristen. He remained a friend of Kristen after the 24 hour supervised visitation provision was lifted. Matt testified to the court, as Bern did to the evaluator, he never found any problem with Kristen as a mother even under the difficult situations Bryce could create. These men had spent more than a hundred times the hours Rob had with the boys and Kristen.

Kristen would also have her parents as witnesses. Kristen gave up her career and became a stay at home mom when receiving Bryce as a foster child at age 6 months. A year later she gave birth to Trey. Handling Bryce by that time would become a full time job. Adding Trey, Kristen would get the needed help from her mother. Harry would work more hours. While he worked the needed help for the boys came from her parents. Perhaps, the fact that we, her parents, were able to give that attention to the boys was a point of contention with Harry. He may have said openly that he appreciated what we did for the boys, but secretly it became a point of jealousy. We felt from our experience with the boys we understood their needs almost as well as Kristen and perhaps better than Harry. I hope much better than Harry. After all, Harry had said Bryce was just an average active boy who did not need to be treated differently. He had no special needs. We knew better. Eventually, Harry would agree with the experts. He would brag to friends that he knew from an early age Bryce was different. More importantly, we would not talk of "cunningly devised fables" as Harry had done. We would be able to testify as "eyewitnesses" of things we observed. Mary Lynne knew from where Bryce came up with the idea of a "blue bowl." I knew of Harry's lie in the stairwell and consequent directive in the hallway. We both knew of Harry's call about the bite. We both knew whose holiday was Easter. We knew what life was like for the boys on the farm. We knew the Rob Chalmers story. Kristen showed both of us the $2000 when she first received it from Mike Spadafora. We thought he was the "Christmas Angel". We could testify to some of the accusations by Harry against Kristen. It is difficult to testify about accusations made that are based on lies. If something did not happen, how can you talk about? That is why it is difficult to find a defense for a lie. That is why a lie is simply "evil." If Judge Lash was interested in the facts of the case, Mary Lynne and I had many to give.

Harry would be his only witness, but Kristen would be her best witness. She would finally be given the chance to refute Harry's accusations. She had not been given the chance in the first PFA. She signed the papers without her testimony of what had occurred. She did not get a chance to talk to any of the doctors from Reading Pedes about the "blue bowl" incident, the "squirty bottle" incident, or the "biting" incident. Children's Services convicted Kristen of child abuse without hearing anything from Kristen. They convicted her based on the testimony of a five year old storyteller diagnosed with "Asperger's". She would be able to explain her relationship with the so called evil men: Bern, Rob, and Mike. She needed Bern as a supervisor and someone to share the rent. She thought Rob was the solution to her problem in finding a man who would be a good choice as husband and helper with the boys. She took the money from Mike rather than give up the fight to keep her children. She could tell about the real evil man in her life, Harry Hall the second.

I thought it was odd that Dr. Peter Thomas would not be a witness in the trial. Despite his recommendation, there were important details we could use from his report. Jamie, Kristen's lawyer, having read Dr. Thomas' evaluation report, was surprised by his recommendation of primary for Harry. In the first evaluation he had said "it is paramount" that Harry stops his attacks. In the second evaluation he said "it is paramount" that the war cease. In other words, he was admitting that Harry had not ceased his attacks. Dr. Thomas said that Kristen was the "nurturer." He said that she demonstrated more knowledge of Bryce's problems. He questioned the "validity" of Rob Chalmer's testimony to Harry. He described Harry's attempt at suing FPC an "egregious act." Surely, that act would cast doubt on the goodness of Harry's character.

The most important fact we thought we could use in our favor were the details of Dr. Thomas' recommendation. During the school year Kristen would have the boys three weekends a month. In the summer, she would have the boys full time except for a vacation week, the week after school, and the week before school would start again. Custody for weekends would be alternating. Harry would agree to that arrangement. In fact, that is what Harry requested. If Kristen and her parents abused the children, why would Harry recommend that arrangement? Effectually, it appeared that he trusted us with the boys? It would be obvious to anyone that he would save a lot of money with this arrangement. It was all about the money. Or, was it about revenge? Probably it was money and revenge. Kristen, obviously, could not afford this arrangement. More finances are needed to raise children when they are not in school. If Harry received primary, he would no longer have to pay Kristen child support. Under the 50/50 custody agreement, Harry was paying Kristen $600 per month for child support. He was not paying her alimony. If Harry had primary those summer months he would be paying for daycare. The amount Kristen would have to pay for daycare would be nearly equal to her income. That is the amount of money Harry would be saving. During the summer months Harry would still receive the $300 a month from the government as he had since he ripped up the check in Kristen's name and had them put in his. If primary was awarded to Harry according to the recommendation, Kristen could end up it contempt of court for not carrying out her obligation to care for the children in the summer. Surely, Judge Lash would recognize the financial impossibility. Surely, he would recognize that Kristen should be awarded primary. "Surely" plus "surely" equals a "sure thing."

Dr. Thomas' evaluation report was dated as April 22, 2008. The custody trial was to be held on August 26, 2008. We thought the events that occurred between those dates would be the key in turning the verdict for primary to favor Kristen. At the expungement hearing on, May 1, 2008, Bryce pronounced, "Mommy did not hit me on the head, Trey did." A second hearing was called for July 30, 2008. At that hearing Harry proclaimed that he was satisfied with 50/50. Kristen offered proof that he was lying. The custody trial was all about Harry requesting primary. On August 19, Kristen met with the supposed DEA agents at the St. Joseph's Medical Center. They said that they had been following her for months and found her not to be involved with Mike Spadafora and drugs. Whether real or phony, their testimony could be shown in a favorable light towards Kristen. And the last discover, which was made on the night before the trial, was that Harry's friend wrote a book of "dirty tactics" which Harry used against Kristen. The name of that friend is Guillermo Jalil. Surely, if these facts were told to Dr. Thomas, his recommendation would change to primary for Kristen. Judge Lash would get to hear these facts and make the change. It was a "sure thing."

We had the facts in our favor. Also, we thought we had a "just" judge. In spite of the child abuse charge be called "founded", Judge Lash had kept the 50/50 custody agreement in place up until the custody trial. That agreement had been based on the recommendation from the first evaluation. Keeping the 50/50 agreement in tact gave us the hope that Judge Lash would be discerning in the custody trial. We had other reasons for that hope. Judge Lash had to be "just" because he was a Christian. More than eight years before the trial, Mary Lynne and I had met Judge Lash at a meeting with my Gideon Camp. He was introduced at the meeting. To a Gideon that meant he qualified to be a member and was a potential candidate for membership of Gideons International. He was also introduced as a candidate running for judgeship. He did not become a Gideon, but he was elected judge. My wife and I would get to meet with Judge Lash and his wife a few years after that meeting. It was at a meeting of the Reading Berks Conference of Churches held in February of 2003 at what is now called the Lincoln Plaza Hotel. I was at the meeting to receive a "City on the Hill Award" for organizing and directing Brass in Praise. In addition to a few others, Judge Lash and his wife were seated at our table. In August of 2007, a new tradition would be started at FPC, Frist Presbyterian Church. Each month the name of a different public official would be introduced from the pulpit. A prayer would be offered for that public official each Sunday of that month. Guess who was the first public official chosen? Lucky guess! I was going to give two hints. A year before he had signed the first PFA. A year later he would be the judge for Kristen's custody trial. May we now talk about a "sure thing?"

Two years before the custody trial, Kristen had been in the same courtroom before Judge Lash for the hearing on the "stoning" incident. When she was called before Judge Lash along with Harry, Judge Lash noted if there was some reason that he should recognize Kristen. She noted that six years ago she had been working for Domestic Relations. I thought it was noteworthy that Judge Lash had remembered Kristen. The day of the hearing, Mary Lynne and I had been waiting with Kristen in the courtroom. Apparently, the three years she worked for Domestic relations left an impression on those with whom she worked. As we sat there, a number of attorneys with their clients passed through the courtroom. When they saw Kristen they recognized her, said "hello," and left seeming to be puzzled as to why she was there. Besides having had a workplace in common with Judge Lash, Kristen wondered if Judge Lash knew that they had a friend in common. Kristen thought this friend was a good guy because he gave her money and called her a "good mom." Judge Lash must have thought he was a good guy because he appointed him to be a guardian for several weeks of a youth who was in trouble. The good guy said he and the judge were buddies. That good guy was Mike Spadafora.

That morning the testimony would begin with Harry on the witness stand. Matt, Mary Lynne, and I would be sequestered outside the courtroom in the hallway. Kristen would have to give us a general idea of what was said in court. The first thing Harry would do was swear to tell the truth. That was the first of many lies. He would repeat the many lies he told to Dr. Peter Thomas in the two custody evaluations. As he was telling his lies, Kristen began to tell her lawyer, Jamie, items to use in the cross examination. Kristen became very busy. At one point Harry complained that he could not hear the questions from his own lawyer because Kristen was too loud in talking to Jamie. If Harry would not have been telling all those lies, she would not have had so much to say to Jamie. Kristen would later explain to us that on a number of occasions Harry would hesitate in his testimony, taking time to "blubber." It was just a "stall tactic." Harry cried with great emotion, "I just want my children to be safe." It is a little trick used by lawyers known as "the fallacy of emotion." I doubt that it impresses judges. Apparently, Mr. Zimmer impressed to Harry that it would. Maybe lawyers try to make their clients think they gave them a good tactic. Surely, Judge Lash would not succumb.

I knew beforehand that many of the things to which Harry would testify he could not have observed. I learned that Harry was asked a number of times for the source of his information. The two main individual sources were Bryce and Rob Chalmers. Bryce said "this," and Rob said "that." Harry's other answer to that question was, "it's all in the reports from the evaluator, doctors, and Children's Services." Now, from where did they get their information? Of course, much of that information in those reports against Kristen was what Harry said that he was told by Bryce and Rob Chalmers. Bryce said "this," and Rob said "that." Help! Get me off this merry-go-round. You have just experienced "circular reasoning." With Harry's testimony, there came many exclamations of "Hearsay!" from Jamie.

Of course, Harry would bring up Mike Spadafora. He said he had learned from Rob Chalmers that Kristen allowed Mike to use her car for "drug deals." Kristen would deny that. There was no proof. Harry had claimed to have talked to a DA. Why did Harry not bring a witness to court to support this claim? Harry's lawyer did bring out a "criminal record" check on Mike. It was bogus. Mike had no criminal record at the time of the trial. No alliance between Mike and Kristen in drug dealing was demonstrated. Harry, on the other hand, clearly demonstrated his "unholy alliance" with Rob Chalmers. I could have said "surely" instead of "clearly."

Kristen told us immediately after the trial that Jamie, in the cross-examination of Harry, was able to use many of the questions she had written down during Harry's testimony. He stumbled over those questions during the cross. Kristen told us Harry did not do well when questioned about Guillermo Jalil and his book. Harry said at first he did not use Guillermo, but then had to recant that testimony later in the cross-examination. He even admitted he hired Guillermo do the criminal record check.

After Harry, Matt got to testify. Matt was only positive for Kristen. Harry's lawyer could do nothing with Matt for his advantage. Mary Lynne got to testify. She demonstrated knowledge of Bryce and his condition that neither Harry, his lawyer, or Judge Lash could argue against. She was also able to express what needed to be done in the best interests of the boys. She also made it known to Judge Lash that she believed Harry to be a liar. The testimony of Harry as a liar would be well corroborated later in the trial through the testimony of Kristen and me. Surely, Judge Lash would get the message. Do you give primary custody to a man who will not tell the truth?

Kristen would finally get to testify on her own behalf that afternoon. The trial was supposed to be over by noon. Harry and Mr. Zimmer should have been in a state of "anxiety." Their "stall tactics" had not completely worked. Kristen was given time to testify. She told the truth about her relationships with Bern, Rob, and Mike. Bern was a needed supervisor. Rob was a possible husband. Mike was the one who made it possible to remain on the farm, and to remain as an active mother for Bryce and Trey. Surely, Judge Lash would be able to discern that Kristen was left with those choices because of Harry's actions against her.

For me, the most important testimony Kristen gave was all the work she had done in behalf of Bryce. Harry had said from the beginning that Bryce's behavior was the result of Kristen's poor parenting skills. He could have blamed it on his not being there to help with Bryce for the four years before he filed that first PFA. Harry has proved his presence would not have helped. Kristen told us she got to give her testimony concerning her efforts with and for Bryce. Surely, Judge Lash had to be impressed. I was when I got to read her testimony in the trial transcript exactly four months after the trial. Of course, I had been impressed with her efforts before the trial. When I began writing this chapter concerning the witnesses for the trial, I thought of the notion that there were no experts, that is, professionals appearing as witnesses. After reading Kristen's testimony, I knew my notion was wrong. Kristen was indeed an expert, that is, a professional. She had a degree in social work with a minor in criminal justice. She had worked three years at the Berks County Youth Center and three more years in Domestic Relations. Her testimony of Bryce's special needs problems and what she did to fight for help for Bryce went on for eight pages of the trial transcript.

Ms. Dautrich: And how old was Bryce when you first took him into your care?

Kristen: Bryce was six months old.

Ms. Dautrich: And at what point in time, was there any indication that Bryce was a special needs child?

Kristen:—from the very beginning showed some special needs.—there was something as far as sensory integration that he was having problems with.

Ms. Dautrich: Now, had you ever worked in an atmosphere with children before?

Kristen: Yes, I worked at the Berks County Youth Center for three years. And a lot of the children up there had, of course, special needs. And a lot of problems that Bryce has, those children had, ADHD, hyperactivity problems, impulse control problems, you know. So I was aware of what it was like to work with children with special needs.

Kristen would go on to testify how she could modify her knowledge of "passive restraint" to use with Bryce to keep him safe from hurting himself or his younger brother. She told of mentioning Bryce's problems at 18 months old to a doctor. He shrugged if off as Bryce just being a boy. A year later the good doctor would be proven wrong—so much for professionals. She did get Bryce some speech therapy shortly after that visit with the doctor. It was with Easter Seals. In a few months, Bryce proved that was not the problem. He seemed to appear very smart, very intelligent. Kristen never referred to Bryce as being a "moron" as Harry claimed. Maybe she was referring to Harry. Kristen told how she looked into getting Bryce involved with BCIU, Berks County Intermediate Unit, even before starting in school in the Oley Valley School District. Kristen planned to remain a stay at home mom. At three and a half, she had Bryce evaluated and they thought he was not behind socially or verbally. Kristen still suspected a problem. Bryce at 4 years old would be accepted into a special program at BCIU. At the time of Harry's filing the first PFA, she had an important evaluation for Bryce which Harry cancelled. She got a new appointment and with the prescribed medicine Bryce was helped to some degree. Kristen fought to help Bryce and earned $300 a month thru that effort. Harry fought to get that $300 a month for himself. (Four years later, Harry still gets the entire $300 a month.) Harry accomplished that after the first PFA by destroying the check in Kristen's name and having them written in his. Surely, after hearing Kristen's testimony, Judge Lash would know who understood Bryce's needs. The only thing Harry could say was, "I put Bryce in time out!"

Kristen did have another professional who testified. However, he was not given much time to testify. That witness would be me. The day before the custody trial, I started my forty-second year of teaching mathematics. Four of the last five years were for the YMCA in its Youth Outreach Program. It was an alternative education program for students of junior high and senior high school age. Those children were similar to those Kristen had dealt with years before at BCYC. I felt if she could have success with them, then so could I. For most of my summers, I worked with children of a younger age. They were mostly volunteer positions. My first real paying job in working with young children was as the Children's Ministry Director at FPC. Of course, that was the job from which I resigned when Harry threatened to sue the church because of my letter.

I did not realize, when I got on the witness stand at 4:00 pm, my letter had already been discussed in testimony. I did not want it discussed. I knew it was not proposed by either party to be an exhibit. I was surprised when Mark Zimmer brought it up to me. I had thought it would not be brought up in the trial because it would make Harry look bad. What conclusion would you make of someone's character who tried to sue a church? Add to that question the additional information that the church was not involved with the incident. Forget my question, additional information, and go with the next thought. Dr. Thomas had called Harry's act of suing the church an "egregious act." So, why would Harry's lawyer bring up the topic of my letter? Surely, that "egregious act" would demonstrate a flaw in the character of Harry Hall.

Judge Lash would spend the last minutes of my testimony time to inform me that my letter was inappropriate. Does that mean Judge Lash believed Harry's attempted suit of the church was appropriate? Maybe a verdict in our favor was not a "sure thing."

CHAPTER 37 – DISPARITY

Decision and Order

The Decision and Order for the custody trial written by Judge Lash was dated September 5, 2008. We did not expect to hear from the judge that quickly. It had been more than a month since Kristen's second evaluation hearing and we still had no results. That hearing was about one bump on the head. The custody trial had many items to consider yet the results were received in ten days. I was thinking Harry would be arrested for "perjury." At the least, Kristen would receive primary. I was wrong.

This chapter contains statements by Judge Lash in the 20 pages of his Decision and Order. All quotes in block form are from his report. The following two quotes are from the last paragraph on page 17 and a quote from page 7.

> The Court will accept Father's request, which provides for Mother to have primary custody in the summer and three weekends out of the month during the school year. We caution that if Mother's side of the family and Bryce become further alienated, we may revisit the Order, particularly to revise the summer schedule. On the other hand, if Mother and her side of the family can move past the problems that Bryce

can cause and the fact he is not the natural child of the parties, and provide unconditional love to Bryce as they do to Trey, the Court would also entertain modifying the Order to provide for a 50/50 arrangement.

Father expresses the importance of offering unconditional love to Both Minor Children. Of course this is an essential concern of parenting. Father raises this as an issue because he perceives that Mother treats the Minor Children in a disparate manner, showing favoritism to Trey and treating Bryce poorly.

Disparate is an adjective meaning "distinct in quality or character." Disparity is the state of being disparate. I get it. The three of us, my wife, my daughter and I, had just been found guilty of not showing unconditional love and showing disparity. I never realized that the witnesses could be pronounced guilty. I thought it was only the defendant that could be found guilty. In addition, we are cautioned that we could become further alienated from Bryce. Is being cautioned something like being threatened? Is Judge Lash threatening us? We have complained that it was Harry who was trying to alienate Kristen and us from the boys.

How is it that a man who tries to sue a church knows about unconditional love? How do you show unconditional love? How has Harry shown unconditional love? Did he show it to Kristen in all the PFA's and PSR's against her? Maybe you can show unconditional love by accusing someone without facts. How have we not shown unconditional love to Bryce? How have we shown unconditional love to Trey? Please tell us so we know what we have to do to win 50/50.

The report I am reading has been annotated my daughter. I admit that I can not improve upon many of her notes written along the sides. Kristen writes, "I was a stay at home loving mother for four years. Harry never reported a problem with my parenting until we separated. For the past two years he has no idea how I treat the children."

In what way was it proved that we have shown disparity in our treatment of Bryce compared to Trey? I know of a great example of disparity. It is in Judge Lash's writing in reporting the testimony of this case. He demonstrates disparity in accepting Harry's lies as truth and ignoring the truth of our testimony.

> In making a determination, this court considered the testimony of the parties, the maternal grandparents, Mary Lynne and David Rathman, Mother's friend, Matthew Folk, the written evaluations performed by Dr. Thomas, and the Exhibits submitted by the parties.

In Christendom, we talk of the sins of commission and the sins of omission. A direct lie is an obvious sin of commission. There are also lies told by lacing the facts with the arsenic of deception. The more devious lie is the sin of omission. A particular egregious act is to know a fact or truth, as in this case, and keep it hidden. I define the sin of omission as knowing what could be done for the good and not doing it. That is my motivation for writing this book. Judge Lash, in his report, told direct lies, lies of deception, and lies of omission. Judge Lash claims he considered the testimony of Matthew Folk. Matt had been a supervisor during the illegally enforced supervised visitation. He remained a friend of Kristen after that. His time of supervision had ended a year before the custody trial. He had seen her with the boys at different times up until the time of the trial. He testified that he never saw anything wrong with her parenting and that she was a good mother. He testified that he never saw disparity in the treatment of the boys. Judge Lash omits that testimony in his report. Judge Lash states I got to testify. He notes nothing of my testimony in his report. He omits my testimony that I caught Harry in the stairwell of the courthouse lying to Kristen. That was the lie that was substantiated by Bill Clemons.

> According to Father, the disparate treatment had manifested itself in Mother's discipline methods. Mother's punishment of Trey is reasonable but of Bryce is excessive on occasion. This includes the incidents giving rise to the Protection from Abuse Petitions and the Children and Youth Service Investigations. In some situations, mother has implemented what she calls the "passive resistance" technique to control Bryce's

behavior, a technique she believes is appropriate for handling a child with Asperger's syndrome, but which Father believes is excessive and cruel.

Here is a perfect example of Judge Lash's use of the lie of deception. Upon reading the above, you would think that BCCYS was investigating Kristen's use of the "passive resistance" technique. Your thinking would be wrong. The only things investigated by BCCYS were the two bumps on the head. The first bump incident should not have been brought up in the trial because it was called "unfounded." It was never determined that the incident was an act of punishment. She did not cause the bump. Neither was the second bump determined to be an act of punishment. Judge Lash would not allow me to testify about the second bump. Harry, Mark Zimmer, and Judge Lash knew that I was going to tell the truth that Bryce said, "Mommy did not hit me, Trey did." In this, Judge Lash deceived and omitted. Again, Judge Lash purposefully omits Kristen's testimony that she used a modified version of the "passive restraint" technique in order to keep Bryce from hurting himself or his brother. He omits that Kristen testified learning the technique from her experience and training in her work at BCYC. She should have only said training. In three years at BCYC she never had to use the technique. She gained that much respect from the youth. There was only one PFA filed in reference to Bryce. Upon reading the report, Judge Lash uses the plural of the word "petition." Therefore, I declare Judge Lash a liar. What was that one petition? Judge Lash should have known. It was the one where Harry said that Kristen was going to hit Bryce with a stone. Where are the examples that demonstrate that Kristen's discipline methods are reasonable for one and excessive for the other? Judge Lash offered no examples in his report. Nor were any examples offered as evidence in the trial. Is Judge Lash fair and balanced, or did he just demonstrate disparity?

Father also believes that Mother has questionable judgment on her social choices. For an extended period of time, she had a roommate who had a criminal record. She accepted money from another individual, who Father believes also is being sought by the law. In this situation, it is unclear why this individual, who previously did not know Mother, would voluntarily give her money. Mother claims he was simply being benevolent. A third individual Mother was dating eventually began engaging stalking behaviors and damaged her vehicle after she broke up with him.

Why is it that Judge Lash writes about these men from Harry's testimony and not Kristen's? It seemed like he only listened to Harry. His facts are laced with lies. Kristen knows all three of these men. Harry only knows a little about one of them. These men have names. Is Judge Lash trying to hide something in not revealing their names? These men were not social choices. They were choices of necessity and need. In knowing the truth about these men, the deception would clearly be revealed. Bern was not a roommate. They did not share a room. They shared the rent. Kristen needed someone who would be willing to act as an overnight supervisor because she was on supervised visitation. Bern had been in jail from age 18 to 27. He had been out of prison nearly 9 years and was gainfully employed. Kristen trusted Bern because his brother had been befriended by Kristen years before she met Harry. Key facts concerning Bern were left out of Judge Lash's report. These would illustrate the deception by the judge. Bern, much to his surprise, was accepted by BCCYS as a supervisor. Bern testified before Dr. Peter Thomas that Kristen was not only a good mother to her own children, but she was to his also. Judge Lash also left out the fact that once the year lease for the farm house was up, Kristen moved to an apartment of her own. It was not for an extended period of time as Judge Lash suggested. She no longer needed a supervisor. You could say that Kristen's association with Bern was caused by Harry in issuing that bogus Easter Holiday PSR. He helped Kristen with that "mission impossible."

Harry did not say in testimony that he believed that Mike Spadafora was being sought by the law. Judge Lash lies. Harry said, in testimony, that Mike was a "bad dude" with a "long criminal record." Mark Zimmer went on in court to produce that bogus criminal record check. Why is that bogus criminal record check not mentioned in Judge Lash's report? Where is the mention of Guillermo Jalil, the man who did the criminal report? It was weird how Judge Lash took a recess when that testimony was getting interesting. Where is the mention of Harry's stumbling all over himself in his testimony concerning his use of Jalil? And why, Judge Lash, did you agree to let Mike Spadafora be a temporary guardian for the youth that was supposed to go to boot camp? If you thought Mike was a good guy, why should Kristen not think the same? Why is it so strange that a person of means would give money to a person without? I call that Christian charity. Perhaps, Kristen had revealed her story to Mike. Perhaps, Judge Lash should have listened to Kristen' story and included that in his report instead of Harry's lies. Mike was not Kristen's social choice. She did not choose Mike. Mike chose Kristen. He recognized her to be, as Mike said, "a good mom." Mike has the discernment that Judge Lash lacks. Mike demonstrated charity, Judge Lash disparity.

Rob Chalmers was not a person she was dating. He was a person she was planning to marry. She was a person she knew from her past. Kristen does not want to live alone. Practically, she knows she needs help financially. He was not a stalker as Judge Lash suggests. In short, everything in that one sentence concerning Rob as testified by Harry and repeated by Judge Lash is wrong. Judge Lash says that in his decision he referred to Dr. Thomas' evaluation. Dr. Thomas suggested a severe problem with Harry's decision to form an "unholy alliance" with Rob Chalmers. This was an important part of Dr. Thomas' conclusion. Did Judge Lash omit this important statement on purpose? Did Judge Lash forget that Rob Chalmers was the one who along with Harry wrote the last charges filed against Kristen? In court, Harry, when asked where he got his information, many times answered it was from Rob. Sometimes Harry said his information came from the evaluator's report. Of course, Harry was referring to those statements which were initially from Rob. Dr. Thomas had also questioned why Harry accepted Rob's statements as valid. I question how Judge Lash could throw Rob Chalmers out of one hearing, and then accept testimony from Rob through Harry as fact only a few months later. So, Judge Lash decides that Rob is a bad choice for Kristen, but Rob is a good choice for Harry. It sounds a bit gay to me. No, it is just disparity.

> Mother's ability to disintegrate during times of stress have impacted her ability to parent. Even while in court listening to Father's testimony, she was unable to sit still, constantly gesturing and communicating with her attorney, providing an unfortunate sideshow. It is certainly not a stretch to believe that she is capable of lashing out inappropriately at a Minor Child when she is angered or frustrated.

Judge Lash, the word "have" in your first sentence, to be grammatically correct, should be changed to "has." And the first statement was based on testimony of what event? That testimony came from whom? Did it come from Harry? If it came from Harry, then it would not be the truth? Harry had no other witnesses, other than himself, for the trial. If the second sentence of the paragraph is supposed to be proof of the first sentence, then the third sentence makes this whole paragraph invalid. The validity of my conclusion can be determined by the discernment of the facts that caused the resulting actions as described in the second sentence. Fact number one, Kristen's lawyer was working "pro bono." Therefore, not much time was spent in preparation. Fact number two, Harry was constantly lying. Therefore, there was constant communication with her attorney to inform her of the lies and give her attorney questions for Harry in the cross. The fact that Kristen could give those questions to her lawyer immediately demonstrates great knowledge of the subject and tremendous composure under extreme conditions. Why does Judge Lash not mention Harry's "blubbering" on the witness stand? Wait! He does mention it.

> Father was clearly upset by the perception that Bryce was not treated as favorably as Trey in Mother's and in the grandparent's households.

Kristen mentioned to us that there were a number of times when Harry broke down on the stand. Apparently this was one of those times. I believe it was an act. It's called the "fallacy of emotion." Mark Zimmer also used the "fallacy of characterization" against me when I was on the witness stand and with my daughter about me before I took the stand. This fallacy is used to have the attention focus on destroying the character of the witness rather than the words of testimony given by the witness. Judge Lash used that technique against me when I was on the stand. I was surprised that he did. Usually, that method is used by unscrupulous lawyers. I've already talked about the "fallacy of cause and effect." Harry's actions against Kristen were the real cause that produced the effect which required Kristen to make choices in finding men to help her. None of those men harmed the boys. They provided the needed help. The "slippery slope fallacy" is used in the paragraph below. That is were you hypothesize what might happen. Normally, that is not recognized as permissible testimony. It is not fact or evidence. It is a technique used to gather evidence.

> Dr. Thomas reiterated several areas of concern. Regarding Mother, her being overwhelmed by her emotions is significant. If these abusive acts Bryce did occur, they likely stem from her inability to cope with her anger and frustration. Additionally, Mother makes "naïve judgments" in her choice of friends, exposing her and Minor Children to risk and harm. Dr. Thomas did not believe that Mother always supervises the Minor Children.

What abusive acts? None were demonstrated anywhere. Harry blubbered in court, Kristen did not. The hypothesis is false. Therefore, it does not matter if the conclusion is true or false. This statement has no validity. Judge Lash and Dr. Thomas need an elementary course in logic. Why was Dr. Thomas not provided as a witness by the plaintiff? The answer is simple. He would not have been a good witness for Harry's case. I would like to ask Dr. Thomas why he believes that mother does not "always" supervisor the Minor Children properly. Did he observe that? He would have to say he learned that from Harry. How does Harry know? Harry would say it's written in Dr. Thomas' report. We would call this circular reasoning. It is used in proofs of evolution. The age of a layer of rock is determined by the age of the fossils in that layer. In turn, the age of a fossil is determined by the age of the layer of rock in which it is found. Sorry for the digression. No one can do "always."

Does Harry "always" supervise the children properly? I would ask, has anyone ever observed Harry in supervision of the children? Actually, I did observe Harry. Bryce escaped from the house and pushed that little truck down the street wearing only his underpants. Kristen was observed by supervisors 24-7 for four months. No problem was ever observed. The time for that supervised visitation could have lasted two more months, but it was deemed unnecessary by caseworkers from BCCYS. Why was that not counted in Kristen's favor? Why does that not discredit Harry's claim? Why does Judge Lash write in his report with such disparity in the statement of the facts?

> Unfortunately, we must take the unusual step of analyzing the best interests of these Minor Children separately, based on ample evidence that Mother does treat the Minor Children unequally. It is noteworthy that Mother testified that she would prefer an arrangement with her having custody of Trey and Father having custody of Bryce, rather than have the Minor children living together with the parties splitting time equally. Given this statement and the evidence already discussed, it is evident Mother is not invested in Bryce as Father.

Evidence was presented that demonstrated that Mother gave far more care to Bryce than to her natural son, Trey. Bryce's condition demanded it. Bryce had 100% of Kristen's attention for 12 months. When Trey was born Bryce demanded much more attention because by then he was 18 months old and very mobile. From that time, it was necessary to keep Bryce from hurting Trey. He did hurt Trey on occasion. It was demonstrated in court how it was Kristen that was, has been, and still is the real advocate for Bryce. She made all the arrangements for diagnosing his condition, and getting special programs. Harry invested nothing in Bryce. The only thing he did concerning Bryce was use him as a witness against his mother. Judge Lash says nothing about the fact that Harry's idea of taking care of children is to put them in daycare for 10 hours a day. Judge Lash gives no credit to my wife and I for those four years before Harry filed the first PFA. Harry was not there for Bryce for those four years. Harry did testify of the time he went six months working seven days a week and giving no help to Kristen with the boys. Kristen only got to give special attention to Trey when we came to help babysit. Kristen has a support system. Harry used daycare. Contrast daycare to life on the farm. There is the evidence of real disparity. Kristen suggested that each parent take one child because she knows from experience that Bryce demands one parent's attention continually. It is unfair to the other child to be treated with the disparity created by Bryce. Judge Lash fails to mention the suggestion of each child be with a separate parent was made by Dr. Peter Thomas. Also, Judge Lash failed to say that it was suggested that the children be together on weekends alternating between parents. That would be excellent because the parent can have support from family to help with the children. If Kristen had primary, she could afford to have the two boys with her. She knows she would also have help from parents. Her suggestion was made based on having the boys with 50/50 custody. That arrangement would leave her short on financial support. Judge Lash demonstrates an extreme lack of discernment in this matter.

Providing a key buttress to this concern was the testimony of the maternal grandmother. Mary Lynne Rathman was called to testify on behalf of her daughter. She did so, considering her daughter to be an excellent parent, and having very little good do say about Father. Significant in her testimony, however was her perspective on Bryce. She babysits Bryce quite a bit and was very critical. She compared Bryce to Father, both mannerisms and in his "poor treatment of women." The impression she left was that watching Bryce was an imposition for her. She concluded her testimony by answering questions from the Court and stating her opinion, Bryce should reside with his Father. For her to say that Father is the substantially inferior parent, but that he should, nevertheless, have primary custody of Bryce, speaks volumes on Bryce's standing with this woman.

This statement by Judge Lash speaks volumes of his condescending attitude towards women. How can a person with this attitude be considered as a judge for family law? Of all Judge Lash's misrepresentations of testimony from the trial, this is the worst. Harry Hall's "verbally abusive alcoholic" father, as described by Harry to Dr. Thomas, was especially condescending to women. Harry said his father had directed his verbal abuse against his mother. Harry may not have taken up his father's alcoholism, but he has continued the tradition of being condescending to women. It is apparent that Judge Lash admires this trait. Harry Hall is passing on that trait to both Bryce and Trey. I have heard Trey say to my wife, "you are not my boss." I believe the most important duty of the father is to teach young boys and men to be respectful of women, especially their mothers and grandmothers. Apparently, Judge Lash does not agree.

There is no statement by Mary Lynne in the trial that she considered her daughter, Kristen, to be an excellent parent. Judge Lash you lied. It is true that she had very little good to say about Harry. I can think of nothing good to say about Harry. Judge Lash says nothing in this report about Mary Lynne's testimony about actual events. She was not there to give opinions. She was there to be a witness to the events to which she could testify. Her testimony demonstrated that Harry lied about the events. Over and over again she had to exclaim that Harry lied. Oh yes! Harry's attorney, as could be noted by his questioning of Mary Lynne, also qualifies him as a member of the "condescending of women" club.

Mary Lynne never said that Father was the inferior parent. We did not say anything about his parenting because we were not there to observe his parenting. We do not ask the boys what Harry does with them. We do not use them as spies as Harry does. Yes, Judge Lash said in his order that the children should not be used as spies. Judge Lash does not mention in his report that indeed Harry did use them as spies. How many times did he use them as spies?

It is easy to pick and choose items to write a report so that it supports your own viewpoint. Judge Lash failed to report that Mary Lynne offered an excellent perspective on her knowledge of Bryce's special condition and needs. She offered that it would be best if Bryce lived with a family where both parents were "on the same page." She expressed clearly, truthfully, and candidly that it would be better for each parent to have one child. Bryce would be increasingly dangerous to Trey as they get older. How does Harry manage when he has the two together by himself? Harry is lying if he says it goes well. Either Judge Lash is far behind my wife in his knowledge of children with special needs or he is simply using disparity in his judgment. Why would it not be recommended that the birth mother be given her natural child? Maybe it should be recommended that Bryce be given back to the birth mother. Ask the birth mother? Mary Lynne and I would not have it that way.

Judge Lash forgot to mention in his report that Mary Lynne said, "We consider all children as God's and not our own. We love all children as God loves us." We believe God gives us the responsibility and privilege of raising children so that they may come to know it was God that gave them life. It has been my life's work to present the knowledge of God to children. In his adoption, Bryce was given the middle name David. I take that as a deep responsibility and privilege to do the best I can for Bryce. One of my reason's for resigning from my CMD position at FPC was so I could be Bryce's children's ministry director. Remember, because of the charge of "child abuse" against my daughter, she did not have the needed clearance to be in the room with the boys for any type of activity, not at church or school.

> At issue is primary physical custody. The paramount concern in a child custody proceeding is the best interests of the child. Costello v. Costello, 446 Pa.Super 371, 375, 666 A.2d 1096. 1098 (1995). A determination of what is in the best interests of a child is made on a case-by-case basis and must be premised upon consideration of all factors which legitimately have an effect upon a child's physical, intellectual, moral, and spiritual well-being. Alfred v. Braxton, 442 Pa.Super. 381, 385, 659 Ad.2d 1040, 1042 (1995).

So where is the supporting data that demonstrates that a single "gay" father, mainly interested in making money and destroying the mother, is better equipped for primary custody than a "loving nurturing mother" with a supporting cast of two God-fearing parents. There was overwhelming evidence that indicated that Harry lied on the stand and throughout this case in his claims of child abuse by Kristen and in his defaming her character. How does that demonstrate that Harry is more capable of affecting the boys morally? The evidence clearly indicated that Harry was indeed involved in an attempt to sue a church. Dr. Peter Thomas considered that to be an "egregious act." Judge Lash says he considered Dr. Thomas' report in awarding primary to Harry. Using logic, we most conclude that Judge Lash and Dr. Thomas both conclude that committing an "egregious act" qualifies a guardian of a child to be of such character that it would be of benefit for the child's spiritual well-being. There was nothing in Judge Lash's report about my letter or the suit of the church. Did Judge Lash allow me on the stand just so he could defame my character? All Judge Lash reported about my testimony is that I did testify.

Maybe Harry impressed Judge Lash with his ability intellectually. He was able to take a book and follow the plan in the book to achieve the ultimate goal of primary custody. Why did Judge Lash not include Harry's testimony, that is, lies, concerning his relationship with Guillermo Jalil? I should get his book and see which "dirty tactics" were used by Harry. Harry had said in his testimony that he was the type of individual who was able to follow plans that were clearly laid out, such as reading instructions and blueprints in his occupation as a pipe fitter. On the other hand, maybe he did not follow it completely on his own. The person that wrote the book was a personal friend. Harry admitted on the stand he did use some of his advice. I believe there is disparity in what he admitted to using. I believe there is disparity in Judge Lash's decision not to write anything in his report concerning Guillermo Jalil. Why?

There were many more paragraphs in the report that started with "Harry believes." There were statements by Kristen included. That was fair. But there was disparity. Harry's testimony appeared to be accepted by Judge Lash and Dr. Thomas as the truth. If that was so, then Kristen's testimony was presented by Judge Lash as lies. Mary Lynne and I testified that Harry lied in his testimony. Also, Harry lied in every accusation against Kristen in the PFA's and PSR's. If Judge Lash does not accept our testimony as the truth, then he is saying that we are the ones lying. Disparity lies in Judge Lash.

Chapter 38 - The Sign of the Covenant

Proving Disparity

Why do I say that Judge Lash and Dr. Thomas accept Harry's testimony as the truth? Read from Judge Lash's report.

> Father's plan would be for him to have custody during the year. In that manner, he can oversee the Minor Children's educational and social development. He proposed that Mother would have primary custody in the summer months, as well as all but one weekend during the school year. In essence, Mother would actually have more "interactive time", meaning time when the Minor Children are awake and not in school. Father also notes that his position is not motivated by the child support. He is willing to forego child support regardless of the amount of time he has with the Minor Children.
>
> Dr. Thomas recommended that the Minor Children reside with Father during the school year, with Mother to have three out of four weekends and Mother to have custody during the summers.

Dr. Thomas gave Harry exactly what Harry wanted. Judge Lash gave the same custody recommendation. The conclusion should be that both Dr. Thomas and Judge Lash believed Harry Hall. Surely, they would not give custody to a liar.

I have a problem with Harry's statement concerning educational and social development. It seems to contradict a statement from Dr. Thomas and written by Judge Lash in his report. Dr. Thomas states, "Kristen has a good understanding and knowledge of the Minor Children's issues, both educational and behavioral." Also, it was stated by Dr. Thomas that Kristen's knowledge was better that Harry's. There is no proof that Harry would do better than Kristen as far as those issues are concerned. None was offered. Kristen has a degree in Social Work. Professionally, she has experience in working with children with special concerns. She became a stay at home mom. Harry admitted in court and to Dr. Thomas that his work compromised him being with the children when he and Kristen lived together. One thing Harry had done for the children since the first PFA was put them in daycare. Maybe that does qualify as overseeing the children's development.

Upon hearing this custody proposal for the first time and even before going to court, I had a thought. It appeared to me that Kristen would actually have more "real time" with the children than Harry. It sounded to me that Harry and Dr. Thomas were both saying that they trusted Kristen with the boys. I thought, surely, Judge Lash would come up with that same conclusion. Before reading the statements above, I thought of using the term "quality time." I do like the term "interactive time." I concluded for each of the three weeks where she had custody for the weekends she would have the boys for 28 "quality hours," while Harry had them 20 hours. Of course, there was a problem in that there would be 13 consecutive days each month that the children would not see Kristen at all. Those days would be torture for Kristen as well as the boys. Also, Judge Lash would certainly understand that with Kristen working in the summer her parents would have to babysit. We were always there during Kristen's custody time when she worked. Apparently, despite the negatives Judge Lash would say about us, Kristen's parents, he felt we were worthy enough to be involved in the care of the boys.

The result of this arrangement would be equivalent to Harry throwing Kristen out of the house and away from her children with a fresh PFA every month. Actually, it is worse. In this case, Kristen never gets to go back to the marital residence. How is it that a father can suddenly take on all the roles of a mother and still be working full time? Harry will have to do all the things necessary during the school week. How will he feed the boys? How will he clothe the boys? Will he have time to help them with their educational development? Will he have time to play with the boys? Will he have time to take them to activities during the week? Will he have time to take the boys to all their appointments? So when does he wash the dishes, wash the clothes, wash the boys, watch the boys, and do the boy's homework? Harry will be "super mommy daddy." Who are the "idiots" that propose that Harry can do all this? Harry has no support system to help him. Kristen does have a support system. Harry has not demonstrated that he can be both father and mother. He was not there to help with the boys when the family was together. This proposal is a recipe for disaster.

In the trial, when Harry was asked about using Jalil for advice on alimony and support, Zimmer objected. His objection was that equitable distribution should not be discussed. In other words, he was saying money should not be discussed. I say if money is not discussed in court, the family law system is a sham. "Sham" is a good word. It could mean trick, deceive, hypocrisy, or a hoax. All these descriptions fit. Judge Lash tends to deceive with a commendation of Harry. But, it is all about the money. Judge Lash says that Harry is not motivated by support. He says that Harry is willing to forego child support. What Judge Lash is trying to say is that Harry will not ask for child support money even when he receives title as primary custodian. The deception is in the fact he does not state that Harry would be able to drop the child support payments he was paying at the present. Harry is not as magnanimous as Judge Lash would have you believe. At the time of the trial and with the 50/50 agreement, Harry was required to pay $600 a month in child support. Harry was also receiving the $300 per month for Bryce from the county. At that time Harry's gross income was at least $6000 per month and Kristen's, $1200. Correcting the monthly amounts for child support and county money, Harry's becomes $5700 and Kristen's, $1800. Now, with Harry as primary custodian, Harry's gross income is $6300 and Kristen's, $1200. Thank you, Judge Lash and Dr. Thomas. I wonder what the amounts would be if Harry sought child support? Maybe what Harry really meant was that he was willing to not pay Kristen child support. What would happen if the whole custody arrangement was reversed? What would be the result if Harry had the three weekends and the summer? Harry would pay Kristen $1200 per month in support and Kristen would be given the $300 a month which she had earned. The net distribution would be $4800 per month for Harry and Kristen, $2900. And yes, Harry would have to pay for daycare for the summer months. Kristen receives no alimony. Kristen receives no child support. She can not receive government support because she does not have primary custody. Did Judge Lash do the math? Does Judge Lash care? Sorry, I forgot that the court is not allowed to consider equitable distribution.

> As stated, Mother recommends that a 50/50 arrangement should continue. She believes both parents are appropriate for rearing Minor Children. In the context of parenting, Mother had no criticism of Father.
> Father states that Mother berates him, even in public, calling him names and cursing at him and does this in front of the children.

Both the statements above appear in Judge Lash's report. Judge Lash says Kristen offered no parental criticism of Harry. She would offer no criticism because she has not seen what Harry does with the children since the first PFA. Nor does Harry know what Kristen does with the children. If Harry says he knows, then he is lying. Our criticism of Harry is his lying. Harry's statement above is another lie. Kristen, Harry, and the boys are not in public together for that to happen. Cursing is a character trait of the Hall family. Harry claimed that for his family in the custody evaluation. If Kristen would berate Harry in public, then why did she not berate him in the custody evaluation or in the court? She used the court time to defend herself against Harry's false accusations. There was plenty of evidence, documents, and testimony offered to prove that criticism. We knew before hand that any negative testimony concerning Harry's parenting would have been touted as "hearsay." That would be correct because we had no solid evidence. We do have suspicions. I don't want to think about our suspicions. We were amazed that the "hearsay" offered by Harry was accepted by Judge Lash as evidence.

I said in my letter to Judge Lash that I did not agree with Kristen in going for 50/50. As seen from the statement by Judge Lash above, that decision left the wrong impression. I do not believe a person of Harry's character should be primary custody of anyone's child. I know Kristen does not believe that Harry's is as appropriate as she. She has a nature which makes it nearly impossible for her to criticize anyone. Actually, she may be guilty of the sin of committing unconditional love. We call that irony. She forgives too easily when she is wronged. It was Kristen's and Jamie's game plan to not say negatives about Harry. Harry was making himself look bad by all the lying negatives he used against Kristen. Obviously, Jamie's and Kristen's plan did not work. They should have used my "list." I sat for two hours one afternoon and made a "list" of negative items describing Harry's parenting. I've tired of numbers so I used letters to track the items. I got thru the alphabet twice. Of course, I had varying degrees of proof for those items of negativity. So, no, I do not feel Harry is as appropriate a parent as Kristen.

Kristen had other reasons for only seeking 50/50. Of course, she said she wanted to be fair. In the beginning she said it would be hard to overturn the custody evaluator's recommendation of 50/50. Harry had, at the time of the first evaluation, only filed two PFA's against Kristen. One was for the "stoning" incident against Bryce, and the other for the "recording" incident against Harry. For the custody trial she would have to overcome a recommendation of primary. She thought it would be an impossible stretch for her to go for primary. Besides, it was Harry's trial and she said legally she could not change her recommendation because of that fact. She does have a minor in Criminal Justice and worked in Domestic Relations. I believe she may also have felt it would be harder to find someone willing to marry her if she had the boys on a full time schedule. She was also reasonable in her assessment that she needed someone to help her financially. Keep in mind, she could still not get a better paying job due to the verdict of "founded" of indicated of child abuse. Kristen does want a husband and helpmate for the boys.

> This Court must note the presumption in the law that favors the rearing of siblings together, being one factor to be considered in determining the best interests of the Minor Children. <u>Nomland v. Nomland</u> 813 A.2d 850, 856 (Pa.Super. 2002)

Sorry, Judge Lash, the above statement does not apply to this case. Sibling is defined as one of two or more persons that have a common parent. Is it true that Trey and Bryce each have two parents in common in Harry and Kristen? Sibling includes in its definition that they are related by blood. Are Trey and Bryce related by blood? Of course, Trey and Bryce are not related by blood. They are not siblings. I have proved my point.

Even before adopting Bryce, Kristen and Harry had discussed when it would be good to explain to Bryce that he is adopted. They both agreed that it should be at an early age. Bryce was adopted at the age two years and two months. He was four and a half at the time Harry filed the first PFA. At the time of the custody trial he was six and a half. In a few months he will be nine. He has not been told that he is adopted. Kristen has not persuaded Harry to tell Bryce he is adopted. Others have recommended Bryce be told. Harry has not told Bryce this "hidden" truth. To the eye it is not hidden. Kristen has blond hair and blue eyes. Trey has blond hair in blue eyes. Bryce has "gorgeous" brown hair and dark brown eyes. That is my wife's description of his hair. Harry does not have brown eyes. Bryce is the offensive tackle and Trey is the slim fleet of foot whatever.

Harry says Bryce and Trey are close. They get along so well together. For most of the time they don't. For a time they did tolerate being together. That was when Bryce learned to play video games. Bryce learned to play quickly. Bryce was about five and a half at the time. Half years make a big difference in children at those young ages. Trey would sit and watch. He was four. Bryce felt in charge. He loved when others watched. Often, I was the one to watch him. I wrote a letter to Harry telling him how playing video games gave Bryce self esteem. Harry would soon get the Wii video game for Bryce. It kept Bryce out of trouble. That meant that Bryce was less apt to knocking down whatever Trey was playing with or building. As I said, in the beginning Trey was content watching Bryce. More than a year later, Trey started to learn how to play video games. Bryce was not interested in watching Trey. I would take Bryce to do other things like mow the lawn. One time we went to the soccer field and played two other kids in full field soccer. Bryce laughed as he watched me run up and down the field like a "nut." It would have been better if I was the squirrel. Anyway, it was amazing to me how Harry was able to manipulate Judge Lash and Dr. Thomas into believing his lies about playing video games against Kristen.

For the most part, Trey and Bryce are as different as the two stars, Arnold Schwartzenager and Danny DeVito in the movie "Twins." Trey uses his imagination to pretend. He likes to build things and pretend as he plays. Bryce would ultimately knock down those things that Trey built. I guess you could say in that way they played together. We would discover one thing the boys liked to do. They both liked riding bicycle. It was not that they liked doing it together. They just liked riding. I was the one who taught both to ride, not Harry. Both boys told Dr. Thomas that they liked to ride bikes. Kristen had a bike rack, mine really, and often took the boys to different places to ride. Harry has dozens of trophies in his basement won for riding bikes. Harry did not take the boys bike riding. I taught Bryce how to ride bicycle many months before Trey. Did I show favoritism to Bryce? Oh, Judge Lash says we treat Bryce with disparity.

I looked up the word presumption. I had thought its meaning had something to do with the word assumption. Most people are aware of the joke using the word "assume." I think a good joke should be made with the word presumption as used by Judge Lash. The following definition is quite apropos. A presumption is a legal reference as to the existence of a truth of a fact not certainly drawn from the known or proved existence of some other fact. Proven facts have been considered irrelevant by Judge Lash in this case.

Preachers often use illustrations from contemporary life to validate a particular thought from the scriptures. I like using illustrations from the scriptures to validate a particular thought I might have about contemporary life. I have a thought about this presumption that it is better that siblings be kept together. For example, let us examine the case of brothers, Cain and Abel. What can be said about Ishmael and Isaac? They were siblings in the true sense in that they were related by the blood of Abraham. Ishmael was sent packing? The descendants are still at war. Then there was Jacob and Esau. Jacob was not sent packing. He ran for his life. His mother, Rebekah, favored him over his brother. Jacob showed favoritism to Joseph, something about a coat. How did Joseph's siblings respond? Imagine how they would have felt if they thought he was adopted. He would not have made it out of the pit. In looking at these stories of siblings we find a simple truth. They all seem to be about the parents committing the sin of disparity. What is the number of the commandment against disparity? Ask Judge Lash. How did Moses' adoption work for Egypt?

It is not necessarily true that keeping siblings together is in the best interest of the children. It is true that the determination has to be made case by case. Judge Lash takes this presumption and gives no reason why it should be applied in this case as a reason to keep the boys together. A presumption in itself is not evidence, fact, or reason. Kristen and Mary Lynne had reasonable arguments for separating the boys. As Trey becomes older, he will come to understand more and more that Harry's use of Bryce kept him from being with his mother for all those days in his young life. I believe Trey already understands that to some degree. Trey's growing resentment will continue as long as decisions keep Trey from being with his mother. Trey has not seen Kristen treat Bryce in a desperate manner as both Harry and Judge Lash claim. It is true Kristen has to discipline Bryce more often than Trey. Discipline may not even be the correct word to use. It may be better to say changing the situation. Is acting in a manner to change a situation a form of discipline? For example, if Bryce is sitting on Trey, is it an act to discipline when he is physically taken off of Trey? This conversation is ridiculous. It is more ridiculous when Kristen is accused of punishing Bryce harshly by hitting him on the head with a "blue bowl" of "squirty bottle."

Speaking of disparity, Harry claimed that Trey gets anything he wants, while Bryce only gets punished harshly. Harry never observed Bryce being punished harshly by Kristen. If Harry observed it, why did he let it continue? Harry is just a liar. Bryce's sixth birthday was about a month before the second evaluation. Kristen asked Bryce what he wanted. He wanted a battery driven monster truck that cost $350. Kristen bought it by pawning her engagement ring which brought $200 and using $150 from her monthly support payment from Harry.

In effect, all the money came from Harry. She knew that four months later she would be moving from the farm to an apartment. She knew that she would be giving the truck to Harry. Bryce got what he wanted for his birthday. Harry said, "Trey gets everything he wants, Bryce only gets punished harshly." The truck is a fact. Kristen's treatment of Bryce with disparity is not.

Are there any facts of disparity against Bryce that can be attributed to Harry? Indeed, there are many facts that illustrate Harry committed the sin of disparity. I will proceed with one example.

What was the sign of the Noahic Covenant? It was a rainbow. You knew that? What is the sign of the Mosaic Covenant? Some would say it is the Ten Commandments. That would be wrong. It is the Sabbath. And last, what is the sign of the Abrahamic Covenant? Do you give up? It was circumcision. Bryce had not been circumcised before he came to Harry and Kristen as a foster child at the age of six months. At the time, Harry said that he would have Bryce circumcised when he was adopted. Twelve months after receiving Bryce, Trey was born. Trey was circumcised. About six months later, Bryce was adopted. Shortly there after, Bryce and Trey were baptized at West Lawn United Methodist Church. Bryce was still not circumcised. Bryce and Trey often bathe together. On one occasion Bryce noted the difference. Bryce said his father told him that he would have an operation to make his the same as Trey's. In a few months Bryce will be nine. He has not been circumcised. Would that be a physical proof of disparity? It his been mentioned that Bryce had said he was Harry Hall the second, because Trey's real name is Harry Hall the third. Sorry Bryce, you are older, it is true, but there is disparity? Ask your father?

Chapter 39 – Toxic to Children

Request for Reconsideration of Order

The date on the Decision of Order of Judge Lash for the custody trial was September 5, 2008. In a few days both attorney's, Jamie and Mark, would receive the report and verdict. Kristen would not hear the verdict from Jamie. She would hear it from Harry. Kristen had completed work and was with the boys in the car. Under the 50/50 custody agreement it was her day with the boys. She called us on the phone. She told us she had just received a phone call from Harry. He told her to meet him immediately with the boys at the exchange point. She had not heard from Jamie that Harry had won primary custody. It was a school day and according to the new order it was now a daddy day. She did not trust that Harry was telling the truth, nor did we. We had been thinking that Kristen had at least kept 50/50. I had thought that Harry would be investigated for "perjury." Kristen called Jamie to find out if Harry was telling the truth. Unfortunately, this time Harry did tell the truth. Jamie apologized to Kristen. She said that the order arrived at her office yesterday. She said that after reading the verdict she was too upset to make the call. After reading Judge's Lash's, "Decision and Order," it seemed to her that he did not listen at all to Kristen's testimony.

It would be understated to say that the five of us, Kristen, the boys, my wife, and I were upset. We had not expected to hear the verdict that Harry won primary. Mary Lynne and I thought it would not be good for Kristen to drive herself and the boys to the exchange point, the Turkey Hill at Breezy Corners. Mary Lynne told Kristen on the phone that I would meet her at the parking lot of her apartment complex and drive her and the boys to the exchange point. I pulled into the parking lot a few spaces from Kristen's car. As I got out of my car, Bryce got out of Kristen's and started walking towards me. He called out loudly, "Daddy said bullshit on the phone." Harry must have emphasized that word because generally the boys can not hear Harry when he is talking on the phone with Kristen. Bryce recognized that word as something different from what he would hear from his maternal grandparents. I got in the driver's seat of Kristen's car. Kristen stayed in the back seat with the boys. That is where Kristen sits when the five of us travel together. Grandma had decided to not go with us because she cannot stand looking at Harry. Kristen had already been in the back seat so she could explain to the boys why she was taking them to their father on a mommy's day. Her proximity to the boys had made it easier for Bryce to hear the expletive.

We arrived at the exchange point on time. It was warm so all of us got out of the car and waited. Harry arrived, late as usual, and parked approximately a hundred feet from us. The adults present did not expect what happened next. Harry got out of the Durango and walked towards us. As Harry approached, Bryce started screaming. He screamed, "You said bullshit on the phone! You are trying to take us from mommy!" He screamed that several times. Harry told the boys to get to the Durango. Trey scampered quickly to the Durango. Bryce would not. Harry had to walk the hundred feet to get next to Bryce. Harry shouts at Bryce, "I will give you to three! One! Two! Three!" Bryce scampers to the Durango. I thought Harry only used timeouts. Kristen and I stood dumbfounded. We said not a word. We just watched in awe. We knew in a moment. A jerk we just saw. Harry got in the Durango and drove across the lot in the opposite direction from Kristen and me. He pulled onto Route 12 and turned to pass us heading south on Route 73. As he passed us we noticed he was already talking on the cell phone. I presumed he was not calling to wish someone a merry Christmas. We thought he was probably calling his lawyer to describe the event with some lies.

Harry did describe the event to his lawyer. However, we could not be sure if it was his lawyer that he called first. Harry's version of the event would be written in an official document. Kristen would receive that document, three weeks after that event. The date written on the document was September 30, 2008. The title of the document was PLAINTIFF'S ANSWERS TO DEFENDANT'S REQUEST FOR RECONSIDERATION OF ORDER OF SEPTEMBER 5, 2008. Obviously, Kristen had filed a reconsideration order and this was Mark Zimmer's rebuttal to Kristen's request. Nineteen points are listed in numerical order. For seven of those points, Harry's lawyer simply writes, "Admitted." Points #10 and #19 refer to the exchange incident.

> 10. Mother's belief is irrelevant as transition of the children to Father has already taken place. It should be noted that Father generously gave Mother additional time to effectuate the transfer of the children to the Father.

What additional time? Harry called Kristen to tell her he won primary. He tells her to bring the children to him immediately. Kristen asked for time. Harry says, "Bullshit." Zimmer lies.

> 19. Father believes that the children's exposure to Maternal Grandparents could continue to be toxic to the children considering Maternal Grandparents obvious dislike for Father and Grandmother's testimony at the trial which led the Court to believe that watching Bryce was an imposition on Maternal Grandparents. It should be noted that Grandfather's presence during recent custody exchanges have been disruptive and combative with Grandfather screaming at Father in the presence of the children.

What recent custody exchanges? There was only one exchange. Harry and Mark Zimmer lie again. I drove Kristen to the exchange to prevent any problems. I have never screamed at Harry. I would never have screamed on a public parking lot. The Turkey Hill at Breezy Corners is very busy. It was chosen as the exchange by Harry not just because of the location. My students at YOP would ask me why I would not yell or scream at a disrespectful student. I said that I didn't get paid enough to yell and scream. I liked working at YOP because I had Barry, my supervisor, take care of the discipline. I guess that was why my salary was much less than half what I received before retiring from BCTC, Berks Career and Technology Center. At YOP, I only had to teach and play basketball. The combatants on the hill were Harry and Bryce. Harry won that little battle with Bryce despite the fact that Bryce told the truth. As in every event Harry describes, he lied. Would Judge Lash believe his lie?

It is difficult to convince people that we, my wife and I, were also declared guilty in Kristen's custody trial. It is difficult to get them to understand we were declared guilty. It is difficult to get them to believe were declared guilty. In point #19, we were declared "toxic" to children. I wonder how many of my co-workers over my forty years of ministry with children would believe that I was declared "toxic" to children. That would not be a good point for me to use in my resume to seek another position in children's ministry. Mark Zimmer would include several more points that would preclude that consequence.

> 15. While it is true the children were cared for by their Maternal Grandparents after school, Father believes it is not in the children's best interests to be cared for by their Maternal Grandparents in light of the disparity in treatment received by the children while in Maternal Grandparent's care.
>
> 16. Denied. The children's relationship with Maternal Grandparents was addressed at the trial and Father believes that until Maternal Grandparents can learn to accept Bryce for the special and unique child that he is and treat Bryce the same way they treat Trey, that a relationship with Maternal Grandparents is not suitable at this time.

Of course, Harry never sees how we treat the boys while they are in our care. He says we treat them with disparity. I have to admit there was some disparity. I taught Bryce how to blow the trumpet. When he was only five, Bryce, in a BRASS IN PRAISE concert, got to play some notes before the trumpet feature selection. I asked him to blow the cobwebs out of my trumpet. He did. The audience applauded. Trey has not gotten that opportunity. Unfortunately, since Harry has had primary custody, Bryce has not improved on that skill. At age three, Bryce and I, alone, went on excursions to places like Roadside America and Cabella's. Trey was left at home with grandma and mother. We did take the three of them on our next excursion to Roadside America. I helped Bryce learn to ride the bike many months before Trey learned. I better stop with the disparity discussion. I'm repeating items.

On the other hand, there is also disparity in how our treatment of the boys compared to Harry's treatment of them. We buy the boys new clothes. This little Harry buys none. Harry thinks Kristen should buy all the new clothes, shoes, coats, underwear, etc. After all, Harry pays Kristen child support. She should use that money to buy the clothes. When Kristen sent the boys back to Harry wearing the new clothes, he made sure they came back to Kristen wearing the old clothes. Sometimes, Harry brought the boys to Kristen with Bryce in Trey's clothes and vice versa. Bryce looked stylish in his outfit with his midriff showing, and Trey looked like he was wearing a nightshirt.

I really enjoyed the oxymoron statement in #16. Bryce is special and unique, therefore, treat them the same. I can not decide who the moron is. Would that be the one who believes it, the one who wrote it, or the judge who considers it? You love them the same, but treat them differently.

Judge Lash included in his "Decision and Order" the following descriptions and comparisons of Bryce and Trey by Dr. Peter Thomas. Dr. Thomas also noted that Bryce has evidence of dysfunction, having been described as having attention deficit hyperactivity disorder, as well as oppositional defiant disorder. He states, "He is a difficult child to manage." Trey is much more composed and peaceful. So Mr. Hall, how can they be treated the same. They have different needs and problems. The $300 a month given for Bryce says that he should be treated differently. They require different treatment. We understand that. Apparently, Mr. Zimmer and Judge Lash do not. Again, I wrote almost a year before Mark Zimmer's ANSWER, the following words. "Now every birth is special, whether a girl or boy. God created each special to bring to all great joy."

There were two other points made in Mr. Zimmer's ANSWER that caught my attention.

3. Mother asserts an anticipatory breach which has no basis in fact and is a product of Mother's paranoia.

4. Mother again asserts anticipated issues which are without present or past factual historic basis and only serve to underscore her paranoid thought process.

Because of my daughter's relationships with abusive men, including Harry Hall, Mary Lynne has read books relating to men abusing women. Of course, she learned of the characteristics of the abuser and abused. She also learned of an alarming trend in family law courts to award primary custody to the man. One of the points made in a book was that these men try to prove that their wives are paranoid. Kristen's case fits this trend perfectly according to the statements above. Is this part of the ploy Harry and his lawyer are using against Kristen? Is this one of the "dirty tactics" described by Guillermo Jalil's book?

And what were those issues which they claimed was a product of Kristen's paranoia? Kristen was talking of the issues of Harry using private eyes and other means of spying on her. They claimed that the meeting with the supposed DEA agents, one named "Scottie", never really occurred. Kristen had claimed that there were other times she felt she was followed. Again they claimed these were all a product of her paranoia. How did they so quickly forget that a month before, Harry on the witness stand admitted that he had Kristen followed by a private eye at the time of the first PFA? Also, there was the time Mary Lynne and I got the license plate number. Jamie called and had it verified it was that of a private eye. The hospital had a surveillance tape of the supposed DEA's. Mr. Zimmer denied that interview occurred. Yet, later in the trial he asked Kristen if that interview changed her opinion of Mike Spadafora? We believe we were followed at times when Kristen was under 24 hour enforced supervision. They tried to catch her without a supervisor when she had the boys.

Kristen won permission in her reconsideration hearing to pick up the boys after school. Harry refused to sign the order issued by Judge Lash. Before signing the order, Harry had us staked out to see if Kristen or Mary Lynne would pick up the boys before Harry signed the order. The private eye was staked out down the street from our house. I walked down the street and knocked on his car window. I said, "Here is some interesting reading for you as you sit here." I slipped an article in his slightly opened car window. It was the one I had just written concerning the incident on the hill and Mr. Zimmer's ANSWER. I wonder if that caused Harry paranoia.

Chapter 40 - Reconsider, Appeal, Conform

Decision to Conform

The first order of business would be to file a reconsideration order. Kristen could not allow the children to have thirteen consecutive days each month without seeing their mother. When Harry filed that first PFA it was fifteen consecutive days without seeing or hearing from their mother. Effectually, Judge Lash's order would have that PFA filed each month. At the time of the first PFA, Trey was three and Bryce four and a half. A year later, Trey announced that mommy should that "mommy should have us 100 days and daddy one." Bryce announced a ratio of ten to one in favor of Kristen. In the reconsideration, Kristen asked that she be allowed to have the children the Thursday evening's prior to Harry's weekend of custody.

The following are Harry's and Mark Zimmer's ANSWER to that request.

> 8. Denied. It is not in the children's best interests that they visit with Mother overnight from Thursday to Friday before Father's weekend. To the contrary, the children need a set schedule during the school week in order to establish continuity in their routines.

9. Father believes it is not in the Children's best interest to spend one evening per week with Mother during the weeks prior to and following Father's weekend with the Children.

Point #8 would have given Kristen two nights a month during the school week to have the boys. Point #9 would have given her four school nights a month. Judge Lash denied request #8 and request #9. But, Kristen had another idea.

17. Bryce attends school all day and is dismissed from school at 3:30 pm, at which time he is dropped off at day care. Father then picks up Bryce from daycare by 4:15 pm. There is not enough time between the completion of school and when Father picks up Bryce for Mother to spend any quality time with Bryce.

18. Father believes that Mother would be unable to spend any one-on-one time with Bryce as she could also have custody of the parties' minor child, Trey, at that time.

To our surprise, Judge Lash did not deny Kristen this request. She would be able to pick up the boys after school. She would have to take them to Harry when he gets home at 4:15 pm. Trey had morning kindergarten. He was then transported to daycare for the afternoon. Kristen's work day at St. Joe's hospital ended at 2:15 pm. She could make it in twenty minutes to daycare to pick up Trey. At 3:30, she would pick up Bryce from school. It would be quality time with the boys. Every day she would get to see the boys. She would buy them a snack. They looked forward to those minutes with their mother, and she with them. Thank you, Judge Lash.

I have a question for Harry concerning point #18. You are a single parent. When do you spend one-on-one time with either of the boys? Kristen has two parents who have been invested in the best interests of the boys from the beginning. Bryce had much one-on-one time with Kristen in the past. In the past, Bryce and I did some one-on-one time in order to free Kristen to give one-on-one time with Trey also. With this arrangement Kristen would be able to give that special one-on-one time Trey had missed because of Kristen's need to watch Bryce continually. Another plus would be that Kristen could keep Harry in line with the school schedule and other appointments. Harry could not do it without Kristen's help.

On the surface, it seems like the best possible arrangement considering that Harry has primary. So why would we still by complaining? One problem is the time when Harry has the boys at home by himself. He then has to be father and mother. He has no live in nanny or grandparent to help in the feeding, clothing, bathing, cleaning, brushing of teeth, etc. In addition, he has to do those chores while supervising both boys, who go in opposite directions, very closely. Does anyone think he can handle those jobs? Does Judge Lash believe he can? I believe he can not. What will happen as the boys get older and Harry has the additional burden of school work and extra activities?

There is a bigger problem with this arrangement. It is a problem similar to that of the United States of America? It's called money. Apparently, Judge Lash does not have common sense. (I wanted to use the word "cents".) Otherwise, he would have recognized it before he gave his Decision and Order. Kristen's income was now reduced to $1200. Her rent is $900 per month. Do the math. Obviously, she needs a higher paying job. There is a problem. She can not qualify for higher pay jobs or other jobs in her expertise due to not having the criminal clearance required. Kristen is a child abuser. That problem came by way of Harry Hall and BCCYS. Where is Mike Spadafora when we need him? And of course, if she took another job it would be unlikely that she would get the hours that would allow her to be with the boys each school day for that short time. She had taken the job with St. Joe's because of the children. Her thoughts are always for the best interests of the children.

Kristen would have to appeal the decision of Judge Lash from the custody trial. To remain involved in her children's lives, she would need the finances necessary. The solution was simple. Kristen should have primary custody and be allowed to do the mothering and child rearing. Father should be doing what fathers do, earn the money.

There is another reason to appeal. For Kristen, to not appeal would be an admission of guilt. She is not guilty of what she has been accused. The verdict was based on the lies of Harry Hall and the lack of discernment, intentional or otherwise, by Judge Lash. The defamation of Kristen's character through this verdict, giving Harry primary, is a life sentence. It is also a death sentence. To the world the old Kristen is dead. A new Kristen has been determined by Judge Lash. We need to destroy this new Kristen as defined by Judge Lash, and resurrect the old. Justice has to be served. It can only be served by an appeal and a change of verdict. A resurrection is necessary.

Jamie Dautrich, Esquire writes a NOTICE OF APPEAL dated October 6, 2008.

> Notice is hereby given that Kristen L. Hall, above-named Defendant, hereby appeals to the Superior Court of Pennsylvania for the Order entered in this matter on September 5, 2008. This sentence has been entered in the docket, as evidenced by the attached copy of the docket entries.
>
> I certify that there is a transcript of the Trial scheduled in this matter before the Hon. Scott E. Lash, and that it will be ordered within ten days.

Judge Lash knows that Kristen does not agree with his verdict of primary custody to Harry Hall. Now he knows, officially, that Kristen is appealing the verdict. He knows we are trying to obtain the trial transcript. Does he how understand how his verdict has and will continue to affect lives? I bet he never thought the trial transcript would be used to write a book. The open court would become much more open. Kristen would receive another letter from Jamie dated November 26, 2008.

> Enclosed please find a copy of the Family and Domestic Docketing Statement, in regards to the above-mentioned matter. Please be advised that I need to receive the Five Thousand Dollar fee for the appeal, so that I can order the transcript of the trial. The transcript is necessary for this appeal and needs to be ordered as soon as possible.

We thought the transcript had been ordered. It said in the October, NOTICE OF APPEAL, that it would be ordered in ten days. Kristen received another letter from Jamie on December 1, 2008.

> Enclosed please find a copy of correspondence that I received from the Superior Court, in regards to the above-mentioned matter.

The following words are from the Superior Court of Pennsylvania for the Hon. Kate Ford Elliot, President Judge, dated November 25, 2008.

> Appellant, mother, has filed a notice of appeal from the custody order dated September 5, 2008. This matter has been designated as a Family Fast Track appeal. The Superior Court's Family Fast Track Program has been implemented to give expedited treatment to certain types of family cases in effort to mitigate the harmful effects of such litigation on children.

Jamie did attempt to put Kristen on Fast Track. However, there was a problem, five thousand dollars worth. Kristen has no credit. She could not borrow the money. She wanted to pay Jamie, but could not. She did give Jamie permission to try to obtain the $11,000 Harry had not paid Kristen as part of her divorce settlement. Jamie was unable to obtain that money. We had borrowed $10,000 to pay for Kristen's rent for a year. We could borrow no more. We needed the money to help Kristen survive financially each month. Kristen would not follow through with the appeal. Kristen would conform to the recommendations offered by Judge Lash. He said in his report that he would reconsider the verdict if she did. Two of those recommendations are two points of the Decision and Order.

> 8. Mother shall engage in psychotherapy with a psychotherapist of her choice. She shall be solely responsible for the cost. Her therapy shall continue until

deemed unnecessary by the psychotherapist or until further Order of the Court.

9. The parties shall continue in counseling with Signature Family Services for purposes of co-parenting counseling. The parties shall share costs equally.

Judge Lash said in his report that Kristen needed psychotherapy to become a "better person" and a "better parent." What exactly would Kristen have to do to make her a better person and parent? What has she done to demonstrate that she was not a good person or parent? Dr. Thomas had also recommended that in both evaluation reports. Both the judge and evaluator based their recommendations on the lies of Harry Hall. Harry Hall admitted to having ten years of psychotherapy. If Harry Hall is an example of what a person does that takes psychotherapy, then I recommend that no one take psychotherapy. If Kristen would have agreed to psychotherapy, then she would have admitted that she needed to become a "better person" and a "better parent." Answer this question with a yes or no. Have you stopped beating your wife? You get the point. Kristen would take psychotherapy to conform to Judge Lash's recommendation. She would not agree that she needed to be a better person or parent. She was doing the best she could. Taking psychotherapy would cost less than the appeal. How does Judge Lash expect she can pay for the psychotherapy? Maybe Michael the angel would pay for her therapy. Kristen would also agree to take Family Signature counseling for the second time. It would cost about $300 for each of two months. How does she pay for that? Perhaps, she can take the money from the children's budget for the daily after school snack.

Kristen did take the course the second time. She had Jess as the teacher again. Jess was perplexed to learn Kristen had lost 50/50 custody. Jess was also supposed to be a witness for Kristen in the custody trial. She had been subpoenaed for that trial. She did not make it to the trial due to an illness. Kristen explained to her that it was her goal to have a modification trial and she had to complete the course again as a recommendation by Judge Lash. Jess told her she would refuse to have Harry as a client again. She did. Kristen completed the course again. We learned that Harry never completed the course the second time.

He had a different instructor and only went to four of the fourteen sessions. Harry did not think he needed the instruction. After all, he was awarded primary by Judge Lash. Jess also told Kristen that she would be a witness on her behalf for the modification trial.

There was only one other recommendation by Judge Lash.

> If Mother and her side of the family can move past the problems that Bryce can cause and the fact that he is not the natural child of the parties, and provide unconditional love to Bryce as they do to Trey, the Court would also entertain modifying the Order to provide for a 50/50 arrangement.

So, Kristen is not the only one that has to do some work. How can we show that we provide "unconditional love" to Bryce? How did we show that we did provide "unconditional love" to Trey? I do not know the answer to either question. I did teach, more than thirty years ago for children in Junior Church for ages 4 to 8, the difference between "conditional" and "unconditional" covenants. The difference is based on the little word "if". Maybe that's a clue.

CHAPTER 41 - WHAT IF

Uncovering the Mastermind

Harry had no witnesses other than himself take the witness stand. The last item discussed was Harry's knowledge and use of Guillermo Jalil. Harry had admitted he asked Guillermo for advice from the start. He admitted he hired Guillermo to do a "criminal record" check on Mike Spadafora. Why didn't Harry use his lawyer, Mark Zimmer, to do the check? Harry also stated that Guillermo went to the Exeter Police on behalf of Harry to give and obtain information about Mike Spadafora. Why did Guillermo go to the Exeter Police? This answer becomes stranger when Guillermo's relationship with drug enforcement entities is "uncovered." Who is this man that he would have influence with the law? Why does it seem that Judge Lash abruptly halted that line of testimony? After reconvening, there was no more discussion of Jalil. The line of testimony concerning Guillermo Jalil is conspicuously absent from Judge Lash's report.

The last important event before the custody trial was Kristen's meeting with the presumed DEA agents concerning Mike Spadafora. Was Guillermo involved with setting up that meeting? If they were real DEA agents, was he the one informed them of Kristen's relationship with Mike Spadafora? If they were phony agents, did Guillermo supply them with fake credentials, badges? These are two big "ifs." Harry admitted to using Guillermo from the start culminating with the criminal record check. What if Guillermo was the "mastermind" behind Harry's plan to win primary?

Kristen, as said previously, had met Guillermo at Harry's 20th class reunion for the class of 1985 for Exeter High School. So Guillermo and Harry probably might know people from the Exeter Police Department. However, it is apparent that for some reason Guillermo had influence with someone in the department. There was someone with whom he could give or get information. At the class reunion Harry and Guillermo spoke of their camaraderie in cycling. Harry has dozens of cycling trophies. The item of interest to Kristen at the reunion was that Guillermo had worked in the county as a juvenile probation officer. Kristen had thought about that as a possible career choice. Guillermo was familiar with family law. What if he had a connection with Scott Lash?

Who is Guillermo Jalil? In questioning Harry, Jamie asked him if he knew the book that Guillermo Jalil wrote. Judge Lash quipped, "He wrote a book?" Jamie said she was referring to the book, <u>ASSET PROTECTION FROM DIVORCE</u>. Harry said on the witness stand that he never read it, used it, or knew of its existence. I would discover its existence via internet. The email ad described the contents of the book, but did not give information about its author. I discovered the existence of another book authored by Guillermo Jalil that did tell pertinent facts about its author. Guillermo Jalil produced a video and wrote a book titled, <u>STREET-WISE DRUG PREVENTION</u>. The book is dated 1996. In 1999, he travel 900 miles on bicycle, from Orlando to Virginia Beach, on a Drug Prevention campaign. Kristen remembered correctly that Harry and Guillermo were cycling buddies. He is a volunteer youth counselor, entrepreneur, and former Juvenile Probation Officer. Kristen had remembered correctly about Guillermo being involved in juvenile probation.

The internet article goes on to say that Guillermo gives thanks to local law enforcement and community groups for their assistance. He gives special thanks to the Reading Police Department, Berks County Prison, Manos, Berks Advocates Against Violence, Berks Aids Network, The Caron Foundation, Tom Reese & Associates, and others who prefer to remain nameless. What if one of the others was Judge Lash? Guillermo Jalil's name is associated with the group, Youth Fellowship & Rescue. Guillermo goes on to say that his book may be downloaded for free. It is used by medical schools, federal agencies, schools, churches, and youth programs. How can one person be so magnanimous? Why does Judge Lash not know of such a person so seriously involved with the juveniles of Berks County? Or, does he know Guillermo Jalil?

I know Judge Lash was elected Judge of the Court of Common Pleas of Berks County in the November elections of 1999. Actually, Mary Lynne and I met Judge Lash before the election at a small gathering at a private home in Exeter Township for a Gideon camp meeting of which I was a member. Judge Lash was introduced as a prospective member for the Gideon's International. Also, he was introduced as a candidate for judge. His assignments as judge would include matters in family law, criminal, juvenile, and civil court. Previously, he served as a Juvenile Court Master from 1985-1988. From 1988-1993, he served as a Custody Conference/Hearing Officer. Would Judge Lash be a great source to advise someone about how decisions for custody are determined in family law, especially in his court? If, indeed, Judge Lash advised Guillermo or Guillermo learned from observing Judge Lash in action, would Judge Lash be reluctant in continuing the discussions concerning Guillermo Jalil in a custody trial? I would say that is a big "if."

One book above Guillermo offers for free, the other, not so. You have to pay for the book, <u>ASSET PROTECTION FROM DIVORCE</u>. From the description in the email below, it seems to be worth the price.

> "Some of the tactics and strategies are sneaky, deceiving and down right nasty, but when it comes to money and divorce these traits are a reality. It is our hope that this book will challenge your assumptions, encourage you to examine your finances and facilitate your own plan to protect what is rightfully yours."
>
> An editorial review states: "These are killer divorce tactics that produce a financial victory in your favor in coping with divorce issues such as alimony (spousal support), the family home,—, divorce attorneys, etc. This is not a touch-feely resource for producing a win-win divorce. Make no mistake about it. If you want to protect your assets from divorce, then you've come to the right place."

Did you notice the last sentence started with the word "if?" The ad goes on to talk of common divorce strategies, calling some of them "dirty strategies." The statement in another ad that sent shivers down my spine was, "revenge is a common goal in divorce and obtained through children, money, and assets."

If Harry used information from Guillermo's book or simply his advice, then it is surely worth the price for Harry could not have won any more than he did. He won the family home worth $275,000 for a payment to Kristen of $10,000 which was used for one year's rent. He used the "dirty tactic" on none payment of mortgage to encourage Kristen to not seek alimony. Because he was awarded primary custody, he no longer had to pay child support. With his win in court and the verdict by BCCYS of child abuser, he received his revenge on Kristen and her family through defamation of character. He also made it forever difficult for Kristen to find employment in her field of expertise. His attempted suit of FPC forced me to resign from my position as CMD. Oops! Sorry, Guillermo and Harry, Mark Zimmer takes credit for the attempted suit of the church. If I say more about the book, I would be encouraging the unscrupulous to purchase it.

A few weeks after the custody trial, I did try to buy Guillermo's book online. I got to the ad, but it was said that the book was unavailable. That was puzzling. Jamie was able to get the book online the night before the trial. If Harry informed Guillermo that his book was discussed in the custody trial, would Guillermo have immediately made it unavailable? Jamie had said to Kristen before the trial that morning that in reading only a few pages of the book it appeared to her that it described Harry's plan. I needed to read that book. It was nearly three months after the trial that we asked Jamie if she still had it on her computer and would be willing to transfer it to my computer. It was still not available online. I thought it might never be available again. She said yes to both requests.

It didn't take many pages of reading to discover that it was describing all the actions Harry had used against Kristen. It was a plan. The mastermind of the plan was Guillermo Jalil. So, what? It is not illegal to use a plan from a book. It is not illegal to use advice from an expert. I believe that is why people hire attorneys. The book was more than 200 pages. Many of the last pages were official forms that could be used. I would only get to page 14. A statement appeared on that page that I had to copy. I needed it in print. I would start to copy the book up to that page and stop. The first page the computer printed was a disclaimer. The second page the computer printed was also the disclaimer, but in code. I panicked. I tried to delete the entire transfer for Jamie. I did. My computer survived. I would not try to get the book again.

What did I read on page 14? It was a simple statement that made Harry's plan plain. The statement: "Judges rarely consider 'perjury' in domestic relations cases." Did Harry understand how to apply that statement, or did Guillermo have to expound upon it? If you lie in court and the judge does not consider that to be "perjury," then you may lie to doctors, lawyers, caseworkers, the custody master, the custody evaluator, psychiatrists, BCCYS personnel, friends, Romans, and countrymen. This may be the biggest "if" of all. Harry's plan was simple, lie. A dog can lie about someone, but cannot lie about someone.

I had also been stopped in my reading of the book when I came across the two word phrase, "unconditional love." When I first read it in Judge Lash's report, I thought either Harry, Mark Zimmer, or the judge might have gotten the phrase from my article, "Extra-ordinary Love." I may have been wrong. Guillermo had used that phrase in his book written six years before my article. Did Guillermo write that phrase because of his observance of Judge Lash in court or knowledge of Judge Lash's reports?

There is another word which I believe I had seen in Guillermo's book. If Guillermo did not use it, I would be surprised. My wife, because of her experience with Kristen, has read books on abuse of women. She read of an alarming trend in family law. That is to give primary custody more and more to the man. Friends still say when they first learn that Kristen's ex-husband was awarded primary, "I thought judges almost always give custody to the mother." That may have been the truth at one time. Anyway, the word used often in cases where primary is awarded to the man is "paranoia." Mark Zimmer had used that term in his ANSWER to Kristen's reconsideration attempt. They, Harry and Zimmer, and I should probably include, Guillermo Jalil, said that Kristen had not had all those people follow her. They said that was a product of her "paranoia."

One point considered very important, according to the book, was the choosing of an attorney. Mark Zimmer was not Harry's first choice. Harry had followed Kristen's advice in choosing his first attorney, Jill Koestel. At least we thought she was his first lawyer. Harry said he got a lawyer in June before the first PFA in August. We don't believe he hired Jill that far before the first PFA. Anyway, Kristen did not know when Harry asked the question about who she thought was the best family lawyer that he was planning to hire that choice to use against Kristen. Jill Koestel resigned after a few months, not willing to carry out Harry's unscrupulous plans. Next, Harry hired Jeffrey Karver, Esquire. Harry said he fired him because he was proceeding too slowly. That is funny. In the book, Guillermo suggests using "stall tactics" to push back dates so that your spouse cannot keep up with you financially and may then give up the fight. Harry did have his second lawyer use those stall tactics. I would, however, like to believe that Mr. Karver resigned because he has scruples. Harry had not followed his directive to ask Kristen first. Guillermo suggests that if your lawyer has scruples, find one that does not. That is my paraphrase. I believe that Mark Zimmer was suggested to Harry Hall by Guillermo Jalil. I believe Harry is not the first person to whom Guillermo gave that advice. I also believe that Mark Zimmer was really Harry's first choice, but Harry tried to use the first two lawyers to legitimatize his case.

Mark Zimmer has a reputation that he usually wins his case. I only had a few minutes on the stand to be questioned by him as a witness. I was not impressed. He made no attempt to refute or discredit my testimony about catching Harry in the stairwell lying to Kristen. I don't know why Judge Lash allowed that idiotic line of testimony concerning lying. It was especially self incriminating when he admitted sending my letter to the church. I thought that statement would be a good argument for me to use in suing Mr. Zimmer. After seeing Judge Lash's report, I was extremely anxious to see what had transpired in court the six hours before my few minutes on the witness stand at the end of the day.

Despite all the lies and attempted entrapments of Kristen, I don't believe she lost the case because of the testimony or evidence presented. I believe she lost the case because of relationships. I am not talking of either Kristen's or Harry's relationships. I am talking of the relationships of Guillermo Jalil. What if Mark Zimmer is indeed Guillermo Jalil's lawyer of choice? What if Judge Lash and Guillermo Jalil did more than pass each other casually in the halls of family law? What if Scottie, who posed as a DEA agent, was also known by Guillermo Jalil? After all, Guillermo wrote a book that was used by federal agencies. What if the Scott Erickson, claimed to be from the DA's office by Harry Hall, was directed to Harry by Guillermo Jalil? Harry said Guillermo went to the Exeter police for him concerning Mike Spadafora. Maybe, Guillermo really went to Scott Erickson. What if the two Scotts are the same person? What if Bill Clemons is really an inside agent working in BCCYS for Guillermo Jalil? Is it possible that Bill Clemons was also a Juvenile Probation Officer? It would be not be strange that their paths may have crossed in that they both worked in situations that involve working with youth in trouble. I know it is just a bunch of "what if's."

CHAPTER 42 - THE MASTER PLAN

Hint of a Plan

Kristen, in testimony in the custody trial, hinted of a plan.

Ms. Dautrich: And how did that make you feel about, you know, Harry's motivations with joining up with Mr. Chalmers?

Kristen:—I was like, why would, you know, the father of my—our children get in cahoots with a man to try to bring the mother of his children down just some more, you know. It's been all a plan. All of his accusations of child abuse, it's all a plan just to get primary custody of these children from me. I feel like I've been harassed because there's been a lot of lies about me, and I'm constantly—I have to—it's like I've been defending myself for two entire years. It's been a complete defamation of character, that's what it is.

We always wondered how Harry was so knowledgeable about using the family justice system and Berks County Children's and Youth Services to accomplish his purpose, whatever that may be. We knew Harry's sister, Wanda, had used PFA's on a number of occasions in settling family squabbles. Her sons, his nephews, gave Harry some experience with the law. Each of those nephews had lived with Harry for some time. In a manner of speaking, Harry served as a guardian for both of them. At the time of the first PFA, Jeff was on parole and living in Harry's sister Eileen's home. He was living there at the time Harry's father died. The other nephew, Billy, was serving time at the time Harry filed the first PFA. Kristen believed he was caught making "meth." Clearly, the knowledge gained from his experiences with his family would not have accounted for what Harry was able to accomplish. Also, it could not have been the direction given to him by his first two lawyers. The first had resigned not willing to carry out Harry's plan. We are not sure if his second lawyer resigned or was fired because he was not willing to carry out Harry's plan.

Obviously, Kristen had much more experience in family law than Harry. She had a B.S. in Social Work with a minor in criminal justice from Millersville University. She had worked for the county in the Juvenile Detention Center, Domestic Relations, and Prothonotary. Her knowledge of the things Harry was doing to her and the response by the court may have helped keep her more sane that a person without such experience. What she did not know was the fact that behind Harry's plan was a mastermind with more experience than herself. Guillermo Jalil had an M.S. compared to her B.S. As Kristen, he also had many years of experience working within the same system of family law. However, he did not have the experience as a stay-at-home mom. But, he had critical relationships within the family law system. He gained enough knowledge of the family law system to write a book. It was a book that could be used by someone to gain an advantage in achieving victory in that system. Unfortunately, I did not say in achieving justice. The title of the book is <u>ASSET PROTECTION FROM DIVORCE</u>.

Kristen, as previously noted, had met Guillermo Jalil at Harry's 20th high school class reunion. She remembered when coming back to their table that evening that Guillermo had given Harry something that looked like a business card. That reunion was held in the fall of 2005. In less than nine months, Harry would file the first PFA against Kristen. The master plan may have been put into action even before the reunion. It should be noted that all the steps of that plan as described below had been put into action before Harry hired Mark Zimmer as his third lawyer. At the time Mark came on the scene, Kristen still had 50/50. What follows are twelve steps as carried out by Harry Hall.

STEP 1. Make a lot of money and hide it from your spouse. More than a year before filing the first PFA against Kristen, Harry began working 10 hours a day for 7 days a week. He did this for approximately 6 months. It amazed me to find out that Harry admitted to this time of working many hours to the custody evaluator. He made a lot of money. Kristen did not know how much money. At times she begged Harry to take off to spend time with her and play with the boys. He never did. He did, however, play hide and seek with his money.

STEP 2. Take out a loan using all the equity in the marital residence. Pay off all other loans. Hide the remaining funds from your wife. It can be hidden with relatives you trust. Save some of the funds to use for lawyers, the court expenses, and private eyes. The equity loan was accomplished in March of 2006. Harry had substantial savings to pay for the land and build the house. He saved a lot of money in building the house through what he did himself and with the help of family and friends. I believe his equity at the time may have been as much as $100,000. Kristen had no idea of the true amount of the equity. Harry paid off the Durango and other creditors. He would pay for his soon to be deceased father's pre and post death parties and funeral. After his father's death, Harry set up his mother in a mobile home in a trailer park. Of course, he would use much for lawyer and court fees. After all, he paid retainer fees for at least three lawyers. We know he used private eyes. We wonder how much he paid for advice from Guillermo Jalil. Kristen did receive $10,000 for rental of her apartment the first year. Of course, Harry did receive possession of the marital residence. It was a bargain.

STEP 3. Try to do a little better as a husband and a father. You must make the impression that you are trying to make your marriage work. You must, however, be careful to not be over exuberant in these attempts. Too drastic a change will draw suspicion upon your self. It may take several weeks or even months for the opportunity to arise for which you can make a claim that at least one of your children was threatened by your wife, their mother.

In June of 2006, Harry took the family to the wedding in South Carolina. He even allowed Kristen to be an attendant in the wedding and buy her own dress. He bought Kristen an appropriate Mother's Day card. The family had good times together in July. Kristen thought things had changed. Harry was not hounding Kristen about her parenting of Bryce. He was going to let Kristen go ahead with her plans to have Bryce evaluated in August. It had taken Kristen six months to get the scheduled evaluation. She thought July of 2006 had been the best month for her family. Harry capped off the month with a dozen roses. Harry had pulled off the deception.

STEP 4. File the 24 hour Emergency Protection from Abuse petition with your local District Court Judge. Your story must be such that it demonstrates that the child is in imminent danger. You will not have to prove anything at that time. The judge has to sign the order. The District Judge is not under pressure to sign it because the perpetrator will only be kept from the residence for 24 hours. In addition, that judge will not have to handle a permanent PFA. This will petition will allow you to have your spouse removed from the house.

I do not know if the book gave any suggestions. If no suggestions were given, Harry could give one. You could have one of your children bounce a small stone off the back of the head of the other. Or, you could throw the stone yourself and blame it on the other child. You could say on the petition that the mother was going to throw a stone at the guilty child in retaliation. You could say that you stepped in between to protect your child from the enraged mother. You could write further that the mother, your wife, started throwing stones at you. Kristen did admit to picking up a stone to use as an object lesson. The Oley police did come to remove Kristen from her home. That evening, Harry would be home alone with the boys, which was just what he wanted.

STEP 5. The next day you will follow through with a Protection from Abuse petition. This will be at a court at the county level. This petition should include your story from STEP 4. Be sure to add many points not included in the 24 hour petition. You can work on determining these points weeks before filing the petition. You may get ideas along the way or make up some that you have heard other people use. Remember that they do not have to be true. The facts of your petition will not be investigated. Keep in mind that "judges rarely consider perjury in domestic relations cases." You are free to tell your story, whatever that may be. The judge will sign your PFA. You are in control. To the story of the "stoning," Harry added language that Kristen supposedly used against Bryce. The hearing for the PFA will be held within ten working days.

If you know or suspect that your spouse is having an affair, this is the time to use the money you put aside for a private eye. In many cases, this is the time they will run to that person. Keep in mind, knowledge of the affair will be important information in winning your custody or divorce case. Kristen did not have an affair. She was followed by a private eye. Harry had to admit to that in court. Harry wasted money on that private eye.

STEP 6. At the PFA hearing, insist that your spouse sign "temporary primary custody" over to you as a condition for your dropping the PFA. She will easily be convinced that signing is her best, even her only alternative. In many cases she will have no place to take the children as you have control of the marital residence. If she was a stay-at-home mom she will understand quickly that she has no financial resources to take care of herself let alone the children. If she is not reasonable in signing, use the threat that she will not see the children until another hearing can be scheduled. Tell her it will take months for that hearing to be scheduled and she will not see the children until a decision is made then. Kristen had not seen the children for fifteen days. It was unusual that it took that long for that first hearing. Usually it is done the following week. It took two weeks because Judge Lash was on vacation. She knew from her experience working in Domestic Relations that it was true that she would not see the children if she refused to sign at that hearing. She knew what next steps would have to take place before that hearing could take place. It would be months. She and her lawyer, Jamie, understood that the charges would be thrown out in that next hearing if one could be scheduled. None of the charges could be considered child abuse. They were ridiculous. But Kristen and the boys could not wait for months. Kristen would submit to Harry's request. Judge Lash, in his custody trial report, applauded Harry's gracious willingness to drop his PFA. Obviously Judge Lash never read Harry's charges when he first signed the PFA or at the hearing.

STEP 7. You must secure the marital residence. This is your biggest bargaining point for achieving success in keeping "temporary primary" and eventually "primarily" custody of the children. This should be done before the custody evaluation. The custody evaluator would be reluctant to take children from the only home they had known. It can often be done with a little bit of money. Your spouse will be desperate for money for rent. You could offer to pay rent for a year. You can easily convince your spouse that she would not get that much money for the house because there is little or no equity left. Harry had taken equity out of the house with his loan in March. Kristen did not know how much equity was left. Harry convinced her there was little. Kristen knew she could not keep up with the expenses of a house. She took the $10,000 he offered to give her for rent. She agreed to sign over the rights to the house.

STEP 8. You must file a personal PFA against your wife before she does that to you. This should be done before the custody evaluation. The one to file the first PFA is usually considered to be the innocent party because no accusations up to that time were made against that party by the other. The accused party will be put on the defensive making it difficult to file accusations against you. So file first. Harry did. I called it the "tape recorder" incident. That was when Harry dialed 911. Harry admitted in court dialing 911 at other times. Harry would make up more false accusations against Kristen. Once that first lie concerning abuse by your spouse is accomplished, it is easier to follow with more accusations. Always keep in mind that "perjury" is rarely considered in court. If that is true in court, you can certainly have confidence to lie in every other situation.

STEP 9. You must prepare for the evaluator. Everything you have done to this point has been preparation for the evaluation. If you win the recommendation of primary in the evaluation, you are almost guaranteed to win primary in court. Prepare many lies from partial truths. If you are interviewed first, your spouse will hear those lies and become very angry. She will appear to be very emotional. If you are not interviewed first, in some cases your spouse will not have the chance to refute your accusations. If she is given the chance to hear your lies after your testimony, it will be difficult for her to refute those lies. They will not believe her because she did not bring up those items in her interview.

You have the advantage in that your spouse will go into the evaluation telling the truth and expecting you to tell the truth. You also have the advantage in the fact that you had filed those official PFA's of her abusing the children and you. Harry lied throughout the first evaluation. Kristen did get emotional when hearing Harry's lies. Dr. Thomas did use the fact that she got emotional against her. However, Dr. Thomas in that first evaluation recommended 50/50. It is too bad that Harry was not in his presence when he heard the 50/50 verdict. I am sure Harry would have gotten emotional. Wait! Dr. Thomas reported that Harry did "tear" up when he talked about the safety of the children. Harry was using the "fallacy of emotion", just another little trick.

STEP 10. If your goal of primary custody is not reached through the evaluation process, you will have to use CYS, Children and Youth Services. Through them you will file a PSR, Petition for Special Relief, to accuse your spouse of child abuse. Again, if you make the first accusation with CYS, they will be on your side until you achieve your goal. They will not be willing to admit they made a mistake. Of course, you have to be willing to use your children to accomplish the next step. Younger children frequently get bumps and bruises. It is also easier to get them to go along with a good story. There are books from which you can learn techniques to control what your child may say. You have to be patient and wait for the right opportunity. You have an advantage because you started a history of abuse with the first PFA.

The opportunity came. I called it the "blue bowl" incident. Harry went to CYS. Harry took Bryce to the doctor. The doctor said the bump did not satisfy the description for a "founded" claim of child abuse. Harry's attorney, Jeffrey Karver, gave the directive to both parties to speak to the other before going to an authority about a bump, bruise, or whatever. He did not succeed in arriving at a "founded" verdict on the first try. But he did start the process which could ultimately lead to that verdict because of a "pattern of abuse."

STEP 11. If the first claim of child abuse is called "unfounded", then repeat STEP 10. Repeat STEP 10 until you receive a verdict of "founded" for an indicated charge of child abuse. Harry only needed one more event. I called it the "squirty bottle" incident. The incident occurred in June of 2007. The "blue bowl" incident had occurred in March of 2007. Kristen received the verdict of "founded" of indicated child abuse. The "pattern of abuse" brought about that verdict. Harry made sure he got to talk to the doctor about the previous bump on the head.

STEP 12. Once a verdict of "founded" is reached, you will insist that your spouse be sentenced to 24 hour supervised visitation. If you have established good rapport with CYS, this can be easily accomplished. With proper preparation, your spouse can be tricked into agreeing to these conditions. Generally, the more PSR's you were able to file against your spouse, the easier it will be to get your spouse to agree to the 24 hour stipulation. Many will give up the battle at this point and agree to give you primary. They realize the impossibility of finding supervisors, especially since they have 50/50. If they do agree to 24 hour supervision, then have your private eye ready. This is a good time to entrap your spouse by finding a time when your spouse has the children and no approved supervisor. CYS will have to approve the supervisors. You may try to disapprove of her choices. Kristen signed the agreement with CYS to be under 24 hour supervised visitation in July of 2007.

It had taken Harry less than a year from filing the first PFA to complete STEP 12 of the master plan. At the first expungement hearing held nearly a year later, Kristen was asked, by the administrative law judge, why she signed the paper agreeing to the 24 hour supervised visitation. She told him that Bill Clemons with CYS told her that was the only way she could still have children. She was then told that the 24 hour supervision was only used in extreme cases. It was meant to be a voluntary agreement by the defendant if they realized they can not control themselves and understand that they need help when they are with the child they abused. Harry must have had good rapport with CYS or Bill Clemons. Obviously, we did not. Our rapport problem probably arose from our visit to CYS concerning the "blue bowl" incident. CYS never did get back to us as they said would, but they did get back at us.

Despite the sentence, Kristen would complete the "mission impossible." The 24 hour supervised visitation ended in October of

2007. The 50/50 custody agreement remained intact. The agreement at that time was still based on the custody evaluator's recommendation from the first custody evaluation. Jeffrey Karver was still Harry's lawyer, but that would change in three months. Mark Zimmer, who I believe to be Guillermo's choice for Harry, would take over. Harry continued the battle for primary custody. There were more "dirty tactics" to use. The war was not over. Harry just changed generals. Or did he? The real mastermind was Guillermo Jalil.

Chapter 43 - Self-fulfilled Prophecy

Many Will Know

I wrote a letter to the Honorable Judge Scott Lash. In court he said he did not read it. He was, however, without reading it, able to tell me my letter was improper. He was also able to determine with out reading the letter that he should give it to attorneys, Mark Zimmer and Ms. Jamie Dautrich. Who had the original and who, the copy? Mark Zimmer, in turn, sends my letter to my church. Along with my letter he gives the added information that there is a possibility of a suit of the church because I wrote the letter on church letterhead. My letter finds its way to the law office of John Roland which handles the legal business of the church. How many in that office learned of the existence of my letter? A few weeks before, Mary Lynne and I had spoken to a member of that law office about the possibility of suing Harry Hall. Jonathan Phillips said at that time that we had no case. He said, however, that he would do our will as requested. A week after I wrote my letter to the judge, he said in a letter that he could not do our will due to "conflict of interest." What conflict of interest? Another person from that law office would be with the pastor, church secretary, and me to notify me that I was being suspended without pay because of the intended suit of the church. I would learn from the trial transcript that others had been involved in the discussion of the intended suit of the church. My letter, thanks to the efforts of Judge Lash and attorney Mark Zimmer, was becoming far from remaining a secret.

Now I would have to write a letter to Mark Zimmer. I said that I had not intended for anyone in my church to know of that letter. In my letter to Mark I wrote, "Unfortunately, now many will learn of its contents." I had become a prophet. I predicted that many would learn of the contents of my letter to the judge.

I had not planned to participate in the fulfilling of my own prophecy. I had not spoken to anyone else in the church of my letter up until the trial and learning of the results. My letter was not offered as an exhibit for the trial. It would, however, be brought up. First, Mark Zimmer questioned Kristen about my letter in cross examination. Jamie objected, but Judge Lash overruled. Later in the trial there was a discussion between Mark, Jamie and Judge Lash concerning the attempted suit of the church because of my letter. Mark Zimmer had to admit the attempt. He also admitted that the suit was dropped because they could see that the church was not involved. He also admitted that my resigning from my position encouraged them to drop the suit. The only quote used from my letter in the trial would be, "If only Harry was as good as a dog." It was attorney, Mark Zimmer, who quoted those words. They became part of the court record. Did Judge Lash know Mark Zimmer was going to quote those words? Was that the first time Judge Lash learned of the existence of those words? Judge Lash and Mark Zimmer had become "full" participants in the fulfillment of my prophecy. It was time for me to become a "full" participant.

Organizations send out newsletters. Many individuals involved in Christian ministry send out newsletters to people that support them financially and in their prayers. A growing trend is for individuals, once a year, to send a newsletter concerning their family to relatives and friends. We had received what I call "family newsletters" but had never written or sent a "family newsletter." With relatives, work, our involvement in Christian Ministry, and other organizations we had many acquaintances. A large number of these we would consider more than acquaintances. What do I mean? I am talking about those people to whom you would consider answering with the truth the question,

"How is it going?" These are the people to whom I would consider sending a "family newsletter" with news that was "not so good."

I had to decide to whom I would send my "family newsletter." One of the organizations I remained with for the two years before the trial was the Gideons International. The original Gideon had his army, through a series of tests, whittled from tens of thousands to three hundred. I would have to do something similar. One group that would receive my letter would be members of the brass ensemble which I first organized more than ten years before the custody trial. Some of those brass ensemble members were also Gideons. During those years more than 200 players representing more than 50 churches had performed at some time with the group. At the time of the trial I had 80 active members on my mailing list. My letters would be sent to those active members only a day after what I suspected might be the group's last performance. The performance was for a "pet blessing" held on October 12, 2008. Some pets blessed were dogs. All of them were good dogs. If only Harry was as good as one of them. The following are excerpts from that letter addressed to BRASS IN PRAISE members and friends of BIP

>I thank you for all the "praise" you have given these past ten years. You do not realize, however, how much this has meant to me these past two years. I've had people come to me after concerts saying their "spirit" was down, but while at the concert they had been "lifted" up. That happens to me every concert. Reading the enclosed letters and articles you will understand.

>I know that everyone has "heartaches" and even "doubts" at sometime. Some of these we are not willing to share. I believe the greatest relief we can experience thru these is by giving God our "praise." So again I thank you for your "praise" to God.

>As far as the future of BRASS IN PRAISE is concerned, I do not know. I live by faith, but even then I must recognize reality. I will wait on the Lord for direction.

Another group I had to answer to would be coworkers and friends at FPC. Of course many of those coworkers were also parents of the children. Members of the church staff were not informed of the reasons I had resigned so suddenly. Then, there were the members of "Session" who attended the meeting where I first tried to resign. I had promised them I would remain as CMD as long as they still wanted me. Why did I go back on my promise? For four months my letter to the judge on church letterhead was a well kept secret. The following are excerpts written to those at FPC on October 21, 2008 addressed to friends at FPC. I did not have to send a letter to Dr. Keevil. He knew about my letter. He was there when I was suspended. He received my resignation.

> I thank you for the warm welcome back many of you have given us these past weeks. We have been attending our previous home church, WLUM. It now works out that we can attend both services. I wish I could end this letter here. I can't. The enclosed letters and articles will explain to some degree.
>
> On some occasions you may have seen my daughter attend church with us. She was with us a few weeks ago. You, however, have never seen her there with her boys, now ages 5 and 6. When I started the job in 2007, my daughter was on a 24 hour supervised visitation provision because of a false charge of child abuse. She still is under the false charge. Because of that she was not able to help me with Bible School or any other activity involving children. Therefore, she has not brought them to church. She has had 50/50 custody, but now her husband has been awarded primary custody.
>
> Again thank you for allowing me to be a teacher of your children, God's children. We do need your support and prayers.

To illustrate the effectiveness of the secrecy, I include here excerpts from a letter of a member of the church who was not at the "Session" meeting where I tried to resign.

Today we opened the letter from Dr. Keevil advising us of your resignation as Director of Children's Ministry. We are very sad to get the news because we both felt you were a valuable and effective member of our growing and inspiring staff. We so send along our thanks for the great lift you gave our Children's program. And, we do send along our prayers and blessings that you will find a position somewhere else which will be more gratifying. Will you please send us a list of your "Brass in Praise" performances for 2008? We will anticipate seeing you both at future events.

I guess they may not be as good at prophecy. Would I get a good recommendation from FPC for another CMD position? Ha, and Sarah laughed? What future BIP event? I would send them the letter I had sent to PFC friends which was after the last BIP performance. But, another person learned of the contents of my letter as I predicted.

There would be one other group to whom I would send my "family newsletter". That would be co-participants, co-workers, and friends at WLUM. Being active members for twenty years, many relationships had been formed. My wife and I had participated in many groups involving instrumental and vocal music. I was involved in teaching Sunday school to youth and adults. To whom shall I send? Sixteen of the 45 summer Bible and Sports Schools I directed were at WLUM. I would start my mailing list with those who participated with me in that ministry. They would be especially interested in knowing that I was said to be "toxic" to children. Below is an excerpt from my letter to friends at WLUM written October 23, 2008.

I thank you for the warm welcome back many of you have given us the past weeks. On leaving, I never got to thank you for all the opportunities my family and I had to serve the Lord with you at WLUM. I wish I could end this letter here. I can't. The enclosed letters and articles will explain to some degree the sojourn we have been on these past two years. The remainder of this letter is what I just wrote to our friends and former co-workers in Children's Ministry as FPC.

The letters to each of the three groups above contained the following paragraph.

> I know everyone has "heartaches" and even "doubts" at sometime. Some of these we are not willing to share. I believe God has a purpose for every trial. Sometimes it is hard to see. Maybe for me and my family it is that we humble ourselves and be willing to share our burden with others. Maybe there is a greater purpose. Perhaps we are to use our experience to fight against the "injustices" in our court system where it pertains to "false child abuse accusations." It will take a book to fully describe our situation. I have a good start. I leave you one last thought. For our Children's Christmas Program last year at First Pres I wrote these words with music. "Now every birth is special, whether a girl or boy. God created each special to bring to all great joy!" These words were inspired by my thoughts of Kristen's adopted autistic Asperger's son, Bryce. Now I am accused of not giving "unconditional love" to Bryce.

I had somehow whittled my potential mailing list from a thousand to one hundred fifty. I said in each newsletter that I had included letters and articles with the cover letter. One letter included was my letter to Judge Lash. The other letter was that sent to Mark Zimmer. Have I reached the category of "many" in the number of people that now know the contents of the letter? Have I made another prediction? Did I prophesy that I would write a book? I also included a general letter explaining the results of the custody trial. Excerpts from that letter addressed to friends follows:

> The results are in. Some of you know of the custody battle my daughter, wife, and I have been in the past two years for my daughter's sons. We lost. Primary

custody had been given to our daughter's estranged husband.

The result of the order is that Harry will have the children from Sunday 6 pm to Friday 6 pm. Kristen will have the children for three weekends each month. This is for the school year. In the summer, however, the abusive Kristen and her abusive parents will have the boys full time except for two weekends each month and a week for Harry's vacation. The result is that Harry will no longer pay the $600 per month child support he had under 50/50 custody. Kristen does not, has not, and will not receive alimony payments from Harry. Because of false child abuse charges she cannot use her college degree or experience to get a higher paying job. How do you survive when your rent and income are equal?

The basic arguments by the judge are against Kristen, my wife, and I because we are included as the problem. There are four. First, there is disparity in our favoritism in our love of Harry III compared to Bryce. How does Judge Lash know that? How does Harry? There is disparity in this case. It is in what we have done for the boys compared to Harry.

Next, Harry shows unconditional love to the boys and we don't. How would Judge Lash know? How has Harry shown that? Is it in his destroying their mother? Mary Lynne said on the witness stand that we consider all children "God's" and not "ours." We love both as He loved us. It has been my life's work so show Christ's love to children, even more so to Bryce. Harry has used the boys for revenge.

Third, Kristen was fidgety during Harry's testimony. Therefore, the three of us have anger issues. Yes, we do have anger issues. We hate "injustice" and "abuse."

Last, Kristen makes poor choices in men. I say amen! Indeed, she chose Harry, the worst choice. None of Kristen's other choices hurt the boys. Harry's twenty plus accomplices have.

That's it. I will be writing an article about the trial and the judge's orders. Kristen has been ordered to go to psychotherapy and family counseling. Again, she has to pay high fees for these services. Kristen's lawyer was quite upset over the verdict. She said it was like the judge was not there for Kristen's testimony. In his report, the judge said I got to testify. I did swear in.

Enclosed is my letter to the judge in April of 2008. It still holds true, only more so. It is the best synopsis of the situation. Thank you for reading these letters.

There were two articles enclosed. One was the article concerning the Easter holiday PSR. The other article was described and introduced by the ADDENDUM.

ADDENDUM: I thought the enclosed would be enough, but Harry is still at it. At the present I have list of 35 articles and/or letters I have written to explain our situation. This latest escapade by Harry clearly verifies what I wrote in my letter "Dear Friends." It describes clearly in Harry's statements, his lawyer's statements, and the judge's that their "vendetta" is not just against Kristen, but it is also against my wife and I. Again it includes lies made by Harry, his lawyer, and the judge that can clearly be proved. It includes a direct lie of another incident Harry reported.

The report referred to is THE PLAINTIFF'S (HARRY HALL) ANSWER TO DEFENDANT'S (KRISTEN) REQUEST FOR RECONSIDERATION OF ORDER OF SEPTEMBER 5, 2008.

My article concerning the above report was enclosed with my "family newsletter." I predict that this article will become important in the future. Will that be considered a self fulfilled prophecy? Is self fulfilled prophecy, prophecy?

It seems to me Judges are overly concerned about precedent. I think they should be more concerned about truth. Anyway, is there precedent for self fulfilled prophecy? Jesus said, "Destroy this Temple and in three days I will raise it up." He also told some people that he would not show another sign except the sign of Jonah. Was that a self fulfilled prophecy? I do not know if Kristen will be resurrected from this death caused by—.

CHAPTER 44 - THE INFORMER

News Account of a Tip

In the October 17, 2008, edition of the Reading Eagle the following headline appeared: "Tip Leads to Probe of Drug Making." It stated that a tip from an informant led to the investigation into a large methamphetamine manufacturing operation in southeastern Pennsylvania. It also stated that the investigation began in June of 2007. A Berks County detective said, "We've been receiving information about Mike Spadafora for years." So Mike Spadafora was indeed involved with illegal drug activity. Or was he? Maybe I should read the whole article. After all, my daughter, my wife, and I were convicted of not giving "unconditional love."

For my freshman English composition class at KSC in 1963 I had to write a term paper. My term paper concerned the reliability of newspaper accounts as documents of history. I will let you guess my conclusion. I only remember one newspaper article that I wrote about in my term paper. I kept the clipping for many years. The story tells of a bat, mammal not wood, flying around in the high school auditorium before a band concert. The story concludes with the bat being trapped in a tuba case. It made a cute story, but it was not the truth. I was an eyewitness to the "bat" story which occurred before the Regional Band Concert at Troy, Pennsylvania in February of 1962. The lady that wrote the story was my host for that weekend in Troy. The event happened Friday night, and the story was in the Saturday morning local newspaper. What really happened? The bat landed on the ceiling in the middle of the auditorium. A large ladder was brought into the auditorium. It was not to replace a light bulb. The janitor went up the ladder and with the end of the broomstick, unceremoniously, squashed the bat to the ceiling. Yogh! I think I liked the fictitious story better.

Besides Mike Spadafora, three other suspects were included in the raid. The "tip" article goes on to state that county detectives and federal Drug Enforcement Administration officers joined in the raids of the suspect's homes in August. So, it may have been actual DEA agents that interviewed Kristen on August 19. Maybe the county detective made a mistake when he said they had been investigating Mike since June 2007. Maybe he meant 2008. Maybe the informer was Guillermo Jalil via Harry Hall, II. Harry testified on August 26, 2008 that Guillermo went to the Exeter Police with the knowledge that Mike Spadafora was in the illegal drug business. Harry said in court that it was Rob Chalmers that told him Mike was in the drug business. So what? Guillermo's knowledge came from Harry whose knowledge came from Rob. Therefore the informer was really Rob. How did Rob have knowledge of Mike Spadafora's illegal drug business? Rob's knowledge is based on a statement from Kristen. Rob asked Kristen how she could afford living at the farm. Kristen, without hesitation, said she was able to survive financially because Mike Spadafora gave her money out of the "goodness of his heart." She also told Rob that Mike Spadafora said he earned his money with a vending business, not drugs. Also, Kristen had told Rob that Mike had once asked her if he could borrow her car to collect money from some gaming machines. She said no. Mike did not ask again. When Rob became the jilted ex-fiancee, he turned that statement into one that said Mike used her car for selling drugs. Rob wrote that on the Easter Holiday PSR. That was in March of 2008. At least we know that Harry testified on the stand that it was Rob that made that "car" statement. Rob, however, was not in court to testify to that statement. Did Rob really know about Mike? Or was it a guess?

Two of the other three suspects were a husband and wife. In one of their vehicles was found 170 grams of methamphetamine in a plastic container. On the other suspect's property there was found a meth lab built in a trailer-size shipping container. It had a fully functional lab and all the tools necessary to produce a significant amount of methamphetamine. The officials said that the operation of that lab was shut down before the suspect could produce and distribute any meth. The investigation led to a dismantled lab in Carbon County and to 68 other firearms, including several automatic weapons and handguns equipped with silencers. Among other puzzling items in the article was the preceding sentence. No connection is made between the suspects and the items. The only relationship shown of the four suspects is the husband and wife team. This was not a gang of four individuals working together.

The raid on the husband and wife team was on August 13. The man with the meth lab was raided later. The article does not say it was on the same day. The article goes on to state that agents later raided Spadafora's 13 acre property valued at $500,000. On his property they found a life-size cut out of a police target that had been used for target practice and three rifles. Here comes the "bat" story. Harry said on the stand, "The man is a bad dude." If the man is a bad dude, then why does he not have an automatic weapon or even a handgun for protection? How many hunters have at least three rifles? Kristen knew Mike was a hunter. When the article said the cutout was for target practice, I envisioned a target with many holes all over it. A person angry with a policeman would have enjoyed shooting up the target in many places. A picture of the target was on the next page of the newspaper. It only had a hole where the heart would be. The target appeared to be made of cardboard and yet in very good condition. It supposedly had been gathered up in August and put on display for the picture shoot for that October news article. I would say that was only the second time the target was shot at. Where could Mike have gotten the target? The news article offers no answer. I do not believe Mike shot at the target either time. Mike had no previous record. Why would he be angry with the police? He needed the police for protection as he gathered his money from the gambling machines in the city. He had no beef with the police. Would the police department have such a life-size cutout? Did anyone figure out what policeman was pictured? Does anyone know how to do detective work? I know a person that has lots of influence with police, federal agencies, drug enforcement officials, etc. His name is Guillermo Jalil. I smell a "bat." Harry has a rifle.

Also discovered at the property were meth-making material in the kitchen and a manual titled: YOUR NO NONONSE GUIDE FOR MAKING METH, authored by a "Dr. Practical". I find this hilarious. Later in the article the investigators would say that it appeared Spadafora had been making meth for as long as two decades. Maybe they came to that conclusion because the manual was 20 years old. If Mike had been making meth for 20 years, why does he still need a manual? Dah! Why is the meth-making material lying around in the kitchen? Why do they not mention finding any finished product on the property or his person? There is no mention of Mike selling meth to an informant. That is the most common way to entrap a drug dealer to get a conviction. On the second page of the article it states that Mike was only charged with making the drug. They never mentioned anyone that sold drugs for him. I do not believe that Mike cooks anything. He goes out to eat usually accompanied by a woman, much to the dismay of his wife. I admit that he took my daughter to lunch several times at the hospital and two or three times to dinner elsewhere. I wonder if Guillermo still has his manual on making meth. He may have used it in some of his talks concerning drugs and juveniles. Maybe it is missing. Kristen thought that Billy, Harry's nephew, was in prison for making "meth" at the time of Harry's father's death. He probably isn't missing his manual in prison. Just speculating?

One other thing found in the home of Mike Spadafora was $53,105 in cash. Again I say, "So what!" On one occasion my daughter, still being suspicious, asked Mike how he could afford to give her the money. He said wait. Less than twenty minutes later he came back to the hospital and took her to lunch. He pulled out a wad of twenties that smelled like a bar. No, I did not mean a bear. Kristen has trouble with the smell of cigarette smoke. For those uninformed, including myself, the gaming machines take twenty dollar bills. Kristen did not question Mike about the money again.

It was said in the article that State Attorney General, Tom Corbett, smiled during the press conference when he read an excerpt from the manual. It said that meth manufacturers working full time should be able to outsmart law enforcement officers, who the manual said are mostly dumb. To that Tom Corbett said, "If they want to underestimate us, that's fine." Then why is it that they did not catch Mike making meth when he, supposedly, had been making it for twenty years? Now that is funny.

Seriously, another good thought can be gotten from the subtitle of the "Tip" article. It reads as follows: "Suspect's mother disputes accusations against her son, saying she saw nothing amiss when she babysat her grandchildren." I saw nothing amiss when I babysat my grandchildren. Why don't people respect and accept the testimony of grandparents? Anyway, it was said in the article that Mike Spadafora's mother lives elsewhere in Berks but was at the house Thursday. Maybe the meth ingredients found in the kitchen were her prescriptions. She said she was shocked by Corbett's allegations. She also said her son could not have been involved in such an operation. "My grandchildren live here," she said. "I'm here all the time. There's nothing unusual. There couldn't be anything like that going on. I babysat here." Grandma may cook in the kitchen, but Mike would not. I believe grandma.

The "Tip" article was from page 2. The headline on page 1 is as follows: "Rifle Target at Meth Lab is Cutout of Police Officer." This headline does not agree with that article on page 2. The rifle target was supposedly found at Mike Spadafora's house. The meth lab was at another suspect's house. No meth lab was found at Spadafora's. Grandma would have found it. I conclude that this article is not reliable as a document history. It should be used to collect "bat" droppings.

The page one article states that Mike's operation netted $9,000,000. Who needs a gaming business? Where do they come up with that exorbitant amount? Start with 9,000,000 and divide by 20. Mike's supposed operation was in business for twenty years. So Mike started his business when he was 21 years old. Divide the answer by 12, the number of months in a year. Your answer is $37,500. At $37,500 a month, in twenty years you will come up with a total of $9,000,000. They found $53,105 of cash in the home of Mike Spadafora. That must be the amount of cash he is pulling in from his drug trade per month. Would not some of that money be from his vending business? In the early years he was making much less, so it all averages out. Questions anyone? I have two. Does the money smell like a bar? When does grandma, the babysitter, get to cook in the kitchen? Mike would have been hogging up the cooking time making all that "meth."

Talking about the cardboard cutout target, state Attorney General Corbett stated, "This is a very disturbing picture. I've gone to two funerals now in the last month for police officers killed in the city of Philadelphia." The article states further, Corbett looked again at the cutout next to him and stated simply, "they aimed at the heart." I do not believe a cardboard cutout equates to a policeman. Anyway, what connection does a cardboard cutout have with making meth? There is a statement Corbett makes that is connected with meth. He says there is a large demand for meth. He says, "Somebody's going to try to take this guy's place." Harry, do you know anyone that could take his place?

The name for the sting operation between Federal, state, and Berks County authorities was "Operation Underground." It was dubbed such because Mike Spadafora produced the drug in liquid form and put it in small plastic pipes that he buried on his and relatives' properties. To me it is suspicious that the description in the newspaper accounts of the court records of the items that authorities seized does not include any of those small plastic pipes. Did they find one, a hundred? Maybe it is assumed there are such pipes because that is what the manual tells you to do. Therefore, there is no need to look for such pipes. Why didn't the dog find them? If buried, how are the spots marked so the maker can find them again? Maybe Harry can find them since he is almost as good as a dog.

The next day October 18, 2008, another article appeared with the headline, "Goal is no Drug Money for bail." The bail set for Mike Spadafora was set for $1,000,000. The bail for the other co-defendants was set at $250,000 each. Upon reading the article, I did not understand why the other defendants were called co-defendants. Again, no connection was made between the four. The article goes on to state that Mike ran a large scale meth lab. And this was ascertained from a few chemicals and a how to manual. Was it a bathroom scale? The three were able to make bail. A hearing would be scheduled to make sure that Mike would not use illegal gains, those acquired from selling drugs, to obtain bail. Now wait a minute. It was said the day before that he was arrested for making drugs not selling drugs. At that time, Mike did not make bail. Knowing the amount of time that would be required to run a vending business as Mike's, I don't believe he had the time to make meth. He also took time out to play Santa Clause and Michael the Christmas Angel.

"Speculate: to meditate on, to ponder a subject, to reflect on, to review something casually, often inconclusively." I sound like the robot, "Johnny Five." Often when teaching math, I was heard to say in my robot voice, "Number five is alive." I am sure some of my more than five thousand math students from the past remember. The news articles above contain speculation. May I speculate? I will anyway. Speculation is based on fact. It does, however, go beyond fact. I've said that about faith. Faith should be based on fact. However, what makes it faith is the fact that you go beyond. The scriptures state, "Without faith it is impossible to please Him."

In previous chapters I've stated information from the internet about informer Guillermo Jalil. The Reading Eagle also contains information concerning Jalil. The following is from the edition dated February 16, 1996:

> Guillermo D. Jalil, local author of "Street-Wise Drug Prevention: A Realistic Approach & Intervention in Adolescent Drug Use," will promote the book Feb. 23 to 25 at the Fairgrounds Square Mall, Muhlenberg Township.

The September 27, 1999 edition contains the headline, "Fired Probation Officer Sues Over Termination." The article contains the following statements:

> A former Berks County juvenile probation officer has filed a lawsuit in U.S. District Court in Philadelphia, accusing county officials of improperly firing him because of alleged complaints he was making about the office.
>
> Guillermo Jalil also alleged in the lawsuit county officials fired him March 10 because he is Latino. Jalil is seeking $900,000 in damages.
>
> Jalil alleged in the suit his supervisors discriminated against him by restricting him from speaking to groups

about a book he wrote, and by not allowing him to enter a graduate degree program. In addition, the suit alleges Jalil' supervisors mistreated him after learning that Jalil filed a discrimination complaint against the office with the Equal Opportunity Employment Commission and complained to county officials about the office.

The article goes on to name specific individuals in the suit. Included were the chief juvenile probation officer, assistant juvenile probation officers, court administrator, personnel director, President Judge, and the Judge of the juvenile court.

Those are the facts. I do not know the results of the suit. From the custody trial, I know Guillermo was an informer against Mike Spadafora. At least, that was what Harry said in court. I wonder if Harry informed Guillermo that his name was brought up in the custody trial. I speculate that Guillermo, in helping Harry win over Kristen and her parents, would gain a measure of revenge over the whole family court system of Berks County. The revenge would be much sweeter knowing that the "dirty tactics" he had written in his second book, ASSET PROTECTION FROM DIVORCE, had been used to achieve the victory. Those tactics were learned by himself in the family law system of Berks County. While speculating, could we consider blackmail? Could Jalil have provided more than just information to authorities investigating Mike Spadafora? Could Jalil have a pen name, Dr. Practical? I do not believe, however, that Guillermo considered the possibility that Kristen's father would write about him.

Since I speculated about Guillermo, I might-as-well speculate about Harry Hall, II. Harry admitted to the custody evaluator, Dr. Peter Thomas, that he used marijuana for six months in 1986. Why did he say that? Was he thinking that would make him sound like a "cool dude" to the evaluator? Harry knows about drugs. Kristen believed that his nephew Billy was in jail for making "meth" at the time Harry filed the first PFA. Billy did live with Harry before Kristen moved in with Harry. Harry is a member of the pipe fitters union. On occasion he worked in drug companies installing pipes used for making drugs. The meth is stored in liquid form in small pipes. Near the time of the custody trial, Harry installed some type of outdoor cooker for the boys to cook hot dogs over a wood fire. He also put a wood stove in the middle of the breakfast nook. I thought he had a good heating system in the home. It has radiant heat with pipes in the cement floor in the basement and in the ceiling to heat the floor above. Why a wood stove? The boys said he used the stove to dry their underwear. They did not have to tell us, the nose knew. I wonder what else he cooked on the stove. Mike Spadafora said to Kristen that he and Judge Lash were "buddies." State Attorney, Tom Corbett, stated that a lot of meth users would be looking for a new source. I know nothing about cooking "meth." I should get Dr. Practical's manual. I do know speculation.

CHAPTER 45 - CONTRASTS IN EMPATHY

A Good Samaritan Story

I did not send my "letter to friends" to Dr. Keevil, my pastor at FPC. He knew first hand of my letter to Judge Lash on church letterhead. He was in the room when I was notified of my suspension without pay. He sent emails to those in the church that needed to know of my resignation as CMD. However, he did not inform them of the intended suit of the church by Harry Hall, II. At that time, I was alright with that fact. I knew, however, that some day the truth of my indiscretion, writing on church letterhead, would have to be made known. The truth of why I resigned the second time would have to be made known. Coincidently, April 22, 2008, was the date Pastor Keevil sent out notification of my resignation and Dr. Thomas sent out his recommendation that Harry receive primary custody. Dr. Thomas had not known before writing the recommendation that I had resigned because of Harry's intended suit of the church. However, he did know enough to call Harry's act "egregious."

Was I wrong in sending my letter to Judge Lash? Was I wrong in writing the letter on church letterhead? When my wife tells someone about my letter, they always seem to gasp and exclaim, "He should have never written on church letterhead!" That reaction does not bother me. It bothers me that they did not care to know the content of the letter. Dr. Keevil read the letter. He said it was a good letter. I had hoped he would say it was an "epistle," that is, by definition, an eloquent letter. Notice, I said epistle with a small case "e." So far in my book I would have the "epistle to Judge Lash," the "epistle to Mark Zimmer," the "epistle to the Church in Reading," the "epistle to the Church in West Lawn," and the "epistle to members of Brass in Praise scattered throughout Berks County and beyond." There was also the epistle never sent. That epistle was to Harry called, "Abuse of Christianity." There is the need for many more epistles.

I knew some day I would have to speak to Dr. Keevil in person. That conversation would have to take place after the results of the custody trial of August 26 were made known. The results were made known ten days after the trial. We had missed not attending worship at FPC for those five months. We liked every aspect of worship. Mostly, we missed the preaching of Dr. Keevil. I missed the depth of his teaching. Mary Lynne missed his "Welsh" accent. After receiving the results of the trial we started attending again. We shook hands with our pastor after the services. After several months, I was able to arrange a meeting with Dr. Keevil.

By this time we had formulated a plan for the direction we would take in achieving some order of justice. Attorney Mark Zimmer, when I was on the stand, said that he was the one responsible for sending my letter to the church, not Harry. He admitted attempting to sue the church. He admitted that the attempted suit was dropped because I resigned. When I was on the stand he accused me of writing things in my letter that were not there. I believed we had a case for a suit against Mr. Zimmer, defamation of character and loss of income. My letter to Judge Lash was not to Mark. It was not about Mark. I did send a letter to Mark. That was his to do with what he pleased. What right did he have to send my letter to Judge Lash to my church? Alright, maybe he did have a right. It was on church letterhead. But, what was his purpose?

I did not think I needed a long period of time for my meeting with Dr. Keevil. I could give him much information about the injustice that had transpired the past two years. However, that was not my intention. I only wanted to ask two questions. First, why was I not informed that the intended suit of the church had been dropped? I had called the church several times that summer and left messages asking the pastor to call me. The day of the suspension I asked to be updated on the progress of the suit. I was never called. Second, I was going to ask if I could have a copy of the letter from Mark Zimmer that I presumed accompanied my letter to Judge Lash. Once I had that and the trial transcript, I would be on my way to find a lawyer.

We set the meeting for the Peanut Bar. It is a legitimate restaurant, not a bar in the shape of a peanut. It is located about halfway between FPC on 5th Street and RACC on 2nd Street. I had a math class scheduled for noon and could park at my spot at RACC. I would have to leave our meeting by at least 11:45. I suggested the place. My fellow parishioners from the first twenty years of my life would have been appalled. That denomination at one time was called Mennonite Brethren in Christ. Drinking an "alcoholic" beverage, along with "dancing," was one of the deadly sins. Jesus changed the water into grape juice. Anyway, I knew it would be okay with Dr. Keevil to meet me there. After all, he had taken the church staff there for lunch on one occasion. We ordered drinks first. I ordered something bubbly, either diet soda or ginger ale. I knew something was terribly wrong the Welshman did not order a beer.

I did get to ask my two questions. For most of the remaining time I was told to eat my hamburger. He would do the talking. I first asked why I had not been informed that the suit was dropped. He claimed he told me that John Roland said the suit would probably be dropped. That never happened. If I was told that, I would not have run to the church on the day of the trial to find out about the progress of the suit. I would not have left phone messages at the church asking to be called. Also, why didn't John Roland contact me? John Roland's office handled the legal affairs of the church. John was an important person in volunteer functions and boards of FPA. Also, it was someone from his law office that announced the recommendation that I be suspended without pay. I wondered who actually suggested the recommendation. Was it Dr. Keevil or John Roland? At the time it did not matter to me who made it. Actually, from their vantage point, I agreed with it. But, what would I have done if I was the pastor? Ask me.

It is not like I was not acquainted with John Roland. It was his law office that I went to before Easter of 2008 to find a lawyer to help in a suit of Harry Hall. John and I literally ran into each other many times from 1980 to 1995. However, I can not remember many times that we were on the same side. I do remember one time there was blood. I have to admit I probably would have been called for blocking. In high school I fouled out in most of my games. I am 5 feet 11 inches tall. My claim to fame was holding Kutztown High School's all state center, 6 foot 5 inch Jim Snook, to seven points. I would liked to have had 6 foot 4 inch John Roland on my team in those recreational basketball games. The problem was that he and I were often two of the players designated to choose sides. When my wife and I first attended FPC, I saw John and his wife sitting together. I pointed and said to Mary Lynne, "Remember when I came home from basketball with the cut on my eyebrow."

Besides basketball, John and I had another acquaintance in common before I came to FPC. His name was Judge Lash. I met Judge Lash two times in different places. The first time was the Gideon meeting. The second time was in 2003 at the Lincoln Plaza Hotel for a dinner meeting of the Reading Berks Conference of churches. At that dinner, I received the "City on the Hill Award." That was the meeting where Mary Lynne and I sat with Judge Lash and his wife. I attended the dinner meeting in 20004 by myself. I had to pay for the meal that time. At that meeting, John Roland was installed as the new President of the Reading Berks Conference of Churches. The new Vice President installed was Sharon Lash. She was the wife of one of the speakers. That speaker was the Honorable Judge Scott Lash.

I asked Dr. Keevil, "May I have a copy of the letter Mark Zimmer sent to you stating his intent to sue the church?" Dr. Keevil never admitted to the existence of a letter from Mark Zimmer. I was unprepared for what I heard next. It was too long a sermon to remember word for word. However, I got the message. I was told that I should not seek justice. I was warned that if I tried to seek justice, then we, my daughter, my wife, and I would lose the children completely. It sounded like a threat. I believe it was a threat. He went on to say that if he, as judge, would have read the letter, he would seek revenge on that person. Was he saying that Judge Lash was seeking revenge? Was he saying that Harry won primary because of my letter? Why would Dr. Keevil say, "Do not seek justice?" He said my letter was a good letter when he first read it. If I were judge, I would want to hear the evidence from the man who wrote the letter. Judge Lash did not want to hear my evidence?

At the time of our meeting, we still had not obtained the trial transcript. I still had not learned that my letter was previously discussed in testimony before I took the stand at the end of the day. Judge Lash had said earlier that day that once he learned it was from a church he immediately stopped reading it. Dr. Keevil's words seemed to indicate that indeed Judge Lash read my letter. He read it and believed that I was incriminating him with my words. Of course, that was not my intention.

I had to believe Dr. Keevil and John Roland were intent on acting for the good of my family. I can only speculate, but I believe I have an answer. I do not want to believe the verdict and this threat were part of a revenge scheme for a thin-skinned judge. The answer may be Mike Spadafora. Judge Lash may have told John Roland of my daughter's supposed involvement with Mike. John Roland told Dr. Keevil. Dr. Keevil thought he would be protecting me with the warning. He may have thought I knew little of Kristen's involvement with Mike. He may have thought if I pushed for justice, then Kristen's guilt would be discovered. But, I knew the Mike Spadafora story from the beginning. I call it my "Christmas Angel" story. A story is not a story unless it is told. I told it a number of times. It is one that is difficult for me to tell without "choking up" a little. At one time I told the story to Dr. Keevil. I told him how in November of 2007 Kristen was about to give up the battle for at least partial custody of the boys. She needed $1000 for rent. There was a man who brought a patient to the hospital for a procedure. He was sitting in the waiting area watching Kristen at her desk. He was impressed by her treatment of those she received at the counter. He asked if she would join him in the cafeteria for lunch when she had her break. Cut to the chase. Okay. This man became her benefactor. For five months, through his charity, he made it possible for Kristen to keep the boys on the farm. At the time, I did not tell Dr. Keevil the man's name. Doctor Keevil was touched. Maybe, Dr. Keevil heard a different story about Mike and Kristen.

I now had a third question to ask Dr. Keevil. I did not get to ask the question. I will here. What would you do if it was your daughter who was dealt with unjustly? What would you do if it was your daughter who was falsely accused of abusing her child? Would you fight for justice? What would you do if you had evidence that proved your daughter was innocent? Would you try every available means to present that evidence? What would you do if you understood that unscrupulous tactics were used in the family law system against your daughter and would be used in the future against other innocent victims? Would you do anything to try to stop the same injustice from happening to others? I believe that was more than one question. The aspect of our meeting that bothered me the most was that Dr. Keevil never asked about my daughter. He offered no help, only a threat. Where is the empathy?

Mike Spadafora was in the Reading Eagle again, the date, November 13, 2008. The headline was, "Meth-lab Suspect gets Bail Lowered." The subtitle read, "The Exeter Township father of four convinces a judge the money he'll post didn't come from criminal activity." The article goes on to say that his bail was reduced from $1,000,000 to $500,000. The reduction had been objected to by the Deputy Attorney General. He called Spadafora a high level drug dealer with connections to the Warlocks motorcycle gang. The Deputy showed no proof of Mike's connection with the Warlocks. Why were no members of that gang included with the raid on Mike? It is very interesting that the Deputy Attorney General would say, "This is a dangerous individual, not in the general street-level sales. He makes drugs." Why is that interesting? He was never accused of selling drugs. He was never caught selling drugs. Kristen was accused of allowing Mike Spadafora to use her car for the purpose of selling drugs. This article included the same facts from the October articles. The items found in his residence were the guns, chemicals, $53,105, and the life-size cardboard cutout. It should be mentioned the guns were hunting rifles. There were chemicals but no manufactured methamphetamine. At one place in the October article, it said that the life-size cutout was found at the meth-lab. The meth-lab was not found at Mike's residence.

What about the money? One item I did not mention previously. At one time Mike asked Kristen if he could buy her a new car. He said he would put it in her name. He said he would use it only once in a while when he would check and empty his gaming machines in Reading. He said he had enough cash at home to buy it then. He was thinking of a BMW. She said no. He did give her money for four new tires. They were desperately needed. Again the statement in the news article was made that Mike produced the powerful stimulant in liquid form and stored it in small plastic pipes he buried on his and relative's properties. Specific items that were recovered in the raid that day from those three separate residences were mentioned in the article. Mysteriously, there was no mention of any small plastic tubes being recovered. It still sounds like a "frame job" to me.

Mike Spadafora would make bail. Apparently, he was able to prove, to the judge's satisfaction, that the $500,000 he was using was not from the sale of drugs. The next week Kristen would have another "angelic visitation" at work. It was Mike. It was not one of those sightings were only certain people see the individual. Mike could also be seen on the surveillance camera overlooking her desk. Mike was anxious to ask Kristen one thing. He was shocked by the answer. How could Judge Lash, his buddy, award primary custody to Harry Hall? Mike told her that things would work out alright for him. He said he was framed, but would be exonerated. He said he had no dealings with the Warlocks motorcycle gang. He said he hated them as they hated him. He also learned that Kristen was in worse financial state than before. Now she was no longer receiving child support from Harry. At the time Mike was giving her $1000 a month, she was also receiving $600 a month from Harry. Mike said he would like to help. He said he would take her to lunch sometime.

The next morning, Kristen found a small envelope at her desk at work. There was a note card with $300 enclosed. Kristen recognized the smell of the money. It was from Mike. The "Christmas Angel" had struck again. On the note card were printed the words, "YOU ARE A GOOD MOM!" She would not see or hear from Mike again. I am sure Mike decided it would be dangerous for Kristen. Besides, it is rare to get more than two visits from an angel. From where did empathy come? This "good Samaritan" story will be found in the "epistle to Mike."

Chapter 46 – The Christmas Present

Discoveries from the Trial Transcript

It was December 4, 2008, my wife and I were driving into Reading to order our Christmas present to each other. It was the first time in forty-one years of marriage that we agreed to purchase a present for the both us. It was the earliest I had ever completed my Christmas shopping. Most of the Christmas shopping for others was done by Mary Lynne. My Christmas shopping usually amounted to last minute shopping for my wife. We parked in one of Reading's parking garages. The city of Reading had far less Christmas shoppers than the malls or other shopping areas in Berks County. We were surprised, however, that we had to go to 4th level of the garage to find a parking space. We went into the building. The department we needed to make our purchase was on the 2nd floor. There was no line. We proceeded to the clerk and asked for an order form. We were informed that we had to make half of the payment at that time in order to complete the purchase. We paid the $337.50. The clerk told us they were not very busy at the present. The order might possibly be ready in a week or at the most two weeks. We were delighted. We would have our Christmas present before Christmas.

It would take more than two weeks. We called on the 23rd of December to ask if our order was complete. It was. We asked if we could pick up our purchase on the 24th. They said they would be open in the morning. We went into Reading to pick up our purchase and pay the remaining $337.50. The remaining part of our payment turned out to be $504.00. Some people might complain and say, "Keep it." Then, they would ask for their down payment. We did not. We paid the additional $504.00. The clerk apologized for the additional fee stating that there was more to our order than most. The original order had stated, "the Court authorizes the court reporter to transcribe the above-mentioned proceedings as ordered by counsel for the requesting party upon receipt by the appropriate Clerk of Court of one-half payment as indicated below." We took our purchase and proceeded out the Prothonotary Office which was located on the 2nd floor of the Berks County Courthouse. Someone else knew about our "Christmas Present." The Honorable Judge Scott Lash's signature was required on our order for the trial transcript. It was there.

Originally we had planned to use the transcript for an appeal with the State Supreme Court. Upon learning from Jamie that the fee would be$5000 up front, we scrapped that idea. Besides the sheer enjoyment of reading the transcript, we now had two other ideas for its use. Eventually Kristen would glean the information needed for the modification trial. She was already planning to possibly represent herself at the trial. She understood all the preliminary steps that would have to be accomplished before being granted a trial. It took Harry two years to get to the point that he would have a trial to gain primary custody, his ultimate goal. It could take that long for Kristen to obtain a modification trial. The other idea was mine. I would use information from the transcript to bring a defamation of character and a loss of income suit against Attorney, Mark Zimmer. After all, he said in court the he sent my letter to the church, not Harry. He said in court that I wrote in my letter that Harry's father was an "alcoholic". I said no such thing in my letter. Before receiving the transcript, I still had not learned that my letter and the attempted suit had been brought up before I took the stand. Before I took the stand, it was instructed to both parties by the Court that no topics would be repeated. The discussion of my letter had been brought up previously. The Court allowed it to be brought up the first time. The Court allowed it to be brought up again.

I did not realize all that would be included in our "Christmas Present." I thought it would only include the words of testimony in court. I did not know it would include all the exhibits offered as evidence for the trial. There was a wealth of material, easily worth the cost, a bargain. It included both the evaluation reports by Dr. Peter Thomas. The total cost for both parties for those evaluations had been close to $5000. Harry had paid at least $4000 of that amount. The total time spent in interviews for those evaluations was about three hours. Other time was used for taking tests and having the results evaluated. I made only $4000 for teaching two math courses over a four month time period at Berks Campus that fall of 2008. That was for seventy students. May I talk about disparity? Also included were other documents by counselors, caseworkers, psychologists for Bryce, and others. I was also surprised to see the two doctor's reports from Reading Pediatrics. Reports from people from BCCYS were included. Each exhibit was like a separate Christmas present. The court transcript itself with the pages of testimony was copied so that each page of the copy contained four pages of 228 pages of the original. The pages 229-372 were copied the same size as the originals. These pages were the exhibits. There were a lot of pages.

Pages 2-3 contained the index of exhibits. There was one two page exhibit that intrigued me above all the others. The index described it as a photocopy of a letter dated April 11, 2007. That date put the writing of that letter between the "blue bowl" incident and the "squirty bottle" incident. The salutation read, "To whom it may concern." It was a glorification letter of Harry Hall, II. It was written by Nancy Unger. She had been in the courtroom with Harry's sister, Eileen, at the first hearing concerning the "stoning." She described that she had known Harry for twenty years. Her son and Harry had competed in BMX bicycle racing. So that was the name of the racing for which Harry won all those trophies. She said she knew Harry from his late teen years. I did not realize when I first read this letter that Harry said to the evaluator that he did marijuana for six months in 1986. That would put him in his late teens. Maybe Ms. Unger and her husband did the same in the 60's. I'm just speculating. Anyway, she goes on in the letter to extol the virtues of Harry Hall. One particular sentence caught my attention. She states, "The one word that comes to mind is commitment to a course of action that he believes is right – though difficult or challenging." I agree. Dr. Thomas called it being rigid. Once Harry's mind is made up you can not change it. Harry is committed to destroying Kristen as a person and a mother.

So Ms. Unger's letter was included as an exhibit by Harry and his attorney, Mark Zimmer. It is said in Court that the judge will consider all exhibits. In other words, her testimony in her letter will be considered by the judge. The words of my letter would not be considered, except for the words "as good as a dog." She writes, "Then he hit on hard times in his family with his alcoholic father and needed a place to stay for 9 months." So, who stated in a letter that Harry's father was an "alcoholic?" Nancy Unger wrote that statement. On the witness stand I was berated by Mr. Zimmer that in a letter I had called Harry's father an alcoholic. Of course, I did not state that in either my letter to Judge Lash or the letter to Mark Zimmer.

There was a statement in her letter that speaks to the lying character of Harry Hall, II. Harry would lie even to a person he would probably say is his closest friend. She writes, "He saw early on that Bryce might have some learning difficulties and took time to have him tested by the Oley Valley School District. They did indeed find some problems in learning and Bryce and Harry were given guidance and help in dealing with those problems." Kristen noticed problems early on. Harry denied them and blamed Kristen on poor parenting. Kristen made arrangements with BCIU before he started in the Oley Valley School District. Bryce had special classes with BCIU before he was seen by anyone from the Oley Valley School District. Bryce's problems were behavioral. Harry had nothing to do with getting help for Bryce. If Ms. Unger knew anything at all, she would have said that Bryce was diagnosed with ADHD and Asperger's. Harry lied to his friend.

Nancy Unger concludes her letter stating her credentials. She states, "I have been a substitute teacher in the Kutztown School District for 25 years and know a thing or two about young people. Therefore, I feel well qualified to make some observations I have made in this letter." She also included in her letter that "you phone calls are welcome." I would not call her. But, after reading this letter from the trial exhibits,

I would call to my wife across the room. I said to Mary Lynne, "I found a witness for Kristen. You have to read this letter. Harry has Nancy Unger believing a lie that is easy to prove. And get this! She write's that Harry's father was an alcoholic." I would love to ask her some questions of the witness stand.

Kristen, early on, had decided to subpoena Dr. Thomas if she was able to obtain a modification trial. She felt she was not given a fair chance in her interview to refute Harry's lies in the second custody evaluation. Dr. Peter Thomas in his report had said she made poor choices in her relationships. She felt if Dr. Peter Thomas would learn why she made those choices from herself, rather than Harry, he would change his opinion about those choices.

We had in the exhibits both custody evaluation reports. We would be more intent on studying them now than was done before the custody trial. I did not know it contained Harry's description of his family life. Harry had said his father was a "verbally abusive alcoholic." I did not know that Dr. Thomas knew that many of the accusations made by Harry against Kristen were items Harry attributed learning from Rob Chalmers. I did not know that Harry had admitted to Dr. Peter Thomas that he was attempting to sue my church because I "wrote on church letterhead and trashed his family." I said nothing about Harry's family in my letter. I did not know that Dr. Thomas, in his report, called that an "egregious act." I did not know that Harry admitted being in psychotherapy for ten years.

The two custody evaluation reports were contained on 44 pages. Kristen had not read them thoroughly as it made her too angry when reading Harry's lies. She was mostly interested in the final recommendation. For the first evaluation it was 50/50. She was satisfied with that. She would not have to study that report. For the second evaluation it was recommended that Harry receive primary. Kristen was too angry to read the second report. There was one section of the report she should have read. That was the one that included the testimony of the boys. Both boys said to Dr. Thomas that Kristen never hit either of them with an object. Trey said mother did not hit Bryce with a bowl or a bottle. The "miracle" of Bryce's testimony at the expungement hearing, held a week after the interview with Dr. Thomas, would not have been quite as miraculous as we had thought at the time. And Harry had said in the trial that it was in the evaluator's report that the children said Bryce was hit on the head with the squirty bottle. I should note here that at the time of receiving our "Christmas present," we still had not heard from the Pennsylvania administrative law judge as to his verdict for those expungement hearings held in May and July.

Actually, I was surprised that I could be surprised by the surprising discoveries I would make in the record of the testimonies in the trial transcript itself. I knew Harry was on the witness stand a long time that morning. I was surprised at the lack of quality in the rehearsed testimony of Harry from the questioning of his attorney Mark Zimmer. He was spoken of as a great attorney who won most of his cases. It seemed at times that Harry would get mixed up. He would answer a question with the answer that was supposed to be for the next question. I was surprised that Harry would lie in almost every statement. I knew Harry lied with the information he gave in the PFA's, PSR's, custody evaluations, and other places. I thought at least while under oath he would tell some truth. When we obtained the transcript, the three of us were each supposed to read it to find any lies Harry might have told on the witness stand. Kristen and Mary Lynne would read very little from the Christmas Present. It made them two angry. Lies would be easy to find. It was difficult to find truth in Harry's testimony.

I read all of Harry's testimony. I started writing down lines of his testimony that I believed to be lies. I gave up at the number twenty-seven after about eight of his forty pages of testimony. I was writing down most of his testimony. I had thought we may have lost the trial because Jamie was unprepared to cross examine Harry. I was wrong. Jamie was great. I learned later Kristen had been feeding her information all during Harry's opening testimony. It was funny when during Harry's testimony he complains that he can't hear the questions because Kristen was being too noisy talking to her lawyer. The judged warned Kristen. Jamie said, "I can hear the questions." Jamie would go on to cross examine Harry. Over and over, Harry had to recant previous testimony. I was and am still surprised that Judge Lash never concluded that Harry was just a liar.

The evidence for which we have to give all the credit to Jamie for discovering was the knowledge of Guillermo Jalil and his book. I did not realize the great job she had done on Harry in that aspect of Harry's testimony. I was even more surprised by the fact that none of that was discussed by Judge Lash in his report.

Kristen told me that in her time she thought she had gotten to say much of what she wanted to on the stand in order to defend herself. She never did dwell on Harry's negatives, except that he lied about her. That was her intent. It also was part of Jamie's plan. Harry had surely shown himself to be unscrupulous, abusive, condescending, etc. I don't have to say anymore. I described Harry's character well enough in my letter to the judge. The contrast between Harry's and Kristen's testimonies was astounding. Kristen demonstrated knowledge of Bryce that Harry could not. Kristen did do a good job in her testimony. Jamie was correct in asserting her opinion that it appeared that Judge Lash must have not been listening to Kristen's testimony.

I was surprised by a number of events that were brought up by Harry and his attorney in the trial. The one thing they all had in common was that Harry lied in his description of every event of which I had knowledge. The ones of which I had direct knowledge included the Easter Holiday incident, the biting incident, the blue bowl incident, the squirty bottle incident, the attempted Durango hijacking, and the gang of four in the elevator. The important event I knew about that was brought up in court with me on the stand was the incident catching Harry lying to Kristen in the stairwell. That was brought up by Jamie. Harry and Zimmer did not know how to spin that story to favor Harry. After I testified, Zimmer did not know how to refute that testimony. The key event that was not brought up was the directive given by Harry's second lawyer, Jeffrey Karver. Jamie did allude to the directive in a question to Harry. She asked, "Did you not think, when you discovered the bump on Bryce's head, that you should first ask Kristen how Bryce got the bump?" I am waiting for Harry's answer.

It was only when I opened our Christmas Present that I learned that my letter had been brought up in court before I took the stand. I was surprised that it was allowed. Jamie did object. Judge Lash overruled. The first thing I wanted to find in the transcript was where Mark Zimmer exclaimed to me, while I was on the stand, that he had sent the letter to my church. Harry did not send it to the church. I was surprised I could not find that statement. It was important to me because I needed it in my proposed suit of Mark Zimmer. I realized later, that sometimes a Judge will tell the court reporter to strike a comment. Maybe that happened. It was good that I found that earlier in the trial Mark Zimmer did take that credit. I also wanted to find the exact line where I was accused of writing in my letter that I accused Harry's father of being an "alcoholic." I could not find that statement. I did find were Zimmer accused me of being "hateful" for saying that about Harry's father. However, line 17, where Zimmer accused me of using the word "alcoholic" in the trial, was mysteriously blank in the transcript.

Overall, the trial transcript would turn into a gift that "keeps on giving." I would find many points of discussion for the modification trial. I would find other ideas of whom we would have subpoenaed. But, maybe we should have gotten a dog for our Christmas present. After all, a dog can lie about someone, but can not lie about someone.

Chapter 47 - Will Anyone Listen?

Those Who Listened

Kristen found two people to listen. She would, however, have to pay them to listen. They were both necessary for her plan to conform to the orders of the court. First, she would obtain a psychotherapist. She was fortunate to hire someone from Lutheran Services. The cost was less than a quarter of what it could have been. We, my wife and I, were glad that she had made the step to receive professional help. We had wished she would have sought professional help many years ago. She had an abusive relationship in college for many years. We knew she had a problem. However, it was not the problem that Judge Lash described. She did not need a psychotherapist to become a better person. Her problem was being too forgiving, too accepting. She needed a psychotherapist to overcome the abuse created by Harry Hall, the Court, and others involved in the system of family law.

The other person with whom she needed to talk because of the court order was someone from Signature Family Services. The service to be provided, at great expense, was a family counseling course. The sessions were two hours and held weekly at a cost of $46 per hour. It required ten hours of work for Kristen to pay for one of those sessions. I presume the court believes that is fitting punishment for a child abuser. Anyway, the teacher was Jessica Mastrangelo. She was Harry's and Kristen's teacher for the first time they took the course. It is a course designed for both parties to participate together. It did not work the first time because Harry would not cooperate. The sessions had to be held with each party individually. Kristen had perfect attendance. Harry did not. Jess was amazed to learn that Harry had been given primary custody. She was sure that Kristen had not lost 50/50. She was subpoenaed by Kristen for the custody trial. She said a health issue was the reason she did not make the trial. Kristen informed Jess that she was seeking a modification trial. Jess said she would testify on her behalf. Kristen had found someone who listened.

Mark Zimmer announced in court that he was accepting the responsibility for sending my letter to my church and subsequent attempted suit. From that time, I knew my course of action. I would sue Mark Zimmer for libel, slander, and loss of income. He did not announce that he was a Christian; therefore, I would feel comfortable in a suit. Most of my years of teaching and going to church, I wore a suit. That was the way it was in the "old" days. I would feel even more comfortable in filing a suit after seeing his "ANSWER" to Kristen's request for reconsideration. In that writing, it was emphasized repeatedly that according to himself, Harry, and Judge Lash, my wife and I had been found guilty. Specifically, Mary Lynne and I were guilty of not recognizing Bryce as unique and special, showing disparity, not showing unconditional love, and being "toxic" to children. To me, that sounded like defamation of character, especially, for a Children's Ministry Director.

One law office, to which we would not go for a lawyer would be the Law Office of John Roland. We had gone to the office to find a lawyer for an attempted suit of Harry Hall. At the time, we chose that office because I knew John from the past and that he was a member of our church. Now, I believe that is not a good reason for choosing a lawyer. We had gone to his office only a few weeks before I wrote my "infamous" letter. The lawyer that interviewed us that day wrote a few weeks later that he could not do our will due to "conflict of interest." Of course, we also had the awkward circumstance that his office had been involved in recommending my suspension and defending against the suit of the church.

We went to the Berks County Bar Association, as we had for Kristen two years prior, to find a lawyer for our intended suit. We told the receptionist of our intent. We were told it would be difficult to find a lawyer willing to sue another in the same county. We thought that might be the case. We also thought we had a case. She said there was one person that might be willing. Actually, that person was the President of the Berks County Bar Association. We thought, surely a person of that stature would be great. She called and was able to make an appointment for us the next week. Out of curiosity, I asked, "Could I ask the name of the law office with whom he is associated?" She replied, "The Law Office of John Roland." We told a little more of our story. She called to cancel the appointment. We decided to look outside of the county for a lawyer that would fit our suit.

Eventually, after several failed attempts in other counties, we continued our search for a lawyer through the Philadelphia Bar Association. We realized that we had to have a good case in order to find a lawyer who would consider taking it. Also, we had to find a lawyer who was willing to work on a contingency basis. We, the three, discovered it was difficult to find a lawyer that would even consider reading our transcript or the Judge's "Decision and Order." We were given referrals. We made calls without success. I thought, if only I could point out some key points from the transcript and the judge's order I could convince someone we had a good case.

Once we had received our Christmas present and read some of it, we embarked on a journey to Philadelphia to find someone else who would enjoy reading our Christmas present. We had received one positive call in December before we got the transcript. He said he would consider the case, but he would need the trial transcript. We told him it was ordered. It was a few days into January 2009. The lawyer's office was on Race Street near the Delaware River and the Benn Franklin Bridge. We arrived early that morning and found street parking only a block from the office. We took a several block walking tour. We passed through Elfreths Alley. A few more blocks and we came to the door of the office a few minutes before 9:00 am. We peered through the window and noticed that renovations were in process. Perhaps, this lawyer was young and just starting his own practice. We saw no one in the office, but rang the doorbell anyway. A man came to the door. He was the one making the renovations. He said the lawyer would be in later in the day. The lawyer had said weeks before that he would consider our case. So, we acted on faith and left our Christmas present with the hope that he would read it. Maybe someone else would listen. The rest of the day we completed our walking tour on the streets of Philadelphia. We walked Race Street to the National Constitution Center. We went in and stood amidst the great men that wrote our constitution. We continued outside strolling past Independence Hall. I wondered when I would feel like directing BRASS IN PRAISE again in the strains of "God Bless America." Perhaps, I would after there was justice. We took the long way around back to our car on Race Street. We stopped at City Tavern for lunch and pretended that George was seated at the table across the room. I had rabbit stew.

In late November of 2008, I received an unexpected letter. It was very official looking. Opening the letter, I immediately recognized a symbol on it that I had seen on another letter I received a few years prior. That letter was from a State Senator. It was to congratulate me on receiving the "City on the Hill Award." This letter had the same state seal of Pennsylvania but it was from a member of the state House of Representatives. I was not receiving an award. I had been "randomly selected" for a town meeting. The meeting was to be held on Thursday, December 4, 2008 at the Blandon Fire Company. The following words are from that letter describing the purpose of the town meeting.

> Our purpose is to give you an opportunity to let me know what's important to you. You will do the talking, and I will do the listening. I will also be happy to respond to any questions you may have. Please come prepared to speak with me on school district property tax reform, the need to better control government spending or your personnel problem with the red tape of state government. Be assured, no topic is off-limits, but the choice is up to you.

We emailed to reserve a seat. Would we have a chance to speak with David Argall? We certainly felt we had a problem with justice in our county. Kristen still had not received any word on the progress of her expungement hearings held in May and July with the state administrative law judge. We did not know if it was even being considered.

We attended the town meeting. We sat through the meeting and heard David Argall give his thoughts and proceed to answer questions from individuals. Afterwards, as most individuals started for the refreshments, we proceeded to State Representative Argall. He listened for a few minutes as we described our situation. We did ask specifically if he could check on the progress of Kristen's results for the expungement hearings. We also asked if he would consider reading some of my articles and other information. The information included emails describing the contents of Guillermo's book. My articles included one with the title, "Accomplices." In addition to Jalil, that article described briefly the actions of a number of professionals involved in our case. To our surprise, he answered yes to both requests. Six weeks later, we would receive a greater surprise.

Once again I received a letter with the Seal of the State of Pennsylvania. The letter was dated January 13, 2009. It was signed by State Representative, David Argall. Behold the following:

> Thank you for contacting me to share your experience with the Berks County Children and Youth Services office. I appreciate you taking the time to share your thoughts with me on this important issue and regret the circumstances that have prompted you to contact me.
>
> First and foremost, it is important to understand that as a state representative, I have no authority to modify, terminate, or take any formal action on determinations by children and youth agencies or courts. I am able to explain applicable laws and provide you with information and resources that you and your family may find helpful.
>
> With that said, I did have my staff contact the Department of Public Welfare (DPW), Office of Children, Youth and Families to obtain an update on your case. It is my understanding that Berks County Children and Youth is still waiting final disposition from the appeal hearing you spoke of. Unfortunately, this is not unusual and does typically take some time.

However, based upon your information you provided, there appears to be some serious concerns over the conduct of the professionals involved in this matter. Therefore,.

Someone else listened, someone in state government. Where is my baton?

Chapter 48 - The Kidnapping

Abuser be my Babysitter, Part 2

By January of 2009, Kristen was firmly settled in a routine that began in October. Judge Lash's ruling on Kristen's reconsideration request allowed her to see the boys every school day after school while Harry was at work. Monday thru Friday she worked as a receptionist in the heart institute from 5:15 am to 2:15 pm. She started working St. Joseph's Medical Center when it first opened in November of 2006. It was her first job after being removed from her home by Harry's first PFA. Each school day Kristen drove from work to pick up Trey from daycare sometime after 2:30. Trey had kindergarten in the mornings and was bussed back to daycare for the afternoons. At 3:15, she drove to Oley Elementary School to pick up Bryce. She would then drive the boys pack to her apartment in Blandon. Along the way, she would stop for snacks for the boys. Bryce would be able spend a half hour with Kristen and Trey when Harry would call saying he was on his way home from work. Kristen would then drive the boys from her apartment to their home with Harry near Oley. Each leg of the journey includes driving thru the intersection of Route 73 and Route 12. Yes, that it is intersection we call "Breezy Corners", the place of the "infamous" transition where Bryce and Harry had the confrontation. Question number one, how many times does Kristen pass through that intersection on a school day? Question number two, given that the distance between Oley and

Blandon is 8 mile and the distance from work to Oley is 15 miles, what is the total mileage that Kristen drives from 2:15 pm until she arrives at her apartment at approximately 4:30 pm? Did you say that you do not like reading problems in mathematics? Question number three, why did she do that? Finally, an easy question, it was because of her love for the children, both of them.

Did you ever hear the expression, "going the extra mile?" Every school day Kristen went the extra 40 miles. There is something biblical about the number 40. The original court order gave Kristen three weekends each month during the school year. A weekend was defined as Friday 6:00 pm to Sunday 6:00 pm. During the summer Kristen would have full custody except for alternate weekends and a vacation week or two for Harry. With the fact that now she could see the boys every school day, Kristen no longer had a case for parental alienation. That was no longer the problem. The problem rested in the word "primary." That word declared Harry the better parent. That word declared that Harry had the better support system. That word allowed Harry all the advantages financially when filing income taxes. Harry would still receive the $300 a month for Bryce that Kristen had earned. That word meant that the Kristen could not get the financial help normally afforded to single mothers with children. She was treated simply as a single woman and not a mother. To put it bluntly, Judge Lash had set up Kristen for failure. There was no way that she could provide for her children financially during the school year let alone the summer when she was required to have the boys full time. Something would happen that January that would make it more difficult.

Kristen called Mary Lynne from work at 10:00 am on January 26, 2009. She told her that she and many others were being laid off permanently. Kristen had not intended for her $9 an hour job to be permanent. She had hoped that her "child abuse" accusation would be expunged. Until the child abuse charge was expunged, she could not apply for a position that needed criminal clearance. She could not use her College Degree and work experience for a better paying job. Since Harry and BCCYS collaborated to put that child abuse claim on her record, Kristen had been offered jobs that she could not accept because of the lack of criminal clearance. Besides having health insurance and other benefits, the hours for her receptionist job at least allowed her to have that after school time each day with the boys. What would she do for the future? What would she do that very day?

Kristen drove to our home. By that time it was 11:00 am. She knew that Trey would soon arrive at daycare at Frieden's Lutheran Church in Oley. Mary Lynne accompanied her to the daycare. Trey would be pleasantly surprised to see his mother 3 hours earlier than usual. He would also be surprised to see his grandmother. Kristen went into the daycare. They told her Trey had not arrived with the others on the bus. Kristen called the school. Trey was not there, neither was Bryce. They told her Harry had taken the boys from school. Harry had "ripped off" the boys. It was another kidnapping. Kristen and Mary Lynne drove to Harry's sister's house in Exeter Township. They were not there. As they continued driving Kristen received a call from Harry. Harry said he had taken the boys to BCCYS. Kristen immediately headed to Reading and the office of BCCYS.

A caseworker, who Kristen had never met before, came out to meet them. He told Kristen he was planning to call her and ask her to come in. He told her that Harry had been there with the boys. Harry was there to file a report against her claiming that she was not properly supervising the boys on her weekends. He said the boys came to him after the weekends with bumps and bruises that they did not have when they left his house. Christopher Alberts went on to describe that he was shown a small black and blue mark on Bryce's side and one on Trey's shin. When asked how he got his bruise, Bryce exclaimed that he fell off his bed onto a toy. When Trey was asked, he said he got his bruise on the shin when he was tripped at daycare. Chris went on to say that there really was no problem. She just had to sign this paper and she could be off. She signed. A few days later, February 4, 2009, she received a letter from Christopher Alberts. The words are as follows:

> Berks County Children and Youth Services have completed an assessment of the referral dated 1/26/09, regarding Bryce and Harry Hall (Trey). The agency has determined that no further services are required at this time.
>
> However, as I have indicated, Berks County Children and Youth Services does suggest that you

continue to follow the current safety plan that you use appropriate, and safe, forms of discipline (such as time-outs, taking away toys/privileges, etc.), and provide appropriate supervision of the children. This should include keeping the children with-in ear-shot, and eye-shot, at all times.

Thank you for your cooperation in this matter.

Does anyone smell a "dirty tactic?" Harry had gotten BCCYS to work for him again. Kristen had just been convicted again of using improper discipline and not providing appropriate supervision. Mr. Alberts says nothing in the letter about the accusations that led to the writing of the letter. Nothing was said in the letter about the testimony of the boys. Apparently, it is there practice to not give the name of the person that made the referral. I will. It was Harry Hall, II. Did Mr. Alberts tell Kristen of the boy's testimonies in order to trick her into signing that form? Did Harry ask Mr. Alberts to do that very thing? Was Harry starting his plans for the modification trial? I wonder if Mr. Alberts is acquainted with Bill Clemons and Guillermo Jalil. Kristen would not have signed that form if she knew this would be the letter she would be getting from BCCYS. Again, Harry did not follow the directive to call Kristen first about a bump or bruise. Oh, this time he did make the call immediately after taking the boys to BCCYS.

Does anyone believe Harry has the boys in ear-shot and eye-shot at all times when they are in his custody? We know he does let them "wrestle" and "roughhouse." Well, at least he is supervising the wrestling. He probably does that with the expectation that the boys would get bruises that Harry can blame on Kristen's poor supervision.

Kristen would call Harry that evening to inform him on her being laid off. The last days of that week, she would pick up Trey earlier from daycare. The next week Harry called to inform Kristen that he was dropping daycare entirely. She could pick up Trey at school after kindergarten. Harry would save hundreds of dollars a month by not paying daycare. Now Kristen's income, from unemployment would be less than what she pays in rent. Once again, Harry was saying, "abuser be my babysitter." This time, however, it would not be at the marital residence as it was the first time she babysat for free. She would pick up Trey from school and provide lunch. She would pick up Bryce after school and provide snacks to both. And later, she would deliver the boys safely to their father. After all, he is only interested in their safety. Can you imagine having a babysitter who works for nothing and even provides food, shelter, transportation, and love?

CHAPTER 49 - NARCISSISTIC PSYCHOPATH

Gathering Witnesses for Modification

A few weeks after the custody trial, Kristen received a letter dated September 17, 2008. The first paragraph reads as follows.

This letter serves as a confirmation that our agency will provide court-ordered curriculum based parenting service to you. Signature Family Services is pleased to provide the services of Jessica Mastrangelo, Caseworker to facilitate these sessions.

This would not be the first time Kristen and Harry were required to take the course. This is not the first time I am telling this story. I am a teacher. Review is good. Kristen and Harry are told to take a refresher course. When the couple took the course the first time Harry was not cooperative. Most of the sessions had to be held individually. Jess had planned to witness for Kristen, but did not make it to the trial because of health issues. She was surprised to learn from Kristen that Harry was awarded primary custody. She said she would witness in Kristen's behalf for a modification trial. She said she would refuse to be Harry's teacher this time. She did. Harry started with another teacher from Signature Family Services.

After a number of sessions, Jess informed Kristen that she had spoken with Harry's teacher. In this case, I did not think it was wrong for the two caseworkers to discuss their clients. Their clients were supposed to be cooperating together. That could be a "back door" way of trying to get the parents "on the same page." Harry's teacher told Jess that she thought Harry was a very nice man. She exclaimed to Jess how nice it was that Harry allowed Kristen to pick up and see the boys after school every day. Jess said that she set the record straight with the other teacher. It was not that Harry allowed Kristen to see the boys. It was a court order that Kristen be allowed to see the boys. Kristen won that from the court in her reconsideration request. Harry, in the reconsideration order and Zimmer's "ANSWER," argued against Kristen pick-ups being allowed. Harry manages to find a lie to tell to anyone with whom he talks. Kristen completed her 14 sessions. Jess told Kristen that Harry completed about 4 of his sessions. After all, Harry was not the child abuser. Besides, Harry remembered everything from when he took the course the first time.

Kristen, on the witness stand, had complained that she only had fifteen minutes for her interview with Dr. Peter Thomas in the second evaluation. Would a person who worked with Kristen in a one-on-one situation for fourteen hours come to a better understanding of her character? Double that time, Kristen took the course twice.

I said Jess did not make it to the custody trial. I did discover many months after receiving our "Christmas present" that the name Jessica Mastrangelo appeared in testimony.

Ms. Dautrich: How many times did you take Bryce to the doctor— take Bryce to the doctor for injuries without discussing it with Kristen?

Harry: Three times.

Ms. Dautrich: So you didn't think it would be important to discuss with Kristen—being the other parent—the injuries that Bryce had received?

Harry: Bryce is a very intelligent, perceptive child who was very—

Ms. Dautrich: Is that a no, you didn't think it was important to discuss the injuries with Kristen and inform her?

Harry: It's not the words I would choose, but I'll have to say no.

Ms. Dautrich: And you indicated that there was a time that you had taken Bryce to the doctor on a Sunday night when it was time to transfer custody?

Harry: Uh-huh.

Ms. Dautrich: And that was about he had gotten sick, and you thought it may because of an injury he received by an accident at Kristen's home? Correct?

Harry: That's correct.

Ms. Dautrich: And you didn't tell Kristen that you were not bringing him back at that time, at the scheduled Sunday exchange?

Harry: Oh, before I called Kristen, I called Jess Mastrangelo. She was the CYS person from Signature counseling that was involved in our case. And with the situation, yet another head injury, taking Bryce to the hospital, I didn't want mom to be there because of the potential drama. So I called Jess Mastrangelo, who was basically overseeing our communications through CYS. And I asked her if I could not call mom. And I knew I was going to have to anyway. I was just trying to avoid some drama. So I had to call mom. She showed up. There was drama. That's when she hit me.

What had really transpired? Bryce did bump his head falling on the steps at Kristen's apartment. It was not much of a bump. Later that day, she transitioned the boys for Harry's weekend which began Friday evening at 6:00 pm. Harry was supposed to transition the boys to Kristen at 7:00 pm on Sunday evening. For 48 hours Harry did not a problem with Bryce and a bump. It was 7:20 pm Sunday evening and Harry had not arrived at the transition and had not called Kristen. Also, he had not answered his cell phone when Kristen called. Kristen called Jess. Jess called Harry. At 7:30 pm, Harry called Kristen from the hospital. Kristen went to the hospital. Harry's testimony continues.

Ms. Dautrich: So if Miss Mastrangelo were to testify that she had to contact you to find out where the kids were, that would be—she'd be mistaken?

The Court: Who's she? Can you rephrase that?

Ms. Dautrich: Okay. You indicated you called the parenting coordinator from Signature, Ms. Mastrangelo?

Harry: That's correct.

Ms. Dautrich: So you're saying she didn't—she, meaning the parenting coordinator, was not the one to contact you to see where the children were when they weren't returned to Kristen?

Harry: I believe I called her. Because it was just after 7:30, it was real close to transition time when I called Jess Mastrangelo. I'm pretty sure I called Jess Mastrangelo.

Ms. Dautrich: So with the transition being—

Harry: Because I asked a very specific question, do I have to contact mom. She said, yes, you do. So I did.

Ms. Dautrich: So the transition time was seven. And around 7:30, you called Miss Mastrangelo?

Harry: Seven-twenty, seven-thirty. Because I actually I think I left the house at seven, but I was going the wrong way to get to mom. I was going the opposite direction, because mom lived in the opposite direction of the hospital.

Harry is always going the wrong way. He is always going the opposite direction, away from the truth. So why did Harry take Bryce to the hospital at the time the transition was to take place and not at any other time during the weekend? Why is there no report of this bump? Why doesn't Harry say how this bump occurred? Why is there no report from CYS concerning this bump? Harry says first in his testimony that he did not want Kristen to know he went to the hospital. Why? In a way he was saying that Jess, without knowing of the directive to Harry by his second lawyer, was agreeing to the premise of that directive. Why didn't he call Kristen before 7:00 pm? Then why would he have called Jess? He did not call Jess. Jess called him. Does Judge Lash understand that this testimony demonstrates another lie by Harry? Jess could have been an excellent witness to this event if she would have made it to the custody trial. But, we could have an excellent witness for the modification trial.

Harry, in his testimony above, said, "I believe." So, I will say what I believe. I believe the bump was like the others, not noteworthy, too small to be considered. I believe he took Bryce to the hospital because he was acting like someone who had a concussion. Or, had Harry tried to hypnotize Bryce too close to the time of transition? We had suspected that Harry used conversational hypnosis to control the boys. Before Harry started his campaign against Kristen, he talked about his interest in hypnotism and mind control. Perhaps, his session with Bryce had gone awry. He was having trouble snapping Bryce out of his sleep. Maybe he thought he could convince the hospital that Bryce had a concussion. Maybe he was scared because, as a hypnotist, he was only an amateur. So call me crazy. Some of the actions we had seen by the boys were bizarre. Trey had said to Dr. Thomas that it was "in a dream" that he saw Harry hit Bryce. Maybe Bryce was in a hypnotic trance? Maybe I am crazy. Maybe, like Kristen, I need a psychotherapist.

So, who was the first to recommend that Kristen take psychotherapy? It was Harry Hall in the first evaluation with Dr. Peter Thomas held only three months after Harry filed his first lying PFA. That was almost two years before we had discovered that Harry had a plan for this whole affair. The ultimate goal of that plan was to achieve primary custody. There was a mastermind behind that plan. The mastermind had written a book which included "dirty tactics." One of those tactics is to accuse your spouse of mental health issues. Convince the evaluator that you believe your spouse needs psychotherapy to become a "better person" and a "better parent." This is the same mastermind that stated in his book that "perjury is rarely considered in domestic relations cases." Guillermo Jalil had used his experience and knowledge of the family law system of Berks County to write the book. So, when reading what Harry said to the evaluator, it must be with a "grain of arsenic." With this in mind, read the following from Dr. Thomas' report.

> Mr. Hall states that his main goal is to get Kristen help. He states he wanted to do therapy. He wanted to get help. He wanted to have parenting classes. He states, "I wanted to be there for help and us." Mr. Hall states that if his only concern was money or having primary custody, he would have dropped the evaluation. He states that Kristen made him a very generous offer for the children to be with him four days and with her for three days and that financially it would be very good. He states the only hang-up was that Kristen would not go to therapy – "That's why we're here."

So the whole reason for everything is for Kristen to do psychotherapy. If that is all Harry wants, why does Harry not pay for the psychotherapy? Why did he not complete his parenting classes? Kristen never made the offer Harry suggested. It was just another lie. Why would she make that offer? For whom would that be good financially? Harry said in that same evaluation that he was seeking reconciliation. How often does a "gay" man seek reconciliation with his former wife?

Dr. Peter Thomas in both evaluations recommended that Kristen seek professional help, such as a psychotherapist. The problem is the reasons for the recommendations were based on the lies of Harry Hall. Would his opinion have been different if he knew Harry's relationship with Guillermo Jalil?

Following Dr. Peter Thomas' lead, Judge Lash recommended that Kristen take psychotherapy. He said she needed it to become a "better person" and a "better parent." Those are exactly the reasons Kristen said she did not need psychotherapy. If she admitted to needing psychotherapy for those reasons, then she would be admitting to guilt. How did Judge Lash expect her to become "better" through psychotherapy? Should she become less loving, less accepting, less forgiving, and less trusting? She certainly has learned that you can not trust the family law system of Berks County. Would she learn from psychotherapy that she, as well as her parents, should cease fighting for justice? That idea was suggested by Dr. Keevil.

I have to back up. Harry was not the first person to suggest that Kristen would benefit from professional help. Her mother had suggested it to Kristen after learning of the abuse she had endured from a boyfriend while she was in college. Actually, we were glad it was suggested by the court and Dr. Thomas. We did not, however, agree with their reasons for suggesting it. We also felt if the court was ordering it, the court should be paying for it. We believed she needed psychotherapy because of the injustice shown to her by the court and family law system. We agreed with the court that indeed Kristen did choose at least one "abusive" man. That man was Harry Hall, II. He not only abused the mother of his children, he abused the children in alienating them from their mother.

Harry said to the evaluator, "I don't want my children to have the same experiences I had growing up in my family." He said that his father

346

was "verbally abusive," especially to his mother. He said his mother was not there for him. She had to work two jobs because his father did not work at all. Harry has abused his wife in a more despicable manner than his father. He is keeping his children from their mother as his mother was kept from him.

Kristen had 15 sessions, of one hour each, from October 24 to February 9, 2009. Is it possible that her psychotherapist, Ms. Dedra Young, learned more about Kristen in those fifteen hours than Dr. Thomas had learned in that fifteen minute interview in the second evaluation? Dedra asked Kristen early on, "How could Dr. Thomas learn enough about you in those fifteen minutes to make such a recommendation?" Kristen said, "Exactly." That was what Kristen asked the court in the custody trial. That was the reason Kristen subpoenaed Dr. Thomas for the modification trial.

Ms. Young would learn over the weeks of therapy why Kristen needed it. It only took two sessions for her to come to the conclusion that Kristen needed psychotherapy in order to deal with the injustice she had received. During the next several weeks she would learn of the many accomplices that were involved in dealing the injustice to Kristen. Kristen's anger was not caused by Bryce. It was caused by Harry's lies. Why did Dr. Thomas not think that her anger towards Harry Hall was justified? Ms. Young would discover the same problems that I wrote about Kristen. She was too forgiving, too accepting, etc. She gave Kristen assignments to work on her problems.

In the fourteenth session, Kristen told Dedra that she had just been laid off from work. Kristen told her that Harry had taken the boys to BCCYS again with false claims. Kristen told her that Harry had dropped daycare so that Kristen could babysit. He wanted the abuser to be his babysitter again. Harry would save a lot of money. Kristen would have to spend more.

Ms. Young exclaimed, "Harry Hall is a narcissistic psychopath and a bully. File for modification now!" Perhaps, Kristen should ask to have her psychotherapist subpoenaed. I know a psychopath is a mentally ill person. I get the idea of what a bully is. Should I look up narcissistic?

CHAPTER 50 - AND JUSTICE FOR ALL

The Blessing of Liberty

It is Christmas Eve and the family and extended family are seated around a table to enjoy a turkey dinner. The father of the house asks Aunt Bethany to say "grace." She is 80 years old and suffers from a slight degree of hearing loss and dementia. Uncle Lewis recognizes a problem. He tells her say "grace." Still, she does not get it. He says, "The blessing! He wants you to say the blessing!" Aunt Bethany begins. She ends, along with everyone else, with the words, "and justice for all."

This may be my favorite movie scene. You may remember the scene and think it was funny. That probably was the intent of the movie makers. I, however, consider it one the most profound truths I have ever heard. It is as profound as the Constitution of the United States. The preamble to the Constitution of the United States is as follows:

> We the people of the United States, in order to form a more perfect union, establish justice, insure the domestic tranquility, provide for the common defense, promote the general welfare, and secure the blessings of liberty to ourselves and our posterity, do ordain and establish this Constitution of the United States of America.

Note that the first thing to be done was to "establish justice." So, you ask, what does that have to do with saying a blessing? In the pledge to the flag, the two words pronounced before, "and justice for all", were, "with liberty." It is stated above, "and secure the blessings of liberty to ourselves and our posterity." Liberty is declared here as containing blessings. We are compelled to seek liberty not only for ourselves but also for our family. Everyone around that table participated in the blessing. I say, "Amen," along with everyone in that scene. You might say, without thinking, that it was not a proper blessing. You would have spoken too soon. It was also exclaimed, "One nation, under God."

I first heard the phrase "black liberation theology" a few years ago. I thought I had a good idea of what it meant. I did not. However, my thoughts of what it might mean would lead me to how I define liberty. I thought blacks in slavery naturally identified themselves with the children of Israel as they were slaves in Egypt. I thought the idea of liberation theology meant Slaves could be free even as slaves. Not only that, it was their master who was the slave. How can that be? I wrote the following verse, the fourth, and chorus for a song I called, "this Promise is to Me."

God then gave the Law to Moses so his promise could not be denied.

But the Law couldn't really free them from sin no matter how hard that they tried.

But Jesus fulfilled all the promises when he died upon Calvary's tree.

Those promises sealed when he rose from the grave, so we can live eternally.

Because from sin he set me free. This promise is to me.

The slave's master could be or was a slave to sin. The slave could have as his master, Jesus, and thus be a slave to righteousness. He would be free from sin. It is said in scripture that "If the Son has made you free, you will be free indeed." I wrote in another song that it is only when Jesus comes to reign that we will have true liberty. To have true liberty, you need a perfect judge who can execute perfect justice. Without justice there is no liberty. To have liberty means to have the freedom to do what you know is just. How is that done?

Uncle Lewis said, as he grits his teeth, "the blessing." He was correct. The source of true liberty is announced as one of the blessings to Abraham. The third verse of the song above is as follows:

God made a promise to Abraham that the world would be blessed thru his seed.
Descendants numbered as the stars, and he'd give them the land that they'd need.

How is the world blessed thru his seed? The blessing is the promise of the Spirit the Christian receives thru faith in Jesus Christ. Living in the Spirit, the Christian becomes a slave to Him and not to sin. The idea of redemption in the scriptures is that the price has been paid so that we no longer have to remain slaves to sin. The book of Exodus is called the book of redemption because of the Israelites being freed from slavery.

I have only written seven original songs that have words with the music. All of these were written to be used in my children's ministries. Five of these are theme songs to be used with the curriculum I developed for summer Bible schools. Each of these has at least one line referring to my thoughts on liberty as expressed in the Bible. I have never published anything so I feel compelled to write those pertinent words here.

From the song, "I See God": I see God in the lives He's changed, and how He set them free.

From "To Be a Christian": Justified, though I was guilty. Redeemed, He purchased me from sin.

And from the song, "By Faith": Without faith, it is impossible to please him. Without faith, he could not our sins forgive. But with faith in Christ, we have a free salvation. And with faith in Him, we'll have the strength to live. For by faith, he made it possible to be redeemed set free from the burden of sin. So look to Jesus Christ the Author and the Finisher for with faith in Him we'll have the victory!

At one time, my favorite song was "The Statue of Liberty." If my brass ensemble was a marching band, then this is the song we would play as we marched down the street. I love the melody. However, the words are more important to me than the tune. The first verse talks about the Statue of Liberty in New York harbor and how it speaks to us of our liberties as citizens. It speaks of the pride we have as Americans because of those liberties. The second verse speaks of the cross being the Christian's statue of liberty and thus we are glad to be called Christians. The final chorus concludes making the analogy that as the statue speaks of our liberties as citizens the cross speaks of the liberty of our souls. I am still glad to be called a Christian. I am having a little trouble with the other.

That is enough theology. Let us learn some logic. Consider the statement, "Tom received justice." The negation of that statement would be, "Tom did not receive justice." Consider the statement, "All persons received justice." You may say, "All persons did not receive justice." Close, there is a clearer statement. That would be, "There exists at least one person that did not receive justice." If one person does not receive justice, then justice is not for all. Of course, it is impossible in the human realm to achieve justice for all. That does not, however, mean that we should give up the attempt. I know of a person that I believe has not received justice. Guess who?

Kristen would continue her fight for justice for herself and her boys. I had to do something with the knowledge I had gained through this whole experience in the system of family law. I had learned that there are books written that describe "dirty tactics" to be used to win in custody cases. Among other things, I learned that lies are used as part of those tactics. Would it be good to write a book warning others of those tactics? I had spoken to a State Representative who listened. If I wrote a proposal for state legislature, would it be considered? I could give it to State Representative, David Argall. I could call it, "Legislative Proposal for Custody Determination." It would be a small step in achieving "justice for all." Whatever was done would have to be done "by faith."

In February of 2009, Kristen received an envelope from the COMMONWEALTH OF PENNSYLVANIA DEPARTMENT OF PUBLIC WELFARE. It was written by Andrew Maloney, Administrative Law Judge and dated, February 19, 2009. He writes the following:

It is hereby recommended that the appeal of the Appellant be SUSTAINED. The Department of Public Welfare and Berks County Children and Youth Services agency should be directed to expunge Appellant's name from the Child Line Registry at the number indicated above.

Seven months after the second expungement hearing, Kristen received the recommendation. It still had to go back to BCCYS. They would have the chance to appeal the recommendation of the administrative law judge. It would be highly unlikely that they would make an appeal. It was possible that it could happen. After all, the recommendation was saying that BCCYS had made a mistake in calling the "squirty bottle incident" a "founded" verdict of indicated child abuse. Kristen did not feel she had to read the report. The verdict was enough. I did read the report. I was wondering if BCCYS was chastised for their part in calling the incident "founded."

Anyway, Kristen was given a huge piece of evidence for her modification trial. We knew it might take a year to have that scheduled. We knew of the many hearings and other steps needed to get to that point. We had gathered many ideas for evidence and persons to be subpoenaed. Financially, we had no idea how we were going to be able to keep Kristen in a place for her and her children. She was supposed to have the boys full time in the summer. We could not afford to pay, as in the previous year, the rent for the whole year in advance. We could not afford it when we did. She would have to move. She could not live with us and her boys in our house as we were in a fifty-five and over adult community. Nevertheless, we would carry on "by faith."

But, we had received justice from the state government. My pride in being an American had just been raised. There was still the question of justice in the family court system of Berks County. In the custody trial, Judge Lash said to me, "you say you are seeking justice." I am.

EPILOGUE

Three Epistles, and a Book, no Two, Maybe Three

Kristen did all the necessary paper work and had the hearings needed to secure a date for the modification trial. It was scheduled for and was held on November 16, 2009. We made a number of attempts in acquiring a lawyer for the trial. We had the transcript of the trial. I had written numerous articles pointing out the flaws in the judge's decision. Some lawyers said she did not have a chance of winning. They would not take the time to read our material. A month before the trial, we thought we might have a law office that would take our case. They said the cost would be between $3000 and $5000. The head lawyer of the law firm who talked to Kristen first could not take the case because of conflict in dates. Another lawyer associated with the office was found for the case. We gave our materials to him to read over the weekend. Kristen met him on Monday. He only read the judge's biased report. He did not read any of the transcript or my articles. The new estimated cost for the trial was $7,000. They said it would be a waste of money and she could not win. Kristen would represent herself. She was preparing all along that she might have to do that.

In the summer Kristen had the required hearing with the Custody Master. For the custody trial theses meetings are usually held with only the lawyers and the Custody Master. They try to negotiate so the expense of a trial can be avoided. For this hearing, Kristen would have to represent herself. She was surprised that Harry was allowed into the hearing with his lawyer. Fifteen minutes is usually the amount of time allowed for these hearings. Kristen was only trying to modify to regain 50/50 custody. I wanted her to go for primary. The first words to Kristen by the Custody Master were, "You wasted a lot of trees." Kristen had to tell her that it was Harry that filed all those charges against her. Her paper work was needed to defend herself. To Kristen's surprise, Harry's lawyer announced that Harry was seeking to modify the Order by taking a weekend from Kristen during the school year. Kristen did not believe that Harry would be allowed to do that because she was the one applying for modification. He should have to make his own modification in a separate hearing. She was surprised that the Custody Master was considering the possibility of allowing Harry to modify. Kristen would have to push on towards a modification trial. Otherwise, Harry would get his modification. Kristen would discover later that the Custody Master was a member of the law office where she almost hired the lawyer.

Kristen went to the modification trial well prepared. We knew the case better than any lawyer could have ever learned. We experienced everything that had happened the previous three plus years since the first PFA. Kristen had four witnesses other than herself. For Dr. Peter Thomas, she planned to offer more information that he had not known when he made his recommendation of primary for Harry. Could she change his opinion? At a pre-trial hearing Kristen said that her psychotherapist had called Harry a "narcissistic psychopath." Judge Lash exclaimed that he wanted to hear her in court. She came as a witness for Kristen. We discovered the real Scott? He became a witness via the telephone. Jess, Kristen's family counselor teacher, was subpoenaed but did not show up for the trial. We have not heard from her since Kristen's last class with her.. However, Kristen had completed the course as required by Judge Lash. Harry did not. Harry had three witnesses besides himself. His sister corroborated with him in his lies. His friend Nancy Unger and her husband spoke highly of Harry and admitted they could not say anything about Kristen. Mary Lynne and I would not take the witness stand. We would watch. We wanted to know if we would have to purchase another trial transcript. We wanted to see if Harry would "blubber" on the stand as he did in the first trial. At the appropriate time he did. I had devised an exhibit to demonstrate the plan of Guillermo Jalil as used by Harry Hall. Also, I devised an exhibit to demonstrate "unconditional love" to Bryce. Kristen had finally agreed with me and this time asked for "primary" in the modification trial.

Kristen received Judge Lash's Order with the date November 20, 2009. The last two sentences of the report are as follows: "We will, accordingly modify the current orders in accordance with Father's request. We will also dismiss the Outstanding Contempt Petition by Mother." At the start of the school year for 2009, Harry refused to follow the Judge's order in the Reconsideration Order which allowed her to pick up the boys when Harry was working. She had filed the Contempt Petition and had a hearing. At the hearing Judge Lash said he would consider it at the modification trial. As seen in his last sentence he did not consider it at the trial. Judge Lash is not man of his word.

I had said in my letters, that is, "epistles," that I had enough information to write a book. I started to write it in June of 2010. I quickly realized there was too much information for one book. At that time, Kristen was in the process of appealing Judge Lash's Order from the modification trial. I decided then that the first book would cover the custody trial. The second book would cover the modification trial and the appeal. It would be presumptuous to say there would be a third book. It is my goal that good would come from our experience with the system of family law. Near the end of 2010 there was an article in the Reading Eagle that caught my attention. It stated that departing Governor Rendell signed a bill concerning family law. I read some of the bill's proposals. I had written a proposal to present to the state legislature eight months before bill above was signed. The points in my proposal were missed. My proposal should be seen. Part of my Book 3 would include my continued battle to have points of my proposal included as amendments to the House Bill 1639.

Before starting on my book, I wrote more "epistles." The first two describe some of the events to be included in Book 2. The first epistle was addressed to a State Senator. As we did a year before, we were again given an invitation to a town hall meeting at the Blandon Fire Company. I got to talk to the now State Senator, David Argall. That

355

meeting occurred January of 2010. I was able to tell him that my daughter's expungement was won almost a year before this town hall meeting. I also had to tell him that she lost her modification trial and was in the process of her appeal. I told him then that I would write a legislative proposal that would combat the injustices that were done to us. The second "epistle" was addressed "Dear Friends." I call it the "Epistle to Everyone." This time I would send out 200 letters informing them of the results of the modification trial. The third epistle would be "The Epistle to the State Legislature." This would be my "Legislative Proposal for Custody Determination."

The Epistle to a State Senator

The following was written to State Senator David Argall on March 9, 2010. The answer to this request will appear in BOOK 2: THE MODIFICATION TRIAL.

I am writing for your help in obtaining an audience with the District Attorney of Berks County John Adams. I have been seeking that since receiving the verdict from my daughter's custody modification trial on November 20, 2009. I believe my meeting with the DA is especially important because my legislative proposal is based on what I perceive to be errors and misconduct in awarding primary custody and then further modification in favor of my daughter's estranged husband. These perceived errors pertain to judges, lawyers, evaluators, doctors, the staff of BCCYS, and others under the jurisdiction of Berks County and the authority of the DA.

On October 6, 2009, I attended a lecture entitled, "Judicial Ethics & Leadership." One panelist was the Honorable Judge, Scott Lash. After the three judges and one lawyer spoke, time was given for a few questions from the audience. I got to ask Judge Lash the following: "I read a book recently on how to achieve victory in custody cased. It was stated in that book that 'perjury' is rarely considered in domestic relations cases." I asked Judge Lash if that was true. Judge Lash said it was partially true. He said that since it was hard to prove it usually is not considered. He said it was not up to the judge to consider perjury. It must be brought up by someone else. He stated that if you believe you have a case for "perjury" you should go to the District Attorney. I did.

The title of the book described above is <u>Asset Protection from Divorce</u>. An email ad for this book states, "Revenge is a common goal in divorce and obtained through the children, money and assets." A more recent ad states, "We are making available to you the dirtiest divorce tactics known." Harry Hall used these against my daughter. The writer of the book, Guillermo Jalil, was a juvenile probation officer in Berks County. I believe his paths may have crossed those of Judge Scott Lash. I believe the DA would want to know that his book was written based on his experience of what goes on in the administering of justice which pertains to custody in the County of Berks. My daughter met Guillermo at her husband's 20th class reunion for Exeter High School held in 2005. Guillermo sat with Kristen and Harry that evening. Harry, Guillermo, and Nancy Unger's son were cycling buddies together more than 15 years ago. Nancy Unger was a character witness of Harry in the modification trial of 2009. It was the night before the custody trial of 2008 that Kristen's lawyer, Jamie Dautrich, discovered the email address on one of Harry's lawyer's papers. Looking up the address, it came to an ad for Guillermo's book. She asked Kristen that night if she knew the name. Kristen remembered Harry's class reunion. In court the next day, Harry was asked about Guillermo. He eventually had to admit on the stand that he used Guillermo for advice but did not know of a book. Judge Lash exclaimed, "He wrote a book?"

In early December of 2009, I started to go to the DA with my charges of perjury against Harry Hall. I also wanted to file complaints of "abuse of power" against Judge Lash. After many attempts, I finally thought by mid January, that I had someone from the DA's office that would read my charges and complaints. I was wrong. The only thing that was read was my letter from then State Representative, David Argall. I believe, from my experience, that others have received injustice in Berks County. I believe we have not been given fairness in our right to be heard. I believe in meeting with District Attorney John Adams justice can be served. Thank you for considering this request.

The Epistle to Everyone

The following letter addressed "Dear friends" was written May 6, 2010.

My daughter's appeal to the Pa. Supreme Court has been reinstated. Her appeal was challenged by Harry's lawyer on a technicality. He knows he can not win in court when the evidence is allowed to be presented and the verdict is judged on that evidence. Kristen went to the law library, found what she needed, and won that battle. Kristen had been her own lawyer since December of 2008. What she did in the modification trial of 2009 was amazing. She won her points. She should have been awarded primary. Harry and his witnesses should be convicted of "perjury."

Kristen did have a lawyer to fight the first baseless PFA filed by Harry in August of 2006. After an initial fee of $1500, her lawyer agreed to work "pro bono." It would be easy to get 50/50 custody. Even with the lies, it would be dismissed. Her lawyer kept with her for more than two years. Kristen would finally achieve 50/50 custody in April of 2007. Before that, in March of 2007, Harry, upon learning that 50/50 was recommended by the evaluator, filed a PSR based on a bump on the head of Bryce. The doctor said it was not enough of a bump. In June of 2007, Harry filed another PSR with BCCYS based on a bump on the head of Bryce. Kristen caused neither bump. That time, however, the supposed child abuse was called "founded" because there was a pattern of abuse. The real pattern is Harry's lies.

Kristen filed an appeal to the state. At that expungement hearing, May of 2008, Bryce says, "Mommy did not hit me, Trey did." It took until March of 2009 for Kristen to achieve that expungement. Kristen was told only 5% of appeals are won. As her own lawyer, she achieved that result. Now she would go into her modification trial seeking primary custody, "pro se." With her lawyer she had lost 50/50 custody in the trial of 2008. She should have won. Harry should have been convicted of "perjury" for all his lies in that trial. Kristen had started the appeal motion for that trial but did not have the $5000 to continue. Since Harry was awarded modification in his favor in her modification trial in November of 2009, she has set the appeal process in motion again. This time the lies were not only by Harry and his witnesses, Judge Lash lied.

Obviously, this is an oversimplification. To get the whole story you will have to read my book, AS GOOD AS A DOG. Since I last wrote to you in October of 2008, my number of articles has increased from 35 to 70, and the number of accomplices for Article #18 from 30 to 70. Page 2, my letter to State Senator, David Argall, describes some of my attempts at achieving justice.

Pages 3-6 (#31B), describe one small event included in the modification trial held on November 16, 2009. Either I am lying, or it is Harry, his sister, and Judge Lash that are lying. Pages 7 and 8, which is Article #31, "Exchange and Putdown," was my description of the same event written over a year before the 2009 trial. That article also describes Judge Lash's condemnation of my wife and me. Article #31 is a small part of the evidence we have for "perjury" by Harry Hall and his sister and our claim of "abuse of power" against Judge Lash. Kristen had #31 in her hand ready to refute that testimony. She was not given the chance to use it because she was not allowed back on the witness stand.

I also inquired with another person running for office as to how to get an audience with the DA. He gave me the name of a County Commissioner to seek out. I did. Again I got no results. The person running for office goes on to state, "You are not the first one to be caught in the system with no way to justice.It is seldom a friend to the family and often, no friend to the truth." The DA's office is afraid of the truth.

It is my goal to make the courts a friend to the family and an instrument that seeks truth and justice. I am asking for your help. I will explain what you can do. (That will be found in BOOK 2)

LEGISLATIVE PROPOSAL FOR CUSTODY DETERMINATION

1. FILING OF A PFA. Statement of problem. There are many books written on how to succeed in obtaining victory in divorce proceedings. Often the initial step is to file a false PFA of abuse of a child or children. Participants our encouraged in doing this with the statement that "perjury is rarely considered in custody cases." Often the first person filing a PFA is the guilty party. The defendent is pronounced guilty and punished without due process. There is no assumption of innocence.

STEPS OF CORRRECTION:

    a) The child or children should be placed in foster care until an initial investigation can be completed. The cost of this care will be paid for by the plaintiff and defendent determined by percent of income. The court will determine who should remain in the residence. Preference should be given to the defendent. If the plaintiff is really serious and truthful they will put up with this inconvience for the long range benefit. (This procedure will eliminate frivolous complaints)

    b) Both parties must be interviewed in the initial investigation within seven to ten days. Both parties should be asssumed innocent in the start of the investigation. Temporary primary custody will be determined by this investigation.

    c) Evaluation by the custody evaluator will be required within 60 days and a court date within 30 days of completion of the evaluation.

2. THE CUSTODY EVALUATOR. Statement of problem. There are books written that tell how the plaintiff can prepare for victory thru this evaluation. Again lying is encouraged by these books. Defendents often lose because they are not aware that plaintiffs believe they can lie during these evaluations.

STEPS OF CORRECTION:

    a) The custody evaluator should be cognizant that the plaintiff is often the one not telling the truth. The evaluator should tell the one interviewed second the claims of the one interviewed first. Then the one interviewed first should here the claims of the second and be given a chance to answer the claims of the one inteviewed second.

    b) The custody evaluator should always be a witness if their testimony and report is used in the custody trial. The fee for the custody evaluator should also include the fee for the evalutor as a witness in the trial.

    c) Their must be a new custody evaluation if a custody trial or modification trial is to be done more than 6 months after a custody evalutation.

    d) Plaintiff and defendent, not their lawyers, should complete evaluation forms demonstrating their perceived fairness in treatment by the custody evaluator in: 1) letting their voice be heard. 2) the presenting of their testimony by the evaluator.

3. DOCTORS DETERMINING INDICATED ABUSE. Statement of problem. A doctor listens to plaintiffs stories of other claims of child abuse in determining a verdict of "founded" or "unfounded" for a single event. The doctor is influenced by that testimony to call it "founded" because there is a pattern of abuse. Considering the event by itself he may have not arrived at that conclusion. The age and reliability of the child are not questioned. The defendent is given no opportunity to say how the event occurred. The doctor does not consider that the plaintiff may be lying.

STEPS OF CORRECTION:

    a) Doctors should make an effort to determine the reliability of the testimony of the plaintiff and the child.

b) Doctors making these decisions should be certified and trained in procedures so they can determine the validity of testimonies of plaintiff and victim. They should be made aware of the fact that lying is taught in books in order to win custody battles.

c) Accusations of child abuse should be thrown out when plaintiff attempts to influence doctor with other stories. Doctors should only consider the particular event.

d) If the plaintiff did not see the event, testimony from the defendant should be considered by the doctor as to how the event occurred.

4. **CHILDREN'S SERVICES ROLE.** Statement of the problem. Once a plaintiff casts the first stone against the defendant they are believed to be telling the truth. When the defendant tries to tell of abuse by the plaintiff that is dissmissed because the defendant is just trying to get even. So the book tells you to win in child custody cases, cast the first stone. It does not have to be the truth. Young children can be especially capable of going along with a good story. Some young children are natural storytellers. Rarely will a Children's Service Organization change its mind as to who is the abusive parent. The defendant is declared guilty and punished without being given the chance to testify on their own behalf.

STEPS OF CORRECTION:

a) In lieu of the increase in "how too" books, Children's Services personnel should be certified thru training as to determining the guilty party. Often it is the one casting the first stone.

b) A decision should not be made in these cases without giving each party equal consideration.

c) For each case, evaluation forms should be completed by both the plaintiff and defendant, not their lawyers, as to the fairness they received in having their voice be heard and the fairness as to how their testimony was represented in the final report.

d) If a 24 hour supervisory conditioned is deemed necessary, it should be made clear why they are being asked to sign the papers to agree to these conditions.

5. **PERJURY SHOULD BE CONSIDERED.** Statement of problem. The book states that "judges rarely consider perjury in domestic relations and custody cases". Why not? One particularly "dirty strategy" to use is to file a false PFA with little lies in order to get an custody evaluation where you can use many more lies and win primary custody.

STEPS OF CORRECTION:

a) Judge's involved in Custody cases should be certified in training as to what is discussed in these "How Too" books which describe winning custody battles through the use of children and finances.

b) Finances should be allowed to be discussed in custody cases. No determination on what finances should be, but it is necessary to know this because of motive and consequences of the verdict given.

c) It should be considered criminal, in custody cases, to lie to doctors, custody evaluators, custody masters, and Children's Services.

d) Judges should be evaluated by completion of a form by plaintiffs and defendents, not their lawyers, as to the fairness into having their voice be heard in testimony and how that testimony was represented by the judge in his or her final report.

362

RESOVRCES

In the Court of Common Pleas of Berks County, Pennsylvania Civil Action Law, No. 06-9244 ID #2, Harry T. Hall, JR. the Plaintiff versus Kristen L. Hall the defendant, these are the "NOTES OF TESTIMONY" for the CUSTODY TRIAL held Tuesday, August 26, 2008 in Reading, Pennsylvania before The Honorable Scott E. Lash, Judge.

Appearances made were for the Plaintiff, Mark E. Zimmer, Esquire, and the Defendant, Jaime A. Dautrich, Esquire. Also present were Harry T. Hall, Jr. the Plaintiff and Kristen L. Hall the Defendant. The Official Court reporter was Karen C. Moran.

The Plaintiff's witness was Harry Thomas Hall, Jr. The Defendant's witnesses were Matthew Folk, Mary Lynne Rathman, Kristen Hall, and David Allen Rathman.

PLAINTIFF'S LIST OF
EXHIBITS TO BE PRESENTED AT TRIAL

Plaintiff, Harry T. Hall, Jr., by and through his counsel, Mark E. Zimmer, Esquire, and Mogel, Speidel, Bobb & Kershner, P.C., hereby submits the following list of exhibits to be presented at trial in the above matter:

1. Exhibit P-1 – Custody Evaluation Report of Peter H. Thomas, Ph.D. (The date for this evaluation was April 22, 2008.)

2. Exhibit P-2 – Doctor's note from Bryce's visit at Reading Pediatric's on June 27, 2007. (This refers to the squirty bottle incident.)

3. Exhibit P-3 – Doctor's note from Bryce's visit at Reading Pediatric's on February 25, 2008. (This refers to the biting incident.)

4. Exhibit P-4 – Letter from Berks County Children & Youth Services dated July 9, 2007 regarding Defendant's indicated report of child abuse.

5. Exhibit P-5 – Letter from the Department of Public Welfare, Office of Children, Youth and Families dated December 17, 2007, regarding Defendant's appeal of the indicated report of child abuse.

6. Exhibit P-6 – Criminal Record Check for Michael Spadafora. (There are three different Michael Spadafora's.)

7. Exhibit P-7 – Letter of Reference. (The letter from Nancy Unger was dated April 11, 2007.)

8. Exhibit P-8 – Pictures of Plaintiff, the children and their home.

The items in parentheses were not in the original document. They were added by the author for clarification.

DEFENDANT'S EXHIBIT TO BE PRESETENTED AT TRIAL

Defendant, Kristen L. Hall, by and through her counsel, Jamie A.M. Dautrich, Esquire, hereby submits following list of exhibits to be presented at trial in the above matter:

1. Exhibit D-1 – Custody Evaluation Report of Dr. Peter H. Thomas, Ph.D., November 22, 2006.

2. Exhibit D-2 – Custody Evaluation Report of Dr. Peter H. Thomas, Ph.D., April 22, 2008.

3. Exhibit D-3 – Signature Family Report of 6/29/07-9/23/07.

4. Exhibit D-4 – Signature Family Report of 9/24/07-1/18/08.

5. Exhibit D-5 – Viaquest Behavioral Health Rehabilitation Services of PA Treatment Plan.

6. Exhibit D-6 – Psychological Re-Evaluation of Jonathan M. Gransee, Psy.D.
7. Exhibit D-7 – Letter of September 27, 2006, from Claire A Malfaro, MA, LPC.
8. Exhibit D-8 – Letter of March 13, 2007, from William Clemmons (BCCYS).
9. Exhibit D-9 – Family Service Plan.

The DECISION AND ORDER of Judge, Scott E. Lash, September 5, 2008 for the Custody Trial of August 26, 2008.

DEFENDANT'S LIST OF EXHIBITS TO BE PRESENTED AT TRIAL

Defendant, Kristen L. Hall, pro se, hereby submits the following list of exhibits to be presented at trial in the above matter:

1. Exhibit D-1 – Internet advertisement for the book written by Guillermo Jalil, Asset Protection From Divorce.
2. Exhibit D-2 – Letter dated June 30, 2008 from the District Attorney's Office RE: Commonwealth vs. Robert Chalmers.
3. Exhibit D-3 – Plaintiff's Answers to Defendant's Request for Reconsideration of Order of September 5, 2008.
4. Exhibit D-4 – Letter from Signature Family Services dated September 17, 2008 RE: Court-ordered curriculum based parenting services.
5. Exhibit D-5 – Letter from David G. Argall dated January 13, 2009 RE: Berks County Children's Services actions regarding the child abuse investigation regarding Bryce Hall.
6. Exhibit D-6 – Letter from Berks County Children & Youth Services dated February 4, 2009 RE: No service needed.
7. Exhibit D-7 – Department of Public Welfare's Recommendation of 2/19/09 and Adjudication of 3/2/09 RE: Child Abuse Expunction.
8. Exhibit D-8 – Community Care's Interagency Service Planning Team Meeting Summary of June 3, 2009.

9. Exhibit D-9 – Letter from Oley Valley Elementary School RE: Parent pick-up schedule.
10. Exhibit D-10 – Pictures of Defendant with the children and her extended family support system.
11. Exhibit D-11 – Time Chart of the history of the above child custody case.

The ORDER of Judge, Scott E. Lash, November 20, 2009, for case No. 06-9244, I.D. #2.